Jørgen Dige Pedersen
GLOBALIZATION, DEVELOPMENT AND THE STATE
The Performance of India and Brazil Since 1990

Markus Perkmann and Ngai-Ling Sum
GLOBALIZATION, REGIONALIZATION AND CROSS-BORDER REGIONS

K Ravi Raman and Ronnie D. Lipschutz (editors)
CORPORATE SOCIAL RESPONSIBILITY
Comparative Critiques

Ben Richardson
SUGAR: REFINED POWER IN A GLOBAL REGIME

Marc Schelhase
GLOBALIZATION, REGIONALIZATION AND BUSINESS
Conflict, Convergence and Influence

Herman M. Schwartz and Leonard Seabrooke (editors)
THE POLITICS OF HOUSING BOOMS AND BUSTS

Leonard Seabrooke
US POWER IN INTERNATIONAL FINANCE
The Victory of Dividends

Timothy J. Sinclair and Kenneth P. Thomas (editors)
STRUCTURE AND AGENCY IN INTERNATIONAL CAPITAL MOBILITY

J.P. Singh (editor)
INTERNATIONAL CULTURAL POLICIES AND POWER

Fredrik Söderbaum and Timothy M. Shaw (editors)
THEORIES OF NEW REGIONALISM

Susanne Soederberg, Georg Menz and Philip G. Cerny (editors)
INTERNALIZING GLOBALIZATION
The Rise of Neoliberalism and the Decline of National Varieties of Capitalism

Helen Thompson
CHINA AND THE MORTGAGING OF AMERICA
Economic Interdependence and Domestic Politics

Ritu Vij (editor)
GLOBALIZATION AND WELFARE
A Critical Reader

Matthew Watson
THE POLITICAL ECONOMY OF INTERNATIONAL CAPITAL MOBILITY

Owen Worth and Phoebe Moore
GLOBALIZATION AND THE 'NEW' SEMI-PERIPHERIES

Xu Yi-chong and Gawdat Bahgat (editors)
THE POLITICAL ECONOMY OF SOVEREIGN WEALTH FUNDS

International Political Economy Series
Series Standing Order ISBN 978–0–333–71708–0 hardcover
Series Standing Order ISBN 978–0–333–71110–1 paperback
(*outside North America only*)

You can receive future titles in this series as they are published by placing a standing order. Please contact your bookseller or, in case of difficulty, write to us at the address below with your name and address, the title of the series and one of the ISBNs quoted above.

Customer Services Department, Macmillan Distribution Ltd, Houndmills, Basingstoke, Hampshire RG21 6XS, England

The Political Economy of Sovereign Wealth Funds

Edited by

Xu Yi-chong
Griffith University, Australia

Gawdat Bahgat
National Defence University, USA

palgrave
macmillan

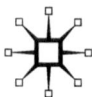

First published 2010 by
PALGRAVE MACMILLAN

Palgrave Macmillan in the UK is an imprint of Macmillan Publishers Limited, registered in England, company number 785998, of Houndmills, Basingstoke, Hampshire RG21 6XS.

Palgrave Macmillan in the US is a division of St Martin's Press LLC, 175 Fifth Avenue, New York, NY 10010.

Palgrave Macmillan is the global academic imprint of the above companies and has companies and representatives throughout the world.

Palgrave® and Macmillan® are registered trademarks in the United States, the United Kingdom, Europe and other countries.

ISBN-13: 978–0–230–24109–1 hardback

This book is printed on paper suitable for recycling and made from fully managed and sustained forest sources. Logging, pulping and manufacturing processes are expected to conform to the environmental regulations of the country of origin.

A catalogue record for this book is available from the British Library.

Library of Congress Cataloging-in-Publication Data
The political economy of sovereign wealth funds / edited by Xu Yi-chong, Gawdat Bahgat.
    p.   cm. — (International political economy series)
    ISBN 978–0–230–24109–1 (hardback)
    1. Sovereign wealth funds.   I. Xu, Yi-Chong.   II. Bahgat, Gawdat.
    HJ3801.P65 2010
    332.67′252—dc22   2010027580

10   9   8   7   6   5   4   3   2   1
19   18   17   16   15   14   13   12   11   10

Printed and bound in Great Britain by
CPI Antony Rowe, Chippenham and Eastbourne

Contents

List of Figures and Tables

Figures

Tables

Acknowledgements

Sovereign wealth funds may be a relatively new topic in academic writing and the issues involved are as old as international political economy as a sub-field of international politics. For the initial ideas of this project, we thank Michael Wesley who may not know much about the detailed issues involved but has an instinct for important subject matters.

This book represents the work of a group far wider than the editors and authors represented here, and we are keen to acknowledge the contribution of all who participated in our workshop and brought with them their insight of the country knowledge and broader issues of politics. We thank Graham Gill (University of Sydney), Les Holmes (University of Melbourne), Gary Rodan (Murdoch University), Matthew Gray (Australian National University), Frank Mols (University of Queensland), John Kane (Griffith University) and Mark Thirlwell (Lowy Institute).

Special thanks to Tim Shaw as the series editor of International Political Economy, Palgrave Macmillan, for his support, participation and comments before and after the workshop, and to Alexandra Webster and her team at Palgrave Macmillan for their enthusiasm for the project and for their attentive assistance.

Our appreciation goes to the Centre for Governance and Public Policy and the Griffith Asia Institute at Griffith University that funded the workshop.

We also thank Keith Whittam, Maureen Todhunter and Greg Burke for editing and assisting the completion of the manuscript, and Natasha Vary for organising the workshop.

Finally, we wish to acknowledge our special appreciation to Pat Weller, as director of the Griffith Centre for Governance and Public Policy, and as a colleague who encouraged and supported this project from the very beginning.

Xu and Gawdat Bahgat
Brisbane
March 2010

Notes on Contributors

Gawdat Bahgat, National Defence University, USA. He is the author of *The Gulf Monarchies: New Economic and Political Realities* (1997), *The Future of the Gulf* (1997), *The Persian Gulf at the Dawn of the New Millennium* (1999), *American Oil Diplomacy in the Persian Gulf and the Caspian Sea* (2003), *Israel and the Persian Gulf: Retrospect and Prospect* (2006) and *Nuclear Proliferation in the Middle East* (2007). In addition, he has published numerous articles on the Persian Gulf and the Caspian Sea in scholarly journals. His work has been translated into Arabic, Farsi, French, German, Italian, Japanese, Portuguese and Russian.

Richard Eccleston, Senior Lecturer of the Department of Government, University of Tasmania, Australia. His recent books include *Regulating International Business* (2008), *Taxing Reforms* (2007) and *The Thirty Year Problem* (2004). He is currently undertaking an ARC-funded research project on international tax regulation in the aftermath of the global financial crisis.

Stephen Fortescue, Associate Professor of the School of Social Science and International Studies, University of New South Wales, Australia. His current research interests include the Russian metals and mining industry, Russian outward foreign direct investment and the policy-making process in contemporary Russia. He is the author of four monographs and many articles and book chapters. The most recent monograph is *Russia's Oil Barons and Metal Magnates: Oligarchs and the State in Transition* (Palgrave, 2006).

John Freebairn, Ritchie Professor of Economics at the University of Melbourne. His main research interests are in the economic analysis of policy options, with particular current interests in the areas of unemployment, taxation, climate change and water. He has published articles in the *Review of Economics and Statistics, American Journal of Agricultural Economics, Economic Record, Australian Economic Review* and the *Australian Journal of Agricultural and Resource Economics*. John has contributed to government policy inquiries, and he is a regular contributor to the media on issues of economic policy.

Liping He, Professor and Chair, Department of Finance, School of Economics and Business Administration, Beijing Normal University, China, has been a member of China Economy 50-Person Forum, a high profile body that meets frequently each year to discuss priority policy issues in the country. He has often undertaken research and consulting projects assigned by Chinese government agencies. He also worked as an independent consultant for research projects sponsored by the World Bank and the Asian Development Bank, among others.

Joseph A. Kéchichian, CEO of Kéchichian & Associates, LLC, a consulting partnership that provides analysis on the Arabian/Persian Gulf region, specialising in the domestic and regional concerns of Bahrain, Iran, Iraq, Kuwait, Oman, Qatar, Saudi Arabia, United Arab Emirates and the Yemen, as well as the Honorary Consul of the Sultanate of Oman in Los Angeles, California. He worked at the University of Virginia, the Rand Corporation, UCLA, and as Hoover Fellow at Stanford University. His publications include *Succession in Saudi Arabia*, (2001), *Political Participation and Stability in the Sultanate of Oman*, (2005), *Oman and the World: The Emergence of an Independent Foreign Policy* (1995). He edited *A Century in Thirty Years: Shaykh Zayed and the United Arab Emirates* (2000), *Iran, Iraq, and the Arab Gulf States* (2001), and co-authored (with R. Hrair Dekmejian) *The Just Prince: A Manual of Leadership* (2005).

Yvonne C.L. Lee, Assistant Professor at the Faculty of Law, National University of Singapore. Her teaching and research portfolios include sovereign wealth funds, company law, administrative and constitutional law, international economic law and public regulation, and corporate governance. She is also an attorney and counsellor of the New York State and an advocate and solicitor of Singapore. Prior to joining academia, she was an in-house counsel of Temasek Holdings and a corporate law practitioner.

Leong H. Liew, Professor and Head, Department of International Business and Asian Studies at Griffith University, Australia. His major area of research interest is China's political economy and he has published numerous journal articles, book chapters and books on China's economic reform and its responses to globalisation. His articles have appeared in journals including the *China Quarterly, China Information, European Journal of Political Economy, Journal of Development Studies* and *Public Choice*. He co-authored with Harry X. Wu *The Making of China's Exchange Rate Policy* (2007).

Jørgen Ørstrøm Møller, after 38 years in the Danish diplomatic service of which 8 ½ as State-Secretary, joined the Institute of Southeast Asian Studies, Singapore as Visiting Senior Research Fellow. He is also Adjunct Professor at Singapore Management University and Copenhagen Business School and has published widely. His major publications in English are *Political Economy in a Globalized World* (2009), *European Integration – Sharing of Experiences* (2008), *A New International System* (2004), *The End of Internationalism or World Governance* (2000), *The Future European Model* (1995), *Technology and Culture in a European Context* (1991) and *Member States and the Community Budget* (1982). He has published in a large number of journals, such as *Futures Quarterly*, *The International Economy* and *Business Horizons*, and contributed columns to numerous newspapers and websites.

Ciaran O'Faircheallaigh, Professor of Politics and Public Policy, Griffith University, Australia. He works with Indigenous organizations on negotiation of mining agreements, and has acted as an advisor or negotiator for the Cape York, Northern, Central, Yamatji and Kimberley Land Councils. He is currently advising the Kimberley Land Council on negotiations in relation to natural gas development in the Kimberley, and is Project Manager for the Aboriginal Social Impact Assessment of the proposed LNG Precinct at James Price Point north of Broome. His publications includes *A New Model of Policy Evaluation: Mining and Indigenous People* (2002), *Environmental Agreements in Canada: Aboriginal Participation* (2006) and *Earth Matters: Indigenous Peoples, the Extractive Industries and Corporate Social Responsibility* (2008), edited jointly with Saleem Ali.

Bent Sofus Tranøy, Associate Professor at the University of Oslo, Norway. As a Senior Researcher at the Institute of Labor Research (Fafo), while on leave from the University of Oslo, has published nationally and internationally on macroeconomic governance, globalisation, European integration and financial instability and housing bubbles. In 2009, he published an article on the Norwegian Government Pension Fund – Global in the journal *Geopolitics*. In 2006 he won the 'Brage prize' for best non-fiction in Norwegian for a book on market power and market fundamentalism. He has worked for the Norwegian Study of Power and Democracy, Advanced Research on the Europeanization of the Nation State (ARENA) and has been a guest researcher at the Wissenschaftzentrum Berlin (WZB).

Xu Yi-chong, Research Professor at Centre for Governance and Public Politics, Griffith University, Australia. Xu publishes in international organisations and energy issues and is the author of *Powering China: Reforming the Electric Power Industry in China* (2002), *Electricity Reform in China, India and Russia* (2004), *The Governance of World Trade: International Civil Servants and the GATT/WTO* (2004) and *Inside the World Bank* (2009) (both with Patrick Weller), and *The Politics of Nuclear Energy in China* (2010).

Abbreviations

ABC	Agricultural Bank of China
ADFD	Abu Dhabi Fund for Development
ADIA	Abu Dhabi Investment Authority
ADIC	Abu Dhabi Investment Company
ADICO	Abu Dhabi Investment Council
ADNEC	Abu Dhabi National Energy Company
ADRPBF	Abu Dhabi Retirement Pensions and Benefits Fund
ADSM	Abu Dhabi Stock Market
ADWEA	Abu Dhabi Water and Electricity Authority
ADX	Abu Dhabi Securities Exchange
AEC	Atomic Energy of Canada
AFC	Asian financial crisis
AMCs	Asset management companies
BAU	Business as usual
BEA	Bureau of Economic Analysis
BIS	Bank for International Settlements
BOC	Bank of China
BP	British Petroleum
BRTI	Badan Regulasi Telekomunikasi Indonesia
CBRC	China Banking Regulatory Commission
CCB	China Construction Bank
CDB	China Development Bank
CDC	Caisse des Dépôts et Consignations
CFIUS	Committee on Foreign Investment in the United States
CIC	China Investment Corporation
CLGFE	Central Leading Group on Finance and Economics
CLGRSS	Central Leading Group on Reforming the Shareholding of SOCBs
CNOOC	China National Offshore Oil Corporation
CRS	Congressional Research Service (US)
CSRC	China Securities Regulatory Commission
EBRD	European Bank for Reconstruction and Development
EEZ	Exclusive Economic Zone
EMAL	Emirates Aluminium Company Limited
EMH	Efficient market hypothesis

EO	Executive Order
ERM	Exchange Rate Mechanism
EU	European Union
FDI	Foreign direct investment
FF	Future Fund
FFR	Fonds de Réserve pour les Retraites
FGF	Future Generations Fund
FHCSIA	Department of Families, Housing, Community Services and Indigenous Affairs
FHLB	Federal Home Loan Bank
FINSA	Foreign Investment and National Security Act of 2007
FIRB	Foreign Investment Review Board
FRB	Federal Reserve Board
GAO	Government Accountability Office (US)
GAPP	Generally Accepted Principles and Practices
GATS	General Agreement on Trade and Services
GATT	General Agreement on Trade and Tariffs
GCC	Gulf Cooperation Council
GDP	Gross domestic product
GFC	Global financial crisis
GIC	Government Investment Corporation of Singapore Pte Ltd
GPF-G	Government Pension Fund – Global (Norway)
GRF	General Reserve Fund
HEEF	Higher Education Endowment Fund
IBRD	International Bank for Reconstruction and Development
ICBC	Industrial and Commercial Bank of China
IEEPA	International Emergency Economic Powers Act
IFC	International Finance Corporation
IMF	International Monetary Fund
Indosat	PT Indosat
IPIC	International Petroleum Investment Company
IWG	International Working Group
IWPPs	Independent Water and Power Producers
KIA	Kuwait Investment Authority
KIB	Kuwait Investment Board
KIC	Korea Investment Corporation
KIO	Kuwait Investment Office
KKP	Kularb Kaew Pcl
KLC	Kimberley Land Council
KOC	Kuwait Oil Company

KPC	Kuwait Petroleum Corporation
KPPU	Commission for the Supervision of Business Competition
LDCs	Less developed countries
LO	National trade union (Norway)
MAI	Multilateral Agreement on Investment
MDC	Mubadala Development Corporation
MENA	Middle East and North Africa
MERT	Ministry of Economic Development and Trade (Russia)
MOF	Ministry of Finance (China)
NBIM	Norges Bank Investment Management
NDRC	National Development and Reform Commission
NGO	Non-governmental organisation
NPLs	Non-performing loans
NPRF	National Pensions Reserve Fund (Ireland)
NWF	National Welfare Fund
OECD	Organisation for Economic Cooperation and Development
OPEC	Organisation of the Petroleum Exporting Countries
PAP	Peoples' Action Party
PBC	People's Bank of China
PPP	Purchasing power parity
SAFE	State Administration of Foreign Exchange
SASAC	State-owned Assets Supervision and Administration Commission
SCB	Siam Commercial Bank Pcl
SingTel	Singapore Telecommunications Ltd
SOCBs	State-owned commercial banks
SOEs	State-owned enterprises
SPC	State Planning Commission
SRI	Socially responsible investment
SRR	Statutory reserve requirement
STT	Singapore Technologies Telemedia Pte
SWFs	Sovereign wealth funds
TAQA	Abu Dhabi National Energy Company
Telekomsel	Telekomunikasi Selular
TRIMS	Agreement on Trade-Related Investment Measures
UAE	United Arab Emirates
UBICO	UAE-Bangladesh Investment Company
UCB	Underlying cash balance

UCS	Underlying cash surplus
UMEP	Union Maroc Emirat de Peches
USCC	US-China Economic and Security Review Commission
WCCCA	Western Cape Communities Coexistence Agreement
WTO	World Trade Organisation

1
The Political Economy of Sovereign Wealth Funds

Xu Yi-chong

A spectre is stalking the world's governments, businesses and press: it is a spectre of a special type of fund, one that buys strategic resources around the world, hollows out companies, gobbles up financial institutions and threatens the sovereignty of the countries in whose resources and companies it invests. It is the spectre of sovereign wealth funds (SWFs) – dedicated government investment vehicles from China, Russia and the Gulf states, among others. These SWFs, critics declare, are the Trojan horse of states that generally are neither democratic nor share the traditions, political systems or legal systems of many OECD countries. They are 'the new bogeymen of global finance' (Plender 2007). To others, SWFs are no more than a financial flare, a fad that will fade quickly as the global financial crisis subsides.

SWFs are not new. Their origin can be traced back to 1816 when France created Caisse des Dépôts et Consignations (CDC) to manage government and overseas tax-exempt funds collected by French savings banks and post offices. Today, CDC invests its deposits to finance public housing, universities and other sustainable development projects. A more recent category of SWF was created in 1953, when, 8 years before its independence in 1961, the Gulf state of Kuwait established the Kuwait Investment Authority (KIA) to manage the country's oil surpluses.

SWFs are not the only investment vehicle at the disposal of governments worldwide: central banks have foreign exchange reserves to manage, and large public pension funds to invest and manage. But none has drawn the same degree of attention and concern as SWFs.

Why the fuss? Four main concerns have dominated debates in countries where SWFs make their investments: (i) the number of countries with SWFs is increasing; (ii) the amount of capital at their disposal is

1

large and rising; (iii) with the government as the owner, SWFs 'might be used for overt or tacit political purposes' (Cohen 2009, p. 713); and (iv) we know little about their investment strategies or how investment decisions are made within SWFs.

Given that more than two-thirds of SWFs are located in countries that are both politically and financially less open than OECD countries, while more than 90 per cent of their overseas investment has gone to OECD countries, there is *fear* that SWFs might threaten the national economy and national security of the recipient countries. Even though 'the threat is more perceived than real' (Lyons 2008, p. 5), the *fear* and *perception* that SWFs might threaten OECD countries have made SWFs particularly challenging in the international political economy because in international politics perceptions are at least as important as reality; they can change quickly, leading either to peace or conflict.

To prevent legitimate concerns from developing into 'illegitimate hysteria' (Bahgat 2008) and to avoid 'fear' becoming a reality require an analysis of the politics in these SWF-holding countries. When and why were SWFs created? How are they organised? What are their mandates? How do they operate? How do they decide their investment strategies? How have they responded to the pressure and action of the recipient countries? These are not only technical but political questions.

In contrast to these common concerns, countries that have established such 'special-purpose investment funds or arrangements that are owned by the general government' (IWG (International Working Group of Sovereign Wealth Funds) 2008, p. 3) vary significantly in size, wealth, development stages and in their political and economic systems. Similarly, SWFs vary in their objectives, investment strategies and operations. In addition, 'SWFs have diverse legal, institutional, and governance structures' (IWG 2008, p. 3). Unpacking the domestic politics of SWFs can help understand their diversity and in turn understand several fundamental questions about the global economy and global politics. Why did the government become an active player in global finance after more than two decades of neoliberal 'triumph'? Why did many SWF-holding countries engage in this 'reverse' global capital flow against a general rule that 'capital historically tended to flow from the core of an economic system to its periphery?' (Hildebrand 2007, p. 4). How does the interaction between SWF-holding countries and the recipient countries shape global politics in the twenty-first century?

Most literature on SWFs focuses on 'concerns' about SWFs from the point of view of the countries where SWFs make their investment. Since much of the fear and unease originates in 'their air of secrecy' of SWFs

(Lyon 2007), this book is designed to bring about an understanding of the domestic politics of seven SWF-holding countries – China, Singapore, Kuwait, United Arab Emirates (UAE), Russia, Australia and Norway. These countries are chosen not only because they are among the world's top ten largest SWF-holding countries, but also because they represent variations in size, wealth and development level in their political, legal and economic systems and their status in geopolitics. They have also drawn the most international attention.

Authors in this book focus their analyses on the domestic politics of SWF-holding countries: why did governments decide to create these investment funds – with defensive or aggressive intentions? What were the domestic political forces behind their creation? How are they organised and operated – hands-off or tight control by the government? Do these funds operate differently from other institutional or private investment funds – with commercial or non-commercial, financial or strategic objectives? What are the benefits of setting up SWFs – domestic engineering or foreign policy aims? How have people in the SWF-holding countries benefited from their investment?

SWFs have been a focus of attention for large countries, for example the USA, and multilateral institutions, such as the European Union (EU) and the International Monetary Fund (IMF). Two chapters will explain the concerns of the countries where SWFs have made their investment. By placing SWFs under the microscope, we hope to provide a better understanding of the changing global economic and political relationship.

SWFs and their holders

There is little consensus on a definition of what an SWF actually is. Often it is easier to define by exclusion. That is, they are government investment vehicles but not foreign reserves managed by central banks; they can cover future public retirement, but do not have direct pension liability. Precise definitions vary from author to author. Similarly, different institutions have chosen to emphasise certain aspects of a SWF's identity. The IMF defines SWFs as government-owned investment funds based on their objectives: stabilisation funds designed to mitigate volatile international market prices on resources/commodities; savings funds intended to share wealth across generations; and reserve investment corporations established to reduce the opportunity cost of holding excess foreign reserves or to pursue investment policies with higher returns. The US Treasury defines a SWF as a government investment vehicle that is funded by foreign exchange assets, and which manages those assets separately from the official reserves of the monetary authorities (the Central Bank and reserve-related functions of the Finance Ministry). At the request of Congress, the US Government Accountability Office (GAO) defines SWFs by four criteria.

1. They are government-chartered or government-sponsored investment vehicles.
2. They invest some or all of their funds in assets other than sovereign debt outside the country that established them.
3. They are funded through government transfers arising primarily from sovereign budget surpluses, trade surpluses, central bank currency reserves or revenues from the commodity wealth of a country.
4. They are not actively functioning as a pension fund (GAO 2008, pp. 2–3).

The EU sees SWFs as state-owned investment vehicles that manage a diversified portfolio of domestic and international financial assets. They can offer a source of investment and market liquidity at a time of real financial crunch. Yet, as state-owned investment vehicles, some can raise questions about the risk that these investments may interfere with the normal functioning of market economies (European Commission 2008, p. 3).

These definitions suggest that SWFs are a heterogeneous group of funds that share one key feature – government ownership. Since late 2008, most discussion has accepted the definition of SWFs agreed upon by the members of the IWG in the Generally Accepted Principles and Practices (GAPP).

> Sovereign wealth funds (SWFs) are special-purpose investment funds or arrangements that are owned by the general government. Created by the general government for macroeconomic purposes, SWFs hold, manage, or administer assets to achieve financial objectives, and employ a set of investment strategies that include investing in foreign financial assets.
>
> (IWG 2008, p. 3)

GAPP also specifies which funds should not be classified as SWFs: 'This definition excludes, *inter alia*, foreign currency reserve assets held by monetary authorities for the traditional balance of payments or monetary policy purposes, state-owned enterprises (SOEs) in the traditional sense, government employee pension funds, or assets managed for the benefit of individuals' (IWG 2008, p. 3). Foreign reserves are excluded from this definition because traditionally they are managed in more conservative ways and can be called upon at any time to meet the balance of payment demands in a country. Yet, increasingly a portion of excess foreign exchange reserves is diversified to more aggressive investment by the central bank or monetary authority, such as in Saudi Arabia, Hong Kong and Russia with its Reserve Funds identified by the GAO. Moreover, the GAPP definition of SWFs excludes those managed for the benefits of individuals, but in this book investment funds owned by sovereign rulers, primarily in the Middle East, Kuwait and UAE, are considered to be SWFs. Even though in these countries 'the line between sovereign wealth and private wealth of the sovereign can be quite blurry' (Rozanov 2009, p. 11), their sovereign wealth funds can benefit from being under the multilateral umbrella rather than standing outside.

The definition of SWFs agreed upon by members of IWG provides a basis for our analysis. This project will include, for example, the China Investment Corporation (CIC), but not the State Administration of Foreign Exchange (SAFE) or the National Social Security Fund in China, even though both are listed by the Sovereign Wealth Fund Institute (a private consulting firm), and the Stabilisation Fund of Russia, but not its Reserve Fund, which is listed as a SWF by the GAO but not the Congressional Research Service (CRS) in the USA.

Even with this agreed definition, a 'typical' SWF does not exist because SWFs differ in their sources and size of assets, structure, governance, risk factors and their objectives. Among them, Kuwait has the oldest SWF: the Kuwait Investment Office later changed into the Kuwait Investment Authority (KIA) and was created in 1953 when the country was still under British rule. It was set up to invest the oil surplus for its future development. Russia has one of the newest SWFs in the group (2008). The Abu Dhabi Investment Authority (ADIA) is the largest SWF in the group with assets of US$625–875 billion in early 2009 and the smallest one is the Russian National Wealth Fund (US$33 billion).

Four of the selected seven countries featured in this book (Kuwait, Norway, Russia and UAE) derive the assets of their SWFs from commodity (oil) exports. Countries that rely on oil and other non-renewable sources for a substantial share of their income face serious challenges: a high level of uncertainty due to the fluctuation of prices and the fact that oil and other non-renewable sources are, by definition, finite. The surge of oil prices in both the 1970s–1980s and the 2000s led to rapidly accumulated oil revenues. The desire to prevent an occurrence of the 'Dutch Disease'[1] – the tendency for large resource revenues to appreciate the real exchange rate, which then damages the non-resource tradable sector – was behind the recycling of oil revenues to the global financial system.

These four resource-based economies, however, have different philosophies behind their SWFs. In Kuwait and UAE, planning against a critical mass of domestic opposition, especially from non-elites/social forces, was one of the driving forces behind the growth of their SWFs (see Chapters 4 and 5). In Russia, inflation had brought the economy to its knees throughout the 1990s, and the desire to control it may have been the sole objective of its stabilisation fund, but the desire of the Ministry of Finance to control how the money was to be used led to the policy preference of very conservative investment (see Chapter 6). In Norway, the long-held democratic-corporatist ideology of socialisation of rights and the pursuit of cross-sector and inter-generational equity were behind the organisation, operation and ethical standards of the Norwegian SWF (see Chapter 8).

Among Asian developing economies, Singapore created its two SWFs before others – Tamesek in 1974 and the Government Investment Corporation (GIC) in 1980. While the two differ in their sources of funding, organisational structure and investment strategies, they are both the product of the strong state capitalism the country's Minister Mentor Lee Kuan Yew has long championed (see Chapter 3). China is among several Asian developing economies that have created SWFs in the last couple of years as they experienced rapid accumulation of foreign reserves. Their emergence corresponded with developed countries as a group running progressively bigger current account deficits, not only in the USA but also in other countries, including Australia and Britain. Yet, it was the notorious bureaucratic competition for control in China that led to the creation of CIC (see Chapter 2).

Australia is the only country in the group where the assets of its Future Fund come from the fiscal surpluses while the country has run persistent current account deficits. The desire to achieve inter-generational equity and to manage competing claims for spending in a system with short electoral cycles is behind the creation of the Future Fund (see Chapters 7 and 8). Indigenous people have gained increasing recognition of their rights by their governments and the international community. With these rights over land and resources, they are obtaining significant potential sources of income that will allow them to pursue inter-generational equity in line with governments in other resource-rich countries (see Chapter 9).

Four main concerns

A recent study shows that in 2001, 89 per cent of investment from SWFs went to emerging economies but by 2006 the share dropped to 37 per cent. In the first quarter of 2008, 94 per cent of the total investment from SWFs went to OECD countries (Monitor 2009). The soaring appetite of many non-OECD SWFs for acquiring large stakes of Western companies, whether financial institutions or resources companies, has led to a series of accusations and concerns in many recipient countries. This section discusses briefly the four major concerns about SWFs: (i) the rapid increase in the number of SWFs; (ii) their growing size; (iii) the government ownership of these funds; and (iv) their lack of transparency. There may be considerable inconsistency in these concerns, yet understanding each will help us appreciate the real issues in changes to the global economy.

The first concern is that the number of SWF-holding countries has increased significantly (Table 1.1). The issue was addressed by Sir John Gieve, former deputy governor of the Bank of England, who in a speech in London in 2008 commented:

Modern sovereign wealth funds are not new. The first, the Kuwait Investment Office, was set up in 1953 just as Edmund Hillary and Tenzing Norgay were setting out to climb Mount Everest. The number of funds has been increasing since then like the traffic on the slopes of Everest.

(2008, p. 197)

This increase raises three questions: (i) how has the role of the government changed so quickly; (ii) why have more non-democratic than democratic countries resorted to this type of investment vehicles; and (iii) why have some of the relatively poor countries become net capital exporters? The first two questions are at the centre of the debate on the rise of state capitalism. As the Cold War stumbled to an end, the belief that governments could micromanage national economies and generate prosperity seemed obsolete. The neoliberal economic policies spread quickly around the world in developed, developing and transition economies.

Table 1.1   Twenty Largest SWFs by Size

Country	Fund name	Year of inception
Kuwait	Kuwait Investment Authority	1953
Singapore	Temasek Holdings	1974
United Arab Emirates	Abu Dhabi Investment Authority	1976
USA (Alaska)	Alaska Permanent Fund	1976
Singapore	Government Investment Corporation	1981
Brunei	Brunei Investment Authority	1983
Norway	Government Pension Fund – Global	1990
Hong Kong	Exchange Fund Investment Portfolio	1998
Algeria	Revenue Regulation Fund	2000
Kazakhstan	National Fund	2000
Ireland	National Pensions Reserve Fund	2001
Nigeria	Excess Crude Account	2004
Qatar	Qatar Investment Authority	2005
Venezuela	National Development Fund	2005
United Arab Emirates	Investment Corporation of Dhabi	2006
Australia	Australian Government Future Fund	2006
Libya	Libyan Investment Authority	2006
China	China Investment Corporation	2007
Russia	Reserve Fund	2008
Russia	National Wealth Fund	2008

Source: GAO (2008), p. 19.

SWFs are viewed as 'a massive and unstoppable shift of influence back to what are in effect state-owned entities'. How has the global financial system got to this stage after 'three decades of policy, propaganda, and hype about "freeing up markets", "reducing the role of the state", and "promoting the private sector" ', asked Professor Fred Halliday from the London School of Economics (Halliday 2008)? SWFs may claim an arm's-length relationship with governments, but state-controlled agencies making investments in other countries challenge the fundamental philosophy of the neoliberal economics. When an increasing number of governments in non-democratic countries decided to create and expand SWFs, the critics particularly question the validity of the existing rules regulating the free market system (Slawotsy 2009).

The second concern about the recent rise of SWFs is their size and the speed of their growth (Table 1.2). 'In 1990, sovereign funds probably held, at most, US500 million' (Johnson 2007, p. 56). In 2008, according to the IMF, their global total was between US$2–3 trillion. In 2007 alone, they grew by 18 per cent (GAO 2008). Morgan Stanley estimates that the

Table 1.2 Market Estimates of Assets under Management for SWFs Based on latest available information (as of February 2008) (US$ billion)

Name of fund		Assets (range)				
		Lower	% of total	Upper	% of total	Es. Year
Oil and gas exporting countries						
UAE	Abu Dhabi Investment Authority	250	11.2	875	28.1	1976
Norway	Government Pension Fund – Global	380	17.0	380	12.2	1990
Saudi Arabia	No designated name	289	12.9	289	9.3	
Kuwait	Reserve Fund for the Future Generations/ Government Reserve Fund	213	9.5	213	6.9	1960
Russia	Reserve Fund for the Future Generations/	125	5.6	125	4.0	2004
	National Welfare Fund	32	1.4	32	1.0	
Libya	Libya Investment Corporation	50	2.2	50	1.6	
Qatar	State Reserve Fund/Stabilisation Fund	30	1.3	50	1.6	2005
Algeria	Reserve Fund/Revenue Regulation Fund	43	1.9	43	1.4	2000
USA (Alaska)	Alaska Permanent Reserve Fund	40	1.8	40	1.3	1976
Brunei	Brunei Investment Authority	30	1.3	30	1.0	1983
Kazakhstan	National Fund	21	0.9	21	0.7	2000
Malaysia	Khazanah Nasional BHD	19	0.9	19	0.6	1993
Canada (Alberta)	Alberta Heritage Savings Trust Fund	16	0.7	16	0.5	1976
Nigeria	Excess Crude Account	11	0.5	11	0.4	

Table 1.2 (Continued)

Name of fund		Assets (range)				
		Lower	% of total	Upper	% of total	Es. Year
Iran	Oil Stabilisation Fund	9	0.4	9	0.3	2000
Azerbaijan	State Oil Fund	2.5	0.1	2.5	0.1	
Oman	State General Reserve Fund	2	0.1	2	0.1	
Timor-Leste	Petroleum Fund of Timor-Leste	1.4	0.1	1.4	0.0	
Venezuela	LIEM – Macroeconomic Stabilisation Fund	0.8	0.0	0.8	0.0	2005
Trinidad & Tobago	Revenue Stabilisation Fund	0.5	0.0	0.5	0.0	
Asian exporters						
Singapore	Government Investment Corp.	100	4.5	330	10.6	1981
China	China Investment Corporation	200	9.0	200	6.4	2007
Hong Kong	HK Monetary Authority Investment Portfolio	140	6.3	140	4.5	
Singapore	Temasek Holdings	108	4.8	108	3.5	1974
Korea	Korea Investment Group	30	1.3	30	1.0	2005
Taiwan	National Stabilisation Fund	15	0.7	15	0.5	
Other countries						
Australia	Australian Future Fund	54	2.4	54	1.7	2006
Chile	Economic and Social Stabilisation Fund	14.9	0.7	14.9	0.5	
	Pension Reserve Fund	1.5	0.1	1.5	0.0	
Botswana	Pula Fund	4.7	0.2	4.7	0.2	
Kiribati	Revenue Equalisation Fund	0.4	0.0	0.4	0.0	
Total		2233.7		3108.7		

Source: International Monetary Fund (2008), p. 7.

amount could reach US$12 trillion by 2015 when investment returns on SWFs will be higher than that of sovereign bond holdings in the official reserves. The size of total assets of SWFs, however, remains small when compared with other types of investment funds and it accounts for only a fraction of the global capital market.

Global capital markets, US$ trillion, 2007

Global bond market	80.0
Asset management industry	55.0
Global equity markets	53.0
Pension funds	21.6
Mutual funds	19.3
Insurance assets	18.5
Global FX reserves	6.4
Hedge funds	6.0
Daily FX turnover	3.2
SWFs	2.9
Private equity	0.7

Source: Weiss (2009), p. 5.

SWFs are less than 15 per cent of global pension funds and less than 5 per cent of global assets under various managements. They are minute compared with 'the global value of traded securities [which] is about US$165 trillion' (Johnson 2007, p. 56). SWFs are also small compared with the US$62 trillion funds managed by private institutional investors. Meanwhile, SWFs and public pension funds share many important similarities: both are very large in terms of assets under management and are autonomous and accountable only to governments or public sector institutions. They are also increasingly investing abroad and moving into alternative assets (Blundell-Wignall et al. 2008).

One key difference is that developing countries hold a minute share of global pension funds. According to one estimate, in 2001 pension funds assets under management in emerging economies accounted for only 3.2 per cent of those in six of the OECD countries (Chan-Lau 2004; Blundell-Wignall et al. 2008). Some developing countries are starting to build their public pension funds and social security funds. For example, the Sovereign Wealth Funds Institute has listed four funds in China as SWFs – the CIC, the National Social Security Fund, the SAFE Investment Company and the China-Africa Development Fund. The National Social Security Fund has bigger assets than CIC, which has been the most scrutinised fund.

While most pension funds are held by OECD countries, which are excluded from the definition of SWFs, the overwhelming proportion of SWFs is held by non-OECD countries. Only 25 per cent of the global SWFs are owned by OECD countries, Norway (18 per cent), Alaska (2 per cent), Alberta (0.76 per cent), Korea (1.4 per cent) and Australia (2.6 per cent). The rest is split between rich oil-producing countries and export-oriented economies. Middle East oil-producing countries control 42 per cent of global SWFs, with UAE, Kuwait and Saudi Arabia taking the lion's share. Russia controls 7.5 per cent and the rest control 4.1 per cent. In Asia, the ownership of SWFs is even more concentrated, with the top three, China, Hong Kong and Singapore, controlling one quarter of global SWFs.

While the total size of SWFs may be small, the size of assets of some individual SWFs is large and some have the backing of unspecified large foreign exchange reserves, such as GIC. The size has become problematic for some who argue that these countries 'have not gained experience as major players in international finance' (Senn 2009, p. 9) and their lack of experience in managing large investment funds can create financial instability. Interestingly, this argument is made by some officials in Switzerland (Hildebrand 2007). With their large foreign reserves backing, it is argued, some of these SWFs have much greater leverage than private investment funds on financial markets.

The assumption is that these SWFs could use national foreign reserves at their disposal. In discussing SWFs, the US Treasury excludes those government investment vehicles funded by foreign exchange assets managed by monetary authorities (the Central Bank and reserves-related functions of the Finance Ministry). If the definition of a SWF provided by the IMF and US Treasury excludes national foreign reserves, it needs to be applied across all countries. It is important to understand the difference among SWFs in terms of the level of traditional foreign exchange reserves (Beck and Fidora 2008). Some countries, such as UAE, Norway, Kuwait and Singapore, have been accumulating foreign assets in SWFs for many years and consequently hold relatively moderate levels of foreign exchange reserves. In contrast, other countries, especially China and Russia, have only recently accumulated sizeable holdings of foreign exchange reserves. SWFs have been created with relatively modest levels of assets under their management (for example, CIC has assets of US$200 billion out of the country's US$1.3 trillion foreign reserves). Would this difference between these SWFs in terms of a country's foreign exchange reserves affect their investment strategies and behaviour in global finance? How can SWFs tap into the foreign reserves in their investment? These are questions demanding investigation rather than being taken for granted. The third concern about SWFs is their identity or, more precisely, public ownership. This characteristic is shared by a host of other entities as well – funds held and managed by central banks, sovereign stabilisation funds, public pension funds, government investment corporations, sovereign saving funds or even state-owned corporations whose capital and profits are managed to generate wealth. Many of these funds have existed in developed as well as developing countries for a long time and have seldom generated major controversies.

The debate over, and scrutiny of, SWFs started in 2007 when they started acquiring large stakes in Western companies. What makes SWFs different from other institutional investors? One distinction is that SWFs normally have no or only limited liabilities and this allows their managers to pursue long-term investment strategies and have a higher risk tolerance and higher expected returns than traditional official reserve managers (Beck and Fidora 2008). The literature on investment has long argued that short-term investment creates financial instability and contagious effects (Strange 1998; Tirole 2002; Byrant 2003; Eichengreen 2003). Why would the long-established argument not be applicable to SWFs?

The public ownership of SWFs is a concern because, it is argued, so long as governments own these investment vehicles, they cannot be managed independently free from political influence; the government could and would use SWFs to achieve its desired macroeconomic, political or strategic objectives. Those who have raised such concerns often do not distinguish between investment made by SWFs and that made by state-owned corporations, as discussed by Lawrence Summers in 2007:

> In early 2007, government-controlled Chinese entities took the largest external stake (albeit non-voting) in Blackstone, a big private equity group that, indirectly through its holdings, is one of the largest employers in the US. The government of Qatar is seeking to gain control of J. Sainsbury, one of Britain's largest supermarket chains. Gazprom, a Russian conglomerate, in effect controlled by the Kremlin, has strategic interests in the energy sectors of a number of countries and even a stake in Airbus. Entities controlled by the government of China and Singapore are offering to take a substantial stake in Barclays, giving it more heft in its effort to pull off the world's largest banking merger, with ABN Amro.
>
> (Summers 2007)

In 2008, French President Nicolas Sarkozy made the point more explicitly, calling non-OECD SWFs 'predators' of Western companies: 'I will not be the French president who wakes up in 6 months' time to see that French industrial groups have passed into other hands', he remarked. Why would the identity of the investor make any difference? For more than three decades, developing countries were urged to privatise state-owned assets, paying little attention to the identity of the buyer, who in some cases was even a foreign government. EdF could go out and purchase utility companies around the world, especially in the developing countries because 'it seemed permissible for a foreign government to own a country's assets, but not the country's own government', and definitely not in a reverse situation when government-owned funds go out and purchase companies in developed countries (Commission of Experts 2009, p. 60).

Should anyone care about ownership by government-controlled entities? For many, ownership is a concern because governments behave differently from private investors. 'State capitalism' preferred by some non-OECD countries is in direct contrast to 'market capitalism' (Goodman and Story 2008). In a market capitalist system, even though private investment vehicles, including hedge funds and private equity companies, have demonstrated higher leverage on the market and shorter investment horizons compared with SWFs, and even though their potential systematic effects are much greater, the serious regulatory debate is still quite a distance away, as Simon Johnson at IMF explained: 'The consensus so far is that while hedge funds deserve considerably greater scrutiny, there are advantages for the allocation of global capital flows if this sector continues to have a relatively light direct regulatory burden' (Johnson 2007, pp. 56–7).

Government ownership is a concern because in a state-capitalist system 'the country is the unit whose value is to be maximised, with a corresponding increase in the role of the national government as a direct participant in and coordinator of the effort' (Gilson and Milhaupt 2008, p. 1346). When SWFs are owned and managed by a government which is not 'like us', many in the market-capital system will automatically assume that the government will not behave in the same way as private investors; it will use its SWFs to achieve overt and covert political and strategic objectives. This raises 'national security risks and the potential for strategically motivated investments' (Cognato 2008, p. 25). For example, if countries with SWFs decide not to finance the US deficit by purchasing government bonds or treasury bills but engage in more aggressive investment for higher rates of returns, how would this affect the dollar position as global currency? Furthermore, according to Morgan Stanley, for some countries, 'assets that promise solid financial returns may not be as interesting as those that embody technology and techniques that cannot easily be "home-grown" or imitated' (3 May 2007, p. 3).

When resource companies in Australia and Canada, or the banking industry in Britain and Switzerland, high-tech companies and 'national champions' in France or the USA become targets of SWF investments, would these investments lead to cross-border nationalisation (Hildebrand 2007; Summers 2007)? If a government can decide to invest in a more aggressive way to seek higher returns, it could also withhold its investment when it is badly needed in the host country, as Benjamin Cohen argues SWFs can refuse to invest in some Western companies when funds are most needed, 'reinforcing rather than resisting market fluctuations' (Cohen 2009, p. 7). Then the question is: would this behaviour be any different from other types of investors, public and private? Is it government ownership that presents the risk to the host country or flows of investment per se?

The fourth concern about SWFs is their transparency. 'We just do not know much about them, their objectives and investment operations', many have claimed. Even if some of these non-OECD SWFs have stated their investment objectives, few in developed countries believe them. Yet, the complicated and entangled relationship of some SWFs and the domestic banking system is a concern. Studies of SWFs tend to correlate transparency with democracy – that is, when SWF-holding countries are operational democracies they are regarded as transparent. Since two thirds of SWFs are in the hands of non-OECD countries and all are categorised as 'flawed democracies' or 'authoritarian regimes', by definition their SWFs are not transparent and therefore are the source of instability for global financial markets.

Transparency is a question for examination also because SWFs that adopt similar investment strategies may differ fundamentally in terms of transparency. It 'varies even within funds controlled by the same sovereign' (Gilson and Milhaupt 2008, p. 1355). If the argument is that the more transparent SWFs are, the more likely their investment creates stability, then we will have to examine each SWF individually: how it is organised, operated and managed and what strategies each adopts in achieving its designed objectives.

The intense debate over transparency highlights several issues. First, claims for increased transparency have to be balanced against the legitimate business interests of investors. There are limits to how much information investors should disclose. Second, transparency has to be reciprocal. Recipient governments need to make explicit their policies on foreign investment without any discrimination against any specific countries or certain investment vehicles. Third, a sensible management of SWF assets in well-functioning financial markets is in everyone's interest. The more transparent the management of these assets, the more difficult it is for any party to misuse them. More importantly, there is the issue of accountability – how can a sovereign wealth fund maintain its politically correct 'arm's-length' relationship with its owner (the government) while making sure its management team does everything possible to protect and enhance the value of its shareholding while being accountable to both the government and the public? Would the new transparency rules help calm public concern that their country would not be gobbled up by a 'rampaging, politically-inspired' SWF? The answer might not be positive for those who argue that the Western-style 'code of practices' or regulation has no purchase in those countries where the rule of law does not exist.

Rules for the global economy

Given that the owner of SWFs is the government and that all governments have political interests beyond the economic domain, it is inevitable for the government of the countries that are targeted by SWFs for investment to demand new rules, regulations and even restrictions. To achieve the 'great tradeoffs' between 'the openness of capital markets and the legitimate national security concerns of individual countries' (Cohen 2009, pp. 713–4), countries have several instruments at their disposal. They can adopt unilateral, bilateral or multilateral measures. For the SWF-holding countries, there is little choice but to comply, partly because OECD countries offer the best markets for their investment, partly because historically they are rule-takers rather than rule-makers, and partly because their exports from which the assets of their SWFs are generated depend on OECD markets.

In responding to concerns about SWFs, several OECD countries have strengthened their existing rules on regulating foreign investment. In the USA, for example, Section 721 of the Defence Protection Act authorises the President to suspend or prohibit mergers, acquisitions or takeovers that could result in foreign control of a US business if the transaction threatens to impair national security. The President then delegated his Section 721 authority to review foreign investment transactions in the USA to an interagency body, the Commission of Foreign

Investment in the United States (CFIUS). In July 2007, at the peak of the debate on SWFs, the US government enacted the Foreign Investment and National Security Act (FINSA), which requires that foreign government-controlled transactions, including investments by SWFs, be reviewed by CFIUS with an additional 45-day investigation beyond the initial 30-day review (GAO 2008, p. 10). In 2009, the Australian government revised and updated its Foreign Acquisitions and Takeover Act 1975. The new policy streamlined some of the reviews carried out by the Foreign Investment Review Board (FIRB) but it re-emphasises that 'The Government determines what is "contrary to the national interest" by having regard to the widely held community concerns of Australians' (Treasury 2009, p. 1).

While wanting SWFs to invest in its collapsing financial institutions and becoming increasingly impatient with multilateral institutions, the US government, as it has been doing for the past six decades or so, engaged in bilateral negotiations with Singapore and Dubai and settled on a set of principles for SWFs (Treasury 2008). What is remarkable is that these principles are no different, and have not advanced, from the existing multilateral, bilateral and domestic regulations on foreign investment. On the multilateral level, the recipient countries of SWFs have decided it is necessary to 'strengthen' the rules to regulate the new phenomenon through existing institutions. At the G-7 Finance Ministers meeting in October 2007, ministers discussed SWFs for the first time and agreed on a communiqué that the IMF, World Bank and OECD should explore best practices for SWFs in key areas such as institutional structure, risk management, transparency and accountability. The OECD is held to be a proper place to set up the new rules because its members are the recent targets of SWF investment. As it is a rich country club, most SWF-holding countries do not have a say in this institution. Others propose the IMF as the appropriate institution to deal with the issue but the legitimacy and relevance of the IMF are in serious question because the rules of the game have been implemented for different countries in different ways by the institution (Linn and Kharas 2008). Some even argue that the World Trade Organisation (WTO) should be the place where the SWF-holding countries and the targeted countries could strike a bargain without having to fundamentally reform the existing multilateral institutions or even the rules (Mattoo and Subramanian 2008).

The pressure to force some SWF-holding countries into bilateral negotiations and the efforts to make rules at multilateral negotiation tables without participation of many SWF-holding countries has brought large

Table 1.3   Total Announced Cross-Border SWF Activity (2000–08)

Year	2000	2001	2002	2003	2004	2005	2006	2007	2008
No. of deals	6	4	3	7	21	32	37	41	29
US$ million	429	52	232	1087	5160	8188	18 298	52 935	32 696

Source: GAO (2008), p. 35.

SWFs together. Between 30 April and 1 May 2008, 26 IMF member countries with SWFs (Table 1.3) formed the IWG. They have subsequently met on three occasions to 'identify and draft a set of generally accepted principles and practices (GAPP) that properly reflects their investment practices and objectives' (IWG 2008, p. 1). The IWG was assisted by the IMF that has acknowledged that SWFs have been playing a positive and 'shock-absorbing role' in international financial markets. The 26 members of IWG acknowledged that new rules were needed so that they would not be discriminated against and in return, they would guarantee the national security and financial stability of the recipient countries. The 'great tradeoff' prescribed by Professor Benjamin J. Cohen was carried out not by recipient countries, as initially suggested, but by the IWG of SWFs.

IWG adopted the GAPP, also known as the 'Santiago Principles', in October 2008 by consensus. In April 2009, the IWG announced the creation of the International Forum of Sovereign Wealth Funds (hereafter the Forum) where they can exchange information about their investment strategies and operations and, more importantly, the changing policies of recipient countries.

To address the rising concerns, the GAPP highlights four objectives of SWFs:

1. To help maintain a stable global financial system and free flow of capital and investment;
2. To comply with all applicable regulatory and disclosure requirements in the countries in which they invest;
3. To invest on the basis of economic and financial risk and return-related considerations; and
4. To have in place a transparent and sound governance structure that provides for adequate operational controls, risk management and accountability. (IWG 2008, p. 4)

By accepting these principles, members of the IWG have committed to make a series of specific public disclosures, including information on the asset allocation, benchmarks, rates of return over appropriate historical periods consistent with investment horizons and their investment policies and the general approach of their risk management frameworks. Many have raised doubts about the real value of GAPP given that these principles are broadly defined and that their implementation would be voluntary. To the members of the IWG, however, the GAPP is a voluntary and non-binding agreement because there is no enforcement agency. Indeed, the principles were accepted by consensus not by states but by a group of sovereign wealth funds. They may be owned by governments, but they are not governments and therefore they cannot negotiate international treaties.

Meanwhile, with the adoption of the Santiago Principles, the public debate about associated concerns of SWFs seems to have died down. After temporary heavy losses in 2007–08 because of the global financial crisis, some of the SWFs have returned to the world financial markets and expanded their investment while other SWF-holding countries are shoring up the assets of their investment instruments. Some observers have argued that with the slowdown of trade, and especially with the decline of the trade deficit in the USA, the issue of SWFs will soon disappear. Yet, so long as 'the United States is sending $800 million every single day of the week in exchange for full tanks of their oil' (Biden 2008, p. 1), commodity-exporting countries will have to continue putting revenues away as a way to prevent the 'Dutch Disease' from occurring in their economies, and to compete with the high savings rates and export-oriented economies among Asian developing countries. SWFs are the by-products of this global financial imbalance and neither the global financial crisis nor the acceptance of the GAPP has addressed this issue. SWFs nonetheless have led to the discussion of some important issues concerning international political economy – the role of the state and markets, and the place of saving in an economy.

A new dawn?

There is an irony about the rising concerns about SWFs: the timing. 2008 witnessed serious fears that SWFs, especially those from non-OECD countries, would be used for 'industrial espionage or geopolitical threats' and to 'promote strategic objectives'. These fears were further stirred up by the media, think tanks and even some academics: 'Do we want the communists to own the banks, or the terrorists', asked by CNBC TV anchor Jim Cramer on 18 January 2008. Politicians and governments in these countries demanded that these SWFs be subject to 'transparent' rules agreed upon bilaterally and through multilateral institutions, the IMF and OECD in particular. Tell us, demanded Joe Biden, still a senator at the time, 'where is the money coming from? Who controls it? Where is it going?' (Biden 2008, p. 2). Less than 2 months later, the worst financial crisis since the Great Depression erupted with the collapse of the Lehman Brothers, which raised similar questions: how could the banking and financial system bring down the whole economy? Why were the rules and regulation inadequate to prevent the crisis? More importantly, both the lenders and borrowers in rich countries demanded that the government take actions to rescue the economy and rethink their rules and laws on transparency and regulation. 'SWFs were (legitimately) *"puzzled that the standards and transparency requirements that others advocate for them go far beyond anything that has been envisaged for the highly leveraged hedge funds and private equity communities in industrial countries"* ' (Avendano and Santiso 2009, p. 9). Even SWFs from well-established democracies, Australia and Norway, were asking about the fuss over their operation and investment, and why they were singled out. Is it their size, speed of growth, targets of their investment, or their ownership?

According to the contributors of this volume, domestic politics in each country drove the creation and operation of SWFs: in Russia, for example, the finance minister was behind the initiative and the policy was never popular because many politicians wanted to see the money invested more aggressively. In China, the central bank and the Ministry of Finance were fighting over the control of the rapidly accumulating foreign reserves and the CIC was created as a way to manage the notorious Chinese bureaucratic infighting. Nonetheless, their existence had great impacts on world politics. Policymakers in both SWF-holding countries and those in which they made their investment could not simply ignore the anxiety in the body politic, no matter how unjustified. While the Santiago Principles were worked out as a collective response of the SWFs, some of them (especially the CIC) that triggered the most concerns were looking for Western fund managers to manage part of their funds as a way to deflect political attention and to learn from Wall Street how to manage large portfolios.

SWFs are here to stay: they have confirmed their place in world financial markets as institutional investors and there has been an increasing recognition that there was 'little evidence that, even from the Middle East and so on, people have actually used the SWFs in order to advance any real strategic political objectives' (Bhagwati 2008, p. 7). Instead, they behaved not much differently from other public and private institutional investors, such as pension or mutual funds in their investment decisions, except that they are accountable to a collective entity – the state. Their public nature makes them more conservative and much less speculative in making investment decisions in global financial markets.

The global financial crisis has confirmed the failure of the neoconservative model that promotes deregulation, reduced oversight, privatisation and consolidation of market power. The crisis also represents a failure of a system emphasising self-supervision of markets with greater reliance on 'personal responsibilities'. Finally, the crisis also shows that countries with large external deficits and large capital inflows suffered much more than those with savings (Bergsten 2009). Few have openly challenged the fundamentals of the capitalist market system and few are willing to suggest a greater role for the state in ensuring its smooth operation. Yet, governments have been busy in rescuing banks and financial institutions, creating jobs with their stimulus packages, intervening in investment and assisting trade flows.

The visible hand of the state has not been this apparent for some time. The multilateral financial institutions, the IMF and the World Bank, for example, seem to have shifted gear in promoting certain active roles of the state and the 'emerging economies' are quick in picking up the messages. Responding to the suggestion of the IMF that SWFs can be an effective instrument to help resources-rich countries save for a rainy day and future generations (Das et al. 2009), some emerging economies including Angola, Brazil, Indonesia, Malaysia, Mongolia, Nigeria and Saudi Arabia have quickly created or expanded this type of structure for managing their national wealth. The debate remains open in others, such as Algeria and India.

Meanwhile, the IMF is reconsidering its long-held position against capital controls. In 1997, during the Asian financial crisis, it even tried to amend its articles of agreement to allow the IMF explicitly to promote capital account liberalisation. It and some rich countries were at odds with the government in Malaysia at the time over the issue of capital controls. The economists at the IMF have long argued that capital controls are costly because they distort resource allocation and are not effective because they can be easily evaded (it is questionable whether capital controls can be both ineffective and distorting). Currently, some economists at the IMF are suggesting that capital controls are sometimes 'justified as part of the policy toolkit' for an economy seeking to deal with surging inflows. They argue that countries with a larger overall stock of debt had bigger credit booms and suffered bigger collapses during the recent financial crisis; so did countries with large foreign direct investment in the financial sector. Countries with capital controls in place suffered much less of a set-back (Ostry et al. 2010).

While economists can debate the economic validities of the argument, the simple fact of the IMF's reconsideration of capital controls suggests that it is re-evaluating the role of the 'state' in the market. It is an exaggeration to argue that 'state capitalism' – 'a system in which the state functions as the leading economic actor and uses markets primarily for political gains' – is replacing 'free-market capitalism' (Bremmer 2009, p. 41). Governments worldwide, however, are rethinking their roles and functions to ensure the smooth operation of a market system. It is not yet clear whether hybrid actors such as SWFs that blur the line between the public and the private can be the recipe for dealing with both the mismanagement of the whole economy and widespread disenchantment with markets in general (Bootle 2009).

The outline of this book

The next five chapters analyse the sovereign wealth funds from five non-OECD countries: China, Singapore, Kuwait, UAE and Russia. Both Singapore and Kuwait see themselves as 'democratic' countries and both have a strong rule of law. China and Russia are occasionally grouped together because both are transition economies. Russian politics remain 'strong-man' politics while China is increasingly known for its bickering bureaucracies. It is the 'political contestation over national policymaking' that provides the special environment for the emergence of the China Investment Corporation. The UAE hosts the world's largest SWF, Abu Dhabi International Authority and Corporation, and along with others, 'its SWFs have proven to be useful, both in currency stabilisation, investment ties throughout the Muslim world' and they 'play a critical role in the *rentier* state system, along with the intrinsic bargains associated with them', argues Joseph A. Kéchichian in Chapter 5.

Norway and Australia have resource-based economies and their SWFs are frequently quoted as examples of transparency. Both the Government Pension Fund in Norway and the Future Fund in Australia were created because of long-term economic considerations, but the decision to create them is also 'a politically savvy response to the circumstances confronting' the government, as Richard Eccleston points out in Chapter 8. Party politics in Norway was at the core of this debate on 'spending today' or 'saving for the future', and politics also explains the principles of their operation: promoting 'ethical obligations' through exercises of ownership rights has to be balanced with the achievement of long-term financial returns.

One consistent argument made by the contributors of these individual SWFs is that they were created predominantly because of domestic politics, whether being bureaucratic contestation as seen in China, or political party competition in Australia or ideological debates as seen in Norway. Their operation consequently must be understood in this contest, even though these large SWFs and their investment may have significant impact on their targeted companies or countries.

The last section of the book deals with the broader implications of SWFs. Chapter 11 by Jørgen Ørstrøm Møller and Chapter 12 by Gawdat Bahgat discuss the responses to SWFs in the USA and among EU countries. Understanding that the 27 EU countries cannot possibly adopt one position, Jørgen Ørstrøm Møller emphasises that even if SWF investments are not necessarily a real threat to European or US economies, it is 'the psychological barrier in acquiescing with the change of power in the global economy' that has created tension. This is the topic of Chapter 13 by Xu Yi-chong on global disequilibria. Has the power really shifted from the West to the East? No, but there are real issues in terms of the patterns of their economic performance. Neither side – those who have occupied the dominant position and have been writing the rules of the game for the international political economy and those who are historically rule-takers – is fully willing to acknowledge the shift and take responsibility to build a new architecture of an international financial system that can accommodate the interests of old and new players. SWFs, their emergence and performance provide only a window for us to understand broader international political economy.

Note

1. The term 'Dutch Disease' originated in the Netherlands during the 1960s when revenues generated by natural gas discovery led to an appreciation of the national currency and to a sharp decline in the competitiveness of the non-booming tradable sector. The revenue windfall served to increase imports to the determent of national production, provoking a sharp decline in economic growth. The resources boom attracts scarce inputs to production such as labour and capital away from other sectors, thus creating a 'triple-whammy' impact on the national economy. This economic paradox has since been recognised as a situation in which a large inflow of foreign currency – whether it originates from a sharp surge in natural resource prices, or from foreign assistance or foreign investment – adversely affects the performance of the non-booming sectors of an economy, and in particular, the non-booming tradable sector (De Silva 1994).

References

Avendano, Rolando and Javier Santiso (2009), 'Are Sovereign Wealth Funds' Investments Politically Biased? A Comparison with Mutual Funds', OECD Development Centre, Working Paper No. 283, DEV/DOC(2009)8, December.

Bahgat, Gawdat (2008), 'Sovereign Wealth Funds: Danger and Opportunities', *International Affairs*, 84(6), pp. 1189–1204.

Beck, Roland and Michael Fidora (2008), 'The Impact of Sovereign Wealth Funds on Global Financial Markets', European Central Bank, Occasional Paper Series, No. 91, July.

Bergsten, C. Fred (2009), 'The Dollar and the Deficits: How Washington Can Prevent the Next Crisis', *Foreign Affairs*, 88(6), pp. 20–38.

Bhagwati, Jagdish (2008), 'Statement on Sovereign Wealth Funds: Foreign Policy Consequences in an Era of New Money', hearing before the Committee on Foreign Relations, US Senate, 110th Congress, 11 June.

Biden, Joseph (2008), 'Opening Statement on Sovereign Wealth Funds: Foreign Policy Consequences in an Era of New Money', hearing before the Committee on Foreign Relations, US Senate, 110th Congress, 11 June.

Blundell-Wignall, Adrian, Yu Wei Hu and Juan Yermo (2008), 'Sovereign Wealth and Pension Fund Issues', *OECD Financial Markets Trends*, pp. 117–32.

Bootle, Roger (2009), 'Redrawing: Rethinking the Role of the State and Markets', *Finance and Development*, March, pp. 34–5.

Bremmer, Ian (2009), 'State Capitalism Comes to Age: The End of the Free Market?' *Foreign Affairs*, 88(3), pp. 40–55.

Chan-Lau, Jorge A. (2004), 'Pension Funds and Emerging Markets', IMF Working Paper, WP/04/181.

Cognato, Michael H. (2009), 'Understanding China's New Sovereign Wealth Fund', *NBR Analysis*, 19(1), pp. 9–36.

Das, Udaibir S., Yinquiu Lu, Christian Mulder and Amadou Sy (2009), 'Setting up a Sovereign Wealth Fund: Some Policy and Operational Considerations', IMF Working Paper, WP/09/179, August.

de Silva, K. Migara (1994), 'The Political Economy of Windfalls, the "Dutch Disease" – Theory and Evidence', John M. Olin School of Business Discussion Paper, Saint Louis: John M. Olin School of Business.

GAO (US Government Accounting Office) (2008), 'Sovereign Wealth Funds: Publicly Available Data on Sizes and Investments for Some Funds are Limited', GAO-08-946, September.

Gieve, John (2008), 'Sovereign Wealth Funds and Global Imbalances', speech presented at the Sovereign Wealth Management Conference, London, 14 February.

Gilson, Ronald and Curtis J. Mihaupt (2008), 'Sovereign Wealth Funds and Corporate Governance: A Minimalist Response to the New Mercantilism', *Stanford Law Review*, 60(5), pp. 1345–69.

Halliday, Fred (2008), 'Sovereign Wealth Funds: Power vs. Principle', *Open Democracy*, 5 March, available at http://www.opendemocracy.net.

Hildebrand, P. (2007), 'The Challenge of Sovereign Wealth Funds', Central Bank articles and speeches, *BIS Review*, 150/2007.

International Monetary Fund (2008), *Sovereign Wealth Fund – A Work Agenda*, 29 February.

IWG (International Working Group of Sovereign Wealth Funds) (2008), 'Sovereign Wealth Funds: Generally Accepted Principles and Practices: Santiago Principles', October.

Johnson, Simon (2007), 'The Rise of Sovereign Wealth Funds', *Finance and Development*, 44(3), pp. 56–7.

Linn, Johannes F. and Homi Kharas (2008), 'Hypocrisy in Financial Crisis Response: East Asia 1998 and the USA 2008', Brookings Institution, April.

Lyons, Gerard (2008), 'Two Hot Topics: Sovereign Wealth Funds and China', Standard Chartered, 11 April.

Ostry, Jonthan, Atish R. Ghosh, Karl Habermeier, Marcos Chamon, Mahvash S. Qureshi and Dennis B.S. Reinhardt (2010), 'Capital Flows: The Role of Controls', IMF Staff Position Note, SPN/10/04, 19 February.

Mattoo, Aaditya and Arvind Subramanian (2008), 'Currency Undervaluation and Sovereign Wealth Funds: A New Role for the World Trade Organisation', Working Paper Series, WP 08-2, Peterson Institute for International Economics.

Morgan Stanley (2007), 'How big could sovereign funds be by 2015?' *Morgan Stanley Research*, 3 May, 2–3.

Plender, John (2007), 'An Unseen Risk in Sovereign Funds', *Financial Times*, 21 June.

Rozanov, Andrew (2009), 'What is "Sovereign Wealth" Anyway'?, paper presented at the Sovereign Wealth Funds: Governance and Regulation Conference, National University of Singapore, 9–11 September.

Senn, Myriam (2009), 'Sovereign Wealth Funds as a Public-Private Challenge For Institutional Governance', paper presented at the Sovereign Wealth Funds: Governance and Regulation Conference, National University of Singapore, 9–11 September.

Slawotsy, Joel (2009), 'Sovereign Wealth funds as Emerging Financial Superpowers: How US Regulators Should Respond', *Georgetown Journal of International Law*, 40(4), pp. 1239–69.

Strange, Susan (1998), *Mad Money: When Markets Outgrows Governments*. Ann Arbour, MI: University of Michigan Press.

Summers, Lawrence (2007), 'Funds that Shake Capitalist Logic', *Financial Times*, 29 July, available at http://www.ft.com/cms/s/2/bb8f50b8-3dcc-11dc-8f6a-0000779fd2ac.html.

Treasury, US (2008), 'Treasury Reaches Agreement on Principles for Sovereign Wealth Fund Investment with Singapore and Abu Dhabi', 20 March, available at http://www.treas.gov/press/releases/hp881.htm.

Treasury, Australian Government (2009), 'Australia's Foreign Investment Policy', September, available at http://www.firb.gov.au/content/_downloads/Australia's_Foreign_Investment_Policy_September_2009_v2.pdf.

Weiss, Martin A. (2009), 'Sovereign Wealth Funds: Background and Policy Issues for Congress', Congressional Research Services, RL34336, 9 January.

2
Contributing to a Harmonious Society: China's Sovereign Wealth Fund

Leong H. Liew and Liping He

Introduction

This chapter[1] examines key factors that led to the establishment and subsequent organisation of one of the world's largest sovereign wealth funds: the China Investment Corporation (CIC), which began operating in September 2007 after an earlier incarnation as a state-owned commercial vehicle, Huijin. In principle, national governments establish sovereign wealth funds (SWFs) to recycle the country's foreign exchange reserves. In China's case, establishment of the CIC was not simply to maximise return from foreign exchange reserves but was also with an eye to the imperative of maintaining a 'harmonious society' (*hexie shehui*).

Establishment of the CIC must be understood, of course, in the context of China's transition from a planned economy to a mixed economy, with introduction of the market and the space for political contestation that this process has opened. Deng Xiaoping, who steered this transition from its takeoff in 1978, likened the process to 'feeling the stones as one crosses the river'. As the transition continues, Chinese political leaders are unsure of the final form of institutions,[2] whose architecture is contestable and yet to be bedded down. Fragmented political authority provides ample scope for bureaucratic organisations to contest policy, compete for long-term influence and power, and thus sculpture the final form of institutions as they take shape in the process.

We see this in the establishment of China's sovereign wealth fund, which itself serves as a guide to the evolution of reform in post-Mao China. The CIC as it stands today is largely a product of the ongoing competition between two of China's key policymaking bodies over which one of them should manage and control the country's sovereign wealth. The contest over the CIC, between China's central bank, the People's Bank of China (PBC) and the Ministry of Finance (MOF), is derivative of the larger battle between them for influence over broad economic policy and control of the country's financial assets. This contest makes it clear that rather than one omnipotent rational actor guiding national development, multiple actors with conflicting objectives determine the shape of China's new national organisations. Overall we see how, in creating space for political contestation over national policymaking, reform has created an environment that must accommodate political as well as economic imperatives; the logic of free market economics must be tempered with the vital need for social and political stability, which requires astute political intervention. Thus, market economics, political pragmatism and the tensions between them create both the context and the parameters for China's transition – to a mixed economy and a stable, 'harmonious society' – as the evolution of China's SWF illustrates clearly.

Sowing the seeds of competition over China's SWF

The huge increases in international trade that are intrinsic to the opening of the Chinese economy since China embarked on its post-Mao reform have produced substantial foreign exchange reserves. Perhaps also inevitably, the growing reserves have inspired struggle within the Chinese bureaucracy over how to manage and control the reserves through the country's actual or de facto sovereign wealth fund, and particularly by whom. Competition between China's key economic policymaking organisations – PBC and MOF – has intensified from the late 1970s, when Deng Xiaoping-era reform opened the political space for contest over influence and implicit rankings within the bureaucratic hierarchy. Before reform, foreign exchange reserves were extremely limited. Under central planning in the Mao period, monetary policy was subservient to the plan. PBC was a state-owned commercial bank that took on the very limited functions of a central bank in a planned economy and did not have ministry status. It was subordinate to MOF, which had ownership rights over all the state-owned commercial banks (SOCBs). PBC was absorbed by MOF as one of its departments during the Cultural Revolution and was granted independence from MOF only from 1 January 1978. PBC continued to act as both a commercial and central bank until 1983, when it was officially designated as China's central bank and granted ministry status.

The status of PBC was elevated considerably during the premiership of Zhu Rongji, who was previously PBC governor. He sought to reform China's banking sector to make it better equipped to serve the modern market economy that China's leaders had decided to create. Premier Zhu's mission to reform the banking sector was given urgent impetus in 1998 by the Asian financial crisis (AFC), which demonstrated the dangers that a weak financial system could pose to a national economy. His concerted effort to reform the banking sector gave PBC an opportunity to raise its status even further in the country's bureaucratic hierarchy at the expense of MOF. The relationship between PBC and MOF over the SOCBs was complicated, and exacerbated the competition among them. PBC as a central bank was supposed to regulate and supervise the SOCBs, but MOF was also the SOCBs' 'owner'.[3]

In 1998, almost a decade before establishment of CIC, seeds for the competition over control of China's SWF were already planted. Banks were undercapitalised and had serious problems with non-performing loans (NPLs). That year PBC estimated the share of NPLs of SOCBs at 20 per cent (Adams et al. 1998, p. 152), but some non-official estimates were as high as 40 per cent, creating a serious threat of insolvency among the major banks. Loss-making state-owned enterprises (SOEs) were the major contributors to the large number of NPLs and as of October 1997, 46 per cent of SOEs were in the red (Lin 1998, p. 176). Reforming SOEs therefore could not be divorced in the long term from banking reform. NPLs became a particularly serious problem in 1992, when bank loans replaced direct government subsidies to assist loss-making SOEs. The rationale behind the switch was that unlike direct government subsidies, bank loans were, in theory at least, only to tide over temporary enterprise difficulties and they had to be repaid. But in reality, many bank loans issued to SOEs were not repaid and as such became de facto subsidies. In this way, the switch from fiscal subsidies to bank loans paved the way for PBC to exert direct influence over the SOCBs, over which MOF enjoyed ownership rights.

Direct fiscal subsidies to SOEs from 1994 to 1997 accounted for about 60 per cent of government budget deficits (Table 2.1). The subsidies as a proportion of deficits fell after 1997, but that was largely due to the massive fiscal stimulus during the AFC. Fiscal support to SOEs was not reduced, and additional support was provided to them in the form of bank loans, largely from SOCBs. Because MOF oversaw a significant increase in the fiscal deficit as a result of the AFC, it was constrained from bearing the major financial burden of recapitalising the banks and cleansing their balance sheets of NPLs, even though it was the sole

Table 2.1   Government Budget Deficits and SOE Subsidies

Year	100 million yuan			Percentage	
	Subsidies to loss-making enterprises	Deficit	GDP	Subsidies/ deficits	Deficits/ GDP
1994	−66.22	−574.52	48197.9	63.7	−1.2
1995	−327.77	−581.52	60793.7	56.4	−1.0
1996	−337.40	−529.56	71176.6	63.7	−0.7
1997	−368.49	−582.42	78793.0	63.3	−0.7
1998	−333.49	−922.23	84402.3	36.2	−1.1
1999	−290.03	−1743.59	89677.1	16.6	−1.9
2000	−278.78	−2491.27	99214.6	11.2	−2.5
2001	−300.04	−2516.54	109655.2	11.9	−2.3
2002	−259.60	−3149.51	120332.7	8.2	−2.6
2003	−226.38	−2934.70	135822.8	7.7	−2.2
2004	−217.93	−2090.42	159878.3	10.4	−1.3
2005	−193.26	−2280.99	183084.8	8.5	−1.2

Source: NBS (2006).

'owner' of the banks. MOF was well aware that the task of resolving the issue of NPLs was also constrained inevitably by the demand of political leaders for a soft and gentle approach to SOE reform. Hence, the task of recapitalising the banks went to PBC rather than to MOF.

Emergence of PBC and kudos at a price

The first step in China's banking reform was recapitalisation of the major SOCBs to increase their seriously undercapitalised capital base so as to raise their capital-adequacy ratios to the Bank for International Settlements (BIS) benchmark of 8 per cent. In August 1998, the capital base of the four major SOCBs[4] – Bank of China (BOC), China Construction Bank (CCB), Industrial and Commercial Bank of China (ICBC) and the Agricultural Bank of China (ABC) – was more than doubled. PBC lowered the statutory reserve requirement (SRR) ratio from 13 to 9 per cent to free up liquidity to the banks for them to purchase ¥270 billion (US$32.5 billion) of bonds from MOF, which then injected proceeds from the sale of the bonds into the banks as equity (Mo 1999, pp. 93–4).

The annual 7.2 per cent coupon rate of the bonds (Lau 1999, p. 73) earned MOF an additional ¥19.4 billion (US$2.3 billion) a year on top of the expected larger dividends from its increased equity in the banks.

Moreover, the capital injection allowed the banks to pay off ¥270 billion of the liabilities they owed to PBC and saved the banks about ¥4 to ¥5 billion (US$481 to US$602 million) in interest costs. Hence, by lowering the SRR ratio, PBC helped to increase the capital base of the banks and to bring their capital adequacy ratios closer to the BIS benchmark. This move also increased the banks' combined, and therefore MOF's, annual income by about ¥24 billion (US$3 billion). This amount almost equalled the estimated ¥27 billion (US$3.2 billion) combined 1997 profit of all the state-owned banks (Mo 1999, p. 94).

MOF's income would have increased even more had PBC not increased the gap between the interest rate of the banks' reserve deposits and the higher interest rate that the banks charged their customers, in a move to compensate for the lower SRR ratio. In 1998, the banks were paid on their reserve deposits annual rates of between 2.7 per cent and 3.42 per cent below what they could charge their customers (ACFB 1999, pp. 408–10). Although PBC earned kudos from its contribution to banks' recapitalisation through a swap of SRR deposits for MOF bonds and a swap of liabilities owed to PBC for MOF equity, in balance-sheet terms MOF was the clear beneficiary at the expense of PBC.

The next step in banking reform was to clean NPLs from the balance sheets of the four SOCBs. In 1999, NPLs worth ¥1.4 trillion (US$173 billion) were transferred at par value from the banks to four state-owned asset management companies (AMCs), in exchange for AMCs' bonds (55 per cent) and AMCs taking over some of the debt owed by the banks to PBC (45 per cent). Paralleling the debt–bond swap was a debt–equity swap scheme (*zhai zhuan gu*) that converted a portion of the SOEs' previous bank debt into AMC-held equity to prevent their bankruptcy. This was designed to give the SOEs time to restructure themselves into ongoing profitable business concerns, before repurchasing their equity stakes from the AMCs.

MOF as the AMC's only shareholder did not explicitly guarantee the AMCs' bonds and questions were raised over the risk and value of these bonds (Ma 2006, p. 15). The ambiguous MOF guarantee together with the transfer to the AMCs of the banks' liabilities owed to PBC once again benefited MOF at the expense of PBC, which saw its balance sheet weakened a second time. This time it was from uncertainty over whether the AMCs could successfully restructure the SOEs such that they would be able to repay their outstanding loans to PBC. Although MOF was the sole owner of the AMCs, it would not suffer loss if the AMCs failed and it did not honour the financial obligations on the AMC's bonds to PBC.

NPLs and the birth of China's SWF

Efforts at restructuring the SOEs' balance sheets exposed severe problems in SOEs that were previously hidden. It became increasingly clear to policymakers that they had vastly underestimated both the size of the banks' NPLs and the difficulty of reducing them. The banks' response to a directive from PBC to reduce their NPL ratios year-on-year highlights the difficulty the authorities faced. The directive gave the banks incentive to increase lending without necessarily reducing the value of their NPLs (Brehm 2008, p. 10). Recognising that the SOEs could not be restructured easily, the authorities concentrated on recapitalising the banks and left to the AMCs the responsibility for disposing of the NPLs. The NPLs were parked in the AMCs for them to dispose of gradually, without causing massive lay-offs and social discontent.

China's leaders were highly sensitive to the political dangers inherent in SOE reform. Scholars in China estimated that 30 per cent of workers in a total SOE workforce of around 100 million were surplus to requirement and could potentially be retrenched in any reform of the SOEs (Xia 1998, p. 46). Jiang Zemin, then Party leader, acknowledged at the 15th Party Congress in September 1997 that in SOE reform it was 'difficult to avoid laying off workers' (*zhigong xiagang shi nanyi bimian de*). Some workers would face a 'temporary period of difficulty' (*yibufen zhigong dailai zanshi de kunnan*), and he expressed fears that this would increase 'contradictions among the people' (*renmin neibu maodun mingxian zengduo*) (Jiang 1998, p. 2; Jiang 1999). The Party was particularly concerned over the numerous illegal organisations that were established to organise protests against SOE reform (Lai 1999, p. 54).

In the Party's view, business could continue as ever just as long as the AMCs did not aggressively dispose of the NPLs through either auctioning the debt to the public or internal restructuring of the SOEs. Business, however, could not continue as before. After a series of tough negotiations, the Chinese and US governments had reached agreement on conditions of China's entry into the World Trade Organisation (WTO), and on 11 December 2001, China was formally admitted into the WTO with US support. The Chinese government had agreed to lift restrictions on the entry of foreign banks into China and Chinese banks had to be strengthened quickly to meet this challenge. MOF was sole owner of the SOCBs, but could not recapitalise them on its own. The projected cost of cleansing the SOCBs of NPLs was not made public at that time, but research published later indicated that cost could be as much as 30 per cent of 2005 GDP (Ma 2006). PBC was not going to come on board and have its balance sheet weakened like before without any quid pro quo. Drastic action was required. The Third Plenum of the 16th Party Congress in October 2003 decided to restructure ownership of the banks. It established the Central Leading Group on Reforming the Shareholding of SOCBs (CLGRSS) under the late Huang Ju, who was deputy premier and vice-chairman of the Central Leading Group on Finance and Economics (CLGFE) in charge of banking and finance.

Past and current PBC officials dominated CLGRSS. PBC governor Zhou Xiaochuan headed the group's administrative office[5] and almost all other members except the finance minister, Jin Renqing, were past or current PBC officials. Hua Jianmin, the vice-chairman, was vice-mayor of Shanghai when Jiang Zemin brought him to Beijing to be deputy director of the CLGFE office and was not associated with either the MOF or PBC. But both Liu Mingkang, the chairman of the China Banking Regulatory Commission (CBRC), and Zhou were highly regarded and influential in China's economic policymaking circles relative to Jin, even though Jin was a full Central Committee member while they were only alternate members. The members of CLGRSS were clearly PBC's people. Hence, it was not a surprise when CLGRSS came up with a plan to restructure the banks that was favourable to PBC.

In December 2003 CLGRSS decided to make PBC a major shareholder of the SOCBs. However, before the plan could be executed, a shell company had to be established to bypass a Chinese law that prohibited PBC from owning any commercial banks. Such was the genesis of the Central Huijin Investment Corporation (*Zhongyang huijin touzi youxian gongsi*). Huijin was not the financial equivalent of the State-owned Assets Supervision and Administration Commission (SASAC), the administrative entity established to assume ownership rights of non-financial central SOEs.[6] Huijin is a corporation (*gongsi*) not a commission (*weiyuanhui*) that indicates ministry status. But unlike other central SOEs, it is a '*zhongyang*' corporation, which signifies it was not an 'independent' corporation, but one that was embedded within a central ministry. Huijin did not have its own offices and was located within the State Administration of Foreign Exchange (SAFE). In law, Huijin was an independent state-owned investment company; in reality it was a PBC-owned company, as SAFE (vice-ministry) is accountable to PBC (ministry). Its CEO was Guo Shuqing, who was concurrently a deputy governor of PBC and head of SAFE, and five of its seven directors and two of three members on its board of supervisors were from SAFE or PBC (Ming 2004, p. 3).

SAFE invested as initial registered capital in Huijin US$45 billion of foreign exchange reserves, which were then channelled as equity to

BOC and CCB. MOF then wrote down completely all its investments in BOC and CCB, thus making Huijin the sole owner of these banks. SAFE transferred additional foreign exchange reserves to Huijin as equity and a year later Huijin bought an 8 per cent stake (US$3 billion) in the Bank of Commerce, followed in 2005 by a US$15 billion investment in another of the four SOCBs, the Industrial and Commercial Bank of China (ICBC), making it an equal shareholder with MOF. The recapitalisation of these banks through Huijin therefore granted increased influence over the banking sector to PBC at MOF's expense.

While there is no single definition of what constitutes a sovereign wealth fund, there is broad agreement that such funds have these features: they consist of assets controlled and managed by sovereign governments; they are commonly funded by foreign exchange reserves, resource revenue or general taxation; they can be invested domestically; and they are used to achieve certain national objectives (Blundell-Wignall et al. 2008).[7] Since Huijin was established with foreign exchange reserves specifically to recapitalise the SOCBs, it can be regarded as a de facto SWF. Even though China did not officially classify it as an SWF, Huijin has the features that identify it as such.

Using foreign exchange reserves to recapitalise the banks was attractive to national policymakers. China had been running a trade surplus and steadily accumulating foreign exchange reserves since 1994. In 2008, China's foreign reserves reached US$2 trillion, which was far more than the amount it required to cover imports and short-term external debt. Investment of foreign exchange reserves in Huijin meant reducing the amount of official foreign exchange reserves in SAFE, which the authorities hoped would lessen external pressures for appreciation of the yuan.[8] Moreover, it avoided enlarging the fiscal deficit and, in the eyes of the public, weakening the government's balance sheet.

From de facto to official SWF

Huijin was a de facto SWF, but pressures were mounting against its de facto status. Huijin could have remained a de facto SWF if foreign exchange reserves were used solely to recapitalise domestic banks,[9] but China's rapid accumulation of foreign exchange reserves since 2005 closed this option. In 2005, there was a massive jump in China's annual net exports, from 6 per cent to 24.1 per cent of GDP, which significantly raised pressure for yuan appreciation. On 21 July that year, China formally discontinued pegging the yuan against the US dollar and announced the yuan would be pegged against a basket of currencies.

The yuan immediately appreciated by 2.1 per cent against the US dollar. PBC had wanted faster appreciation of the yuan to control inflation and discourage foreign inflows of speculative capital, but came up against opposition from the National Development and Reform Commission (NDRC), MOF and other parts of the bureaucracy.[10] NDRC, which began its life as the State Planning Commission (SPC), was a natural supporter of SOEs and MOF as legal owner of the four state-owned AMCs would lose from yuan appreciation. Yuan appreciation would raise real interest rates and adversely affect the SOEs, which were dependent on bank credit. The AMCs would then be affected as they owned equity in SOEs and carried PBC debt formerly owed by the SOCBs.

Since it was unable to have the yuan appreciate quickly, PBC sterilised the monetary impacts of its purchases of foreign exchange through open-market operations and raising the SRR ratio. However, it had to ensure that its efforts to tighten monetary policy did not increase its cost of funds. It therefore kept the statutory reserve deposit rate low and allocated to banks bonds that they had to purchase at a PBC-determined price. Lower interest rates would also serve to discourage additional capital flows into China and prevent even more upward pressure on the exchange rate. But there is a downside. Below market lending interest rates made it difficult for non-SOEs to obtain loans. Profitable non-SOEs that were able to pay higher interest rates were often unable to obtain credit because of credit rationing that resulted from below-market interest rates.[11] NDRC benefited from this, as it opened the door to non-market interventions in the economy, but Chinese households, which held most of their savings in the form of bank deposits, were penalised from loss of interest income. China's policymakers therefore faced the challenge of how to control yuan appreciation without causing inflationary pressures and exacerbating distortions in the credit market.

The failure of policymakers to agree on rapid yuan appreciation shifted PBC's position on the yuan. SOCBs held a substantial amount of US dollar-denominated assets as a result of the capital injection from PBC. Yuan appreciation would lower the yuan value of the banks' US dollar assets. The banks had steadily improved their capital adequacy ratios and would frown on yuan appreciation causing a reversal in these ratios. PBC, with its now enormous and increasing stock of foreign currency assets, would resist any move that would seriously erode the value of its capital, which could see it requiring a capital injection from MOF. In 2006 alone, yuan appreciation had cost PBC 26 billion yuan (US$3.4 billion), according to Stephen Green of Standard Chartered Bank (Soon 2007).

Acquiring assets abroad is one way of spending and de-accumulating the stock of foreign exchange reserves and lowering the pressure for yuan appreciation. But once the decision was made to invest foreign exchange reserves overseas and/or in non-finance sectors, the door was opened for other parts of the bureaucracy to challenge PBC's monopoly on management of the country's foreign exchange reserves. NDRC, for example, could now legitimately have a say in deciding what strategic overseas investments should be undertaken. Huijin could no longer be solely 'owned' by PBC once other bureaucratic players became involved. And a new structure must be established to allow greater investment choice of foreign exchange reserves, since Huijin is restricted in the type of investments it can make.

Rivalry among PBC, MOF and NDRC stretched back to the beginning of reform when NDRC lost its monopoly over economic policy and had to share its influence, first with MOF and later with PBC as well. PBC emerged as 'winner' in the establishment of Huijin, but the quest for a 'harmonious society' under Hu Jintao would see PBC lose influence over Huijin. There was also the issue of conflict of interest between PBC as both a major shareholder in the nation's banks, and a major policymaker and 'regulator'[12] in finance and banking. The former role required PBC to maximise profits; the latter role required it to meet policy targets. This conflict was complicated by the public offerings of shares of the four SOCBs, not just to the public in China but also to foreign investors. Huijin was expected to play an important role with strategic foreign investors, which were welcomed to invest in China's financial sector in exchange for their management expertise, to clean up the banks' balance sheets. But while foreign and domestic non-state shareholders expected the banks to maximise profit, PBC as a policymaker and 'regulator' compromised this expectation. Discussions in the bureaucracy over PBC's inherently conflicting dual role as both bank shareholder and national policymaker and 'regulator' overlapped with the discussion about what to do with China's massive foreign exchange reserves. MOF had lost only the battle over Huijin; it had not lost the much larger war with PBC, of which Huijin was just a part.

Official establishment of China's sovereign wealth fund

The low exchange and interest rate policies not only created problems for China's macroeconomic management and caused inefficient allocation of resources. They also imposed a huge financial cost on the country. China had invested its accumulated foreign exchange reserves largely in US treasury and agency bonds, which offered rates of return that were on the average 2.5 per cent lower than the rates that PBC had to pay to bond holders to sterilise its purchases of foreign exchange (Wu and Seah 2008). The rates of return of the US bonds were made even more unattractive by depreciation of the US dollar against the yuan. The highest yield for a 10-year US treasury bill in 2007 and 2008 was, respectively, 5.3 per cent and 4.2 per cent (US Treasury 2009). The US dollar depreciated against the yuan by 4.6 per cent in 2007 and 8.7 per cent in 2008.[13] The rate of return to US bonds was therefore barely positive in yuan terms in 2007 and became negative in 2008. As early as 2006, MOF and NDRC were questioning these low rates of return. NDRC, strongly disposed towards planning and undisputedly the most powerful economic ministry in the pre-reform People's Republic, was particularly keen for China's foreign reserves to be invested overseas to secure longterm supplies of key natural resources – a vital aspect of national security. The Chinese public was also critical of the US treasury and agency bond investments.

As we noted earlier, although Huijin could be considered an SWF, the Chinese government did not formally designate Huijin as such. The government formally established an SWF – CIC – only when it decided to use its foreign exchange to invest in foreign assets other than foreign government and agency debt. China is unlike other countries that have established significant SWFs.[14] Most other countries with sizeable SWFs are major exporters of oil or small export-oriented industrial countries. These countries generally have a small industrial base, a modest appetite for resources and have less need to regard resource security as a pressing issue. Their SWFs also tend to have limited profitable investment opportunities at home. China, on the other hand, is a large emerging industrial economy, hungry for energy and other natural resources, and theoretically with ample investment opportunities at home. It is therefore natural that its SWF would seek profitable investment opportunities at home and abroad.

However, the goals of China's SWF are not simply to maximise economic returns. These goals are contestable and the use of Huijin to recapitalise the SOCBs had set a precedent of using foreign exchange reserves to support domestic industry. This is a sensitive issue since with China's legacy of socialist planning and state ownership, Chinese officials recognise that China's SWF could easily end up as an instrument for industry support, as well as an instrument for channelling state savings to productive domestic and overseas investments. This was demonstrated at the height of the global financial crisis in 2008 when Huijin bought 2 million shares in the BOC, CCB and ICBC and announced it would purchase more shares in these banks. The move was clearly to boost the share prices of these banks and lubricate confidence in China's stock markets.[15]

NDRC is a natural supporter of SOEs and state involvement in business, and wants a major say in the country's SWF. The position of PBC as monetary policymaker and owner of banks had provided an opening for MOF to seek control of Huijin. MOF proposed that its finance department should take over the ownership and management rights of state-owned financial assets from Huijin. PBC responded that funds for Huijin's investments in the banks came from foreign exchange reserves, which were purchased with PBC's liabilities (BizChina 2007). PBC could not remain a significant bank shareholder, but it was not prepared to hand over control of Huijin to MOF. Huijin was already a de facto SWF and an instrument of industry policy. It would therefore logically form the core of China's official SWF, but the question for China's leaders was how should an officially designated SWF be administered and managed.

PBC would not agree to relinquish its control over management of the country's foreign exchange reserves to MOF. As a compromise, CIC was placed directly under the State Council and made answerable to the State Council; neither PBC nor MOF has ownership rights. In theory, CIC has ministry rank, like PBC and MOF, but in practice it is lower in the pecking order. On 29 September 2007 MOF swapped ¥1.55 trillion bonds with PBC in exchange for US$200 billion of foreign exchange, which it then injected into CIC in the form of a loan (CIC 2009, p. 10). Since it was a loan and not a capital injection, CIC had to pay interest on the US$200 billion.[16] But the loan is highly symbolic; it signals that MOF is not the owner of CIC. CIC used US$67 billion of the US$200 billion to purchase Huijin from PBC, which became a subsidiary of CIC. Another US$67 billion was originally planned for use to restructure and recapitalise two banks – the China Development Bank (CDB) and the Agricultural Bank of China (ABC), one of the four major SOCBs that PBC had earlier helped to recapitalise – leaving the remaining US$66 billion for investment overseas (Zhang 2008, p. 5). The amount allocated for bank restructuring was later reduced and the amount allocated for investment overseas was increased to slightly more than US$100 billion (CIC 2009, p. 11).

Although MOF was not made owner of CIC, officials with MOF backgrounds dominated its board of directors.[17] Lou Jiwei, a former vice-minister of finance was appointed chairman of the board of directors and Party secretary. Lou was promoted to deputy secretary-general of the State Council – a position that carries ministerial rank – in March 2007,[18] a few days before deputy PBC governor, Wu Xiaoling, revealed that Lou was heading a team to prepare for the establishment of the yet unnamed new organisation (CIC) to manage the investment of China's foreign exchange reserves (Xinhua 2007a).[19] The two other executive directors appointed beside Lou were Gao Xiqing and Zhang Hongli. Gao, an official with substantial experience on Wall Street, is a former vice-chairman of the China Securities Regulatory Commission (CSRC) and National Council for the Social Security Fund. He was also appointed CIC chief investment officer. Zhang is a former vice-minister of finance. Only two of the eight non-executive directors have PBC backgrounds. One of them, Hu Xiaolian, is the former head of SAFE. Three have MOF and two have NDRC backgrounds. Liu Zhongli (MOF), one of the two independent directors, is the only director beside Lou who holds full ministerial rank. The other independent director, Wang Chunzheng (NDRC), has vice-ministerial rank. The only non-MOF, non-PBC and non-NDRC representative on the board came from the Ministry of Commerce (CIC 2009, pp.18–19). Especially significant is that former vice-minister of finance and former vice-president of the Asian Development Bank, Jin Liqun, was recalled to serve as chairman of the powerful board of supervisors (*jianshi hui*) of CIC.[20] The board of supervisors are accountable to CBRC, over which PBC has significant influence. CBRC has a member on CIC's board of supervisors – Wang Huaqing, a member of the Party Central Commission for Discipline Inspection, CBRC Party committee member and secretary of CBRC Discipline Inspection Committee (CIC 2009, p. 21). However, Wang is the only one with a PBC background on CIC's board of supervisors. Moreover, it is the Central Organisation Department of the Party that appoints the heads of the boards of supervisors (Heilmann 2005, p. 13) and this means that Jin outranks him.

The senior management team of CIC comprises Lou (CEO), Gao, Jin, Zhang and four others. PBC has only one representative (Xie Ping) among the four. NDRC and CSRC have one representative each. Liang Xiang, counsellor, is independent (CIC 2009). The senior officials in CIC can be described as representatives of other ministries. Gao had informed US-China Economic and Security Review Commission (USCC) commissioners during their 2008 trip to China that CIC board members continue to report to their former ministries (USCC 2008, p. 51).[21] Therefore the links between CIC's board members and their previous ministries have remained strong and unbroken, even though CIC on paper reports directly to the State Council.

After CIC took over Huijin, its board of directors was restructured and the influence of MOF in Huijin increased at the expense of PBC. Unlike the previous board, MOF and PBC now have equal representation. The restructured Huijin board has three executive and two independent directors, with Lou Jiwei as chairman. Li Jiange, former deputy director of the Development Research Centre of the State Council, was appointed Lou's deputy and is the lone non-MOF, non-PBC background official on the board. Ex-officials from MOF and PBC share equally the remaining executive and independent director positions (Li and Hu 2008).

The previous management structure of Huijin was highly favourable to PBC because the leadership group that set it up was dominated by officials with PBC backgrounds. The decision to establish CIC was made at the National Finance Work Meeting in January 2007. Representatives from all the major economic ministries are normally present at these meetings so it is something of a surprise that MOF could have such a 'convincing win' at the January meeting, securing dominance over both the board of directors and the senior management of CIC. A highly credible explanation is that PBC, through SAFE, is still able to invest its holdings of foreign exchange abroad. SAFE has a little-known subsidiary in Hong Kong, which has invested heavily in foreign equities. SAFE Investment Company (SAFE IC) (*Huaan touzi gongsi*) was established in 1997, with a registered capital of HK$100 million that has since grown to US$34.7 billion.

By the end of August 2008, SAFE IC had investments in about 50 British companies[22] worth a total of £3.7 billion (US$6.7 billion) (Cao et al. 2008). SAFE IC had also invested in three of Australia's biggest banks and the French oil company, Total (Anderlini and Kwong 2008; Yu 2008). The establishment of CIC has no obvious impact on SAFE IC. CIC could therefore be just another official investment vehicle, but one controlled by MOF. This signifies an official strategy to diversify risk, but the establishment of CIC is also a compromise that allows both MOF and PBC to manage the country's foreign exchange reserves. However, although MOF has a role in managing the country's foreign exchange reserves, its role at least for the moment is subordinate to that of PBC. CIC has capital of US$200 billion, but only half of the amount is available for investing overseas. This is an insignificant amount compared with the at least US$1 trillion foreign exchange reserves that are at the disposal of PBC for overseas equity investment, after allowing for imports and external debt contingencies.[23] Nevertheless, CIC is likely to be given more foreign exchange to invest in the future as its investments performed much better than those of SAFE IC during the global financial crisis (GFC).[24]

Investment strategy of CIC

CIC's officials on numerous occasions have enunciated the underlying principles that guide its investment strategy. The principles (CIC 2009, p. 28) can be summarised as:

* CIC's investments are long term, sustainable and risk-adjusted.
* CIC is a financial investor and does not aim to gain control of enterprises or sectors through its investments.
* CIC's investment decisions are research driven and based on commercial rates of return.
* CIC is socially responsible. It abides by the laws and regulations of countries that host its investments and avoids investing in socially undesirable industries, such as tobacco and gaming.

These principles were developed in response to international concerns that there would be undue political influences on CIC's investments. They were designed to reassure potential CIC's investment-recipient countries that its investments pose no threat to their national security. CIC so far has concentrated on investing in the finance sector. By the end of 2008 it had made two major investments: US$3 billion in the Blackstone Group and US$5.6 billion in Morgan Stanley. CIC incurred a huge paper loss as a result of the GFC from these investments, but the loss did not prevent CIC from appointing Blackstone and Morgan Stanley in July 2009 to oversee its hedge fund investments, starting with an initial US$500 million allocation to Blackstone (Carew and Strasburg 2009). CIC reportedly also invested US$800 million in a Morgan Stanley global real estate fund in the first quarter of 2009 (Miracky et al. 2009, p. 16).

CIC is expected to play its part in enhancing China's resource security and seeks investment opportunities in this sector, once the global economy has stabilised and begins to recover from the GFC. In two months of 2009 CIC invested US$300 million in a 45 per cent share of a Russian oil company, Nobel, and US$939 million for a stake in a Kazakhstan oil and gas company, JSC KazMunai (Anderlini 2009a, 2009b). CIC's history is short and the GFC has made it invest more conservatively than otherwise. Nevertheless, it is unlikely to deviate from its stated investment principles. Since CIC owns Huijin, which in turn is a major shareholder in the SOCBs, CIC could exert influence to help SOEs secure finance for their foreign investments. It does not have to invest directly to help secure China's supply of key natural resources. SOEs are more likely to be at the forefront of strategic foreign investments, with discreet CIC support through SOCBs. CIC, however, could be expected to play a more prominent role in the future financing domestic industry policy.

Conclusion

The establishment of CIC came about because of competition among China's major economic policymakers over management of the nation's massive stock of foreign exchange reserves. The competition takes place amidst China's desire to better utilise its foreign exchange reserves – to obtain higher rates of return from the state's investments in foreign assets and to seek resource security, especially in energy. There is increased urgency among China's policymakers to invest the nation's foreign exchange reserves abroad because of their reluctance to allow the yuan to appreciate significantly. Investing foreign exchange reserves abroad is seen as a way to reduce international pressure on yuan appreciation.

CIC gives MOF and NDRC influence over the management of the nation's foreign exchange reserves. MOF and NDRC have gained at the expense of PBC, but the loss in influence of PBC may not be that significant. PBC still controls the management of the bulk of China's foreign exchange reserves. It has representatives together with other ministries on CIC's board and in senior management. Furthermore, CIC has formal foreign investment advisors. Hence, CIC's overseas investments will be more transparent than those of PBC, which are largely opaque. PBC wishes no doubt to seek higher returns from SAFE IC investments to compete with CIC and to avoid domestic criticisms, but this is its secondary concern. Its main preoccupation is managing the yuan exchange rate at a level policymakers deem appropriate.

China's domestic political economy will likely see China continue to run current account surpluses into the foreseeable future. These surpluses will have to be balanced by capital outflows. China's political economy suggests that CIC may be entrusted with more foreign exchange reserves in the future to invest and that a sizeable amount of its future investments will be domestic, to assist industry, and not just to maximise returns. After all, China's still underdeveloped economy is enormous and there is still significant state control over the economy – alongside a national commitment to industry policy. SAFE

IC investments, on the other hand, will be focused on highly liquid foreign assets, where managing the yuan exchange rate is more of a concern. Clearly both domestic and foreign policy concerns will continue to shape the conduct of China's SWFs, even in its officially designated form and whichever bureaucratic organisation calls the most powerful shots over managing China's foreign exchange reserves.

Notes

1. Comments from Mark Thirlwell on an earlier version of the chapter are gratefully acknowledged.
2. We make the distinction between institutions and organisations. Institutions are normally defined as 'rules of the game'.
3. In 2003, the China Banking Regulatory Commission (CBRC) was established to take over from PBC the role of bank regulator. This did not reduce the influence of PBC over bank regulation, as most CBRC staff came from PBC. However, it did reduce the tension between PBC and MOF.
4. They then held 90 per cent of all bank assets (Lau 1999, p. 73). At the end of 2004, they still held almost 60 per cent of the assets (Podpiera 2006, p. 1).
5. It has vice-ministerial ranking.
6. SASAC not managing the ownership rights of the SOE financial institutions meant it has less leverage over them to support other SOEs.
7. The US Treasury has a narrower definition. It considers a fund an SWF if its funding comes only from foreign reserves. It defines an SWF as a 'government investment vehicle that is funded by foreign exchange assets, and which manages these assets separately from the official reserves of the monetary authorities (the Central Bank and reserve-related functions of the Finance Ministry)' (US Treasury 2007).
8. Truman (2008) suggested that the foreign reserves took a 'detour' and were returned to SAFE through the banks' purchases of yuan to avoid foreign exchange risk and SAFE's future repurchases of foreign exchange. It is, however, unlikely that all the foreign exchange were returned to SAFE. The foreign exchange assets that these banks received from Huijin became part of their balance sheets. Banks issue foreign currency loans. The more foreign currency they hold, the greater is their ability to issue foreign currency loans and PBC sets for each bank a minimum quota of foreign exchange that they must hold, ostensibly to control bank lending of foreign exchange but also to lower foreign exchange holdings of PBC. Many enterprises were keen to borrow US dollars in anticipation of yuan appreciation (Zhang et al. 2009).
9. Huijin's scope of business as defined in its Articles of Association is 'to accept the authorisation of the State to make equity investments in state-owned major financial enterprises' (Huijin 2008).
10. The export sector and the export-dependent coastal provinces were key opponents of allowing the yuan to appreciate.
11. China has high incremental capital output ratios (ICORs), reflecting the relatively easy access of capital-intensive SOEs to cheap capital.
12. See note 3.
13. Calculated from US$/¥ rates in NBS (2009, p. 724).

14. See Aizenman and Glick (2008, table 1) for a list of the largest SWFs.
15. Hujin bought more shares in 2009 to increase investor confidence. On 11 October 2009, it was announced that Huijin had bought additional shares in ICBC, CCB and BOC, increasing its stakes in these banks to 35.4 per cent, 57.1 per cent and 67.5 per cent, respectively (Bloomberg 2009).
16. 4.3 per cent per year on ¥1.55 trillion (Ouyang and Liu 2009).
17. The relationship between CIC and MOF became clearer when in August 2009 a source revealed to the *Economic Observer* (*Jingji guancha*) that CIC is no longer required to pay annual interest on the ¥1.55 trillion to MOF. The amount is now considered an asset (*zichan*) and not debt (*fuzhai*) (Ouyang and Liu 2009).
18. Later in the year, Lou was elected an alternate member of the 17th Party Congress Central Committee on 21 October.
19. It soon became clear that the promotion of Lou to minister status and the foreshadowing of his appointment as CIC's boss, and the subsequent structuring of CIC as a ministerial level organisation, were connected.
20. The board has 'responsibilities to oversee the company's accounting and financial activities'. It 'also has the mandate to monitor the ethical conduct of the members of the Board of Directors and senior executives' (CIC 2009). CBRC appoints members of the supervisory boards in the country's key financial institutions and oversees the daily operations of the boards. The 2008 *Almanac of China's Finance and Banking* (ACFB) listed the 16 institutions that have these boards and the names of their heads (ACFB 2008, pp. 675–80).
21. The commissioners misidentified Gao as president of CIC.
22. Most of them are in the FTSE 100 stock index and include some of Britain's most established and best known companies, such as British Gas, Cadbury, Royal Bank of Scotland and Unilever (Cao et al. 2008).
23. There are foreign exchange reserves of US$2 trillion in 2008 and reserve cover ratio (FX reserves divided by sum of half-year imports and short-term external debt) of almost 2.5, which is more than double of what is required.
24. Anderlini estimated that as of March 2009 CIC had paper losses of US$4 billion and SAFE US$20 billion from their overseas equity investments (Anderlini 2009a, 2009b).

References

ACFB (1999, 2008), *Almanac of China's Finance and Banking*. Beijing: Zhongguo jinrong chubanshe.

Adams, Charles, Donald J. Mathieson, Garry Schinasi and Bankim Chadha (1998), *International Capital Markets Development, Prospects, and Key Policy Issues*. Washington, DC: International Monetary Fund.

Aizenman, Joshua and Reuven Glick (2008), 'Sovereign Wealth Funds: Stylized Facts about their Determinants and Governance', Center for Pacific Basin Studies, Working Paper 2008-33, Federal Reserve Bank of San Francisco.

Anderlini, Jamil (2009a), 'China Lost Billions in Diversification Drive', *Financial Times*, 15 March, available at http://www.ft.com/cms/s/0/11fa4136-119f-11de-87b1-0000779fd2ac.html (accessed 10 September 2009).

Anderlini, Jamil (2009b), 'China Forex Funds Find Security in Secrecy', *Financial Times*, 15 March, available at http://www.ft.com/cms/s/0/7a29cfde-1185-11de-87b1-0000779fd2ac,dwp_uuid=9c33700c-4c86-11da-89df-0000779e2340.html (accessed 10 September 2009).

Anderlini, Jamil and Robin Kwong (2008), 'Chinese State Investor Buys Australian Bank Stakes', *Financial Times*, 3 January, available at http://search.ft.com/ftArticle?sortBy=gadatearticle&queryText=China%E2%80%99s+State+Administration+of+Foreign+Exchange&y=0&aje=true&x=0&id=080103000433&ct=0 (accessed 10 September 2009).

BizChina (2007), 'Rethinking Financial Role of Central Huijin', *China Daily*, 26 January, available at http://www.chinadaily.com.cn/bizchina/2007-01/26/content_793526.htm (accessed 10 September 2009).

Bloomberg News (2009), 'China's Wealth Fund to Buy Shares in Nation's Three Largest Banks', 11 October, available at http://www.bloomberg.com/apps/news?pid=newsarchive&sid=a8v8Ep92gecc (accessed 17 November 2009).

Blundell-Wignall, Adrian, Yu-Wei Hu and Juan Yermo (2008), 'Sovereign Wealth and Pension Fund Issues', *Financial Market Trends*, OECD.

Brehm, Stefan (2008), 'Risk Management in China's State Banks – International Best Practice and the Political Economy of Regulation', *Business and Politics*, 10, pp. 1–29.

Cao Zhen, Wu Ying and Xu Ke (2008), 'Waiguanju jing touzi jin 50 jia Yingguo shangshi gongsi' (SAFE has Invested in Almost Fifty British Listed Companies), *Caijing*, 8 September, available at http://www.caijing.com.cn/2008-09-08/110010856.html (accessed 5 November 2009).

Carew, Rick and Jenny Strasburg (2009), 'CIC Turns to Friends: Morgan, Blackstone', *Wall Street Journal*, 31 July, p. C2, available at http://online.wsj.com/article/SB124896400764393841.html (accessed 6 December 2009).

CIC (2009), *China Investment Corporation Annual Report 2008*, available at http://www.swfinstitute.org/research/CIC_2008_annualreport_en.pdf (accessed 1 October 2009).

Heilmann, Sebastian (2005), 'Regulatory Innovation by Leninist Means: Communist Party Supervision in China's Financial Industry', *The China Quarterly*, 181, pp. 1–21.

Huijin (2008), Governance, Articles of Association, available at http://www.huijin-inv.cn/hjen/governance/governance_2008.html?var1=Governance (accessed 17 November 2009).

Jiang Zemin (1998), 'Zai jinian dang de shiyijie sanzhong quanhui zhaokai ershi zhounian dahui shang de jianghua' (Speech Commemorating the Twentieth Anniversary of the Party's Third Plenum of the Eleventh Party Congress), *Shenzhen tequbao*, 19 December, pp. 1–2.

Jiang Zemin (1999), 'Jianding xinxin, shenke gaige, kaichuang guoyou qiye fazhan de xin jumian' (Have Confidence, Deepen Reform, Start a New Phase of SOE Development), *Renmin ribao*, 13 August, p. 1.

Lai Rongwen (1999), 'Zhongguo dalu xiagang wenti zhi yanjiu' (Labour Retrenchment in Mainland China), *Gongdang wenti yanjiu* (Research on Party Issues), 25, pp. 54–66.

Lau, Lawrence (1999), 'The Macroeconomy and Reform of the Banking Sector in China', in *Strengthening the Banking System in China: Issues and Experience*, BIS Policy Papers No. 7, October, pp. 59–89.

Li Jing and Hu Yinan (2008), 'Huijin dongshihui gaizu. Lou Jiwei ren dong-shizhang' (Reshuffling Hujin's Board of Directors: Lou Jiwei Appointed Chairman), *Caijing*, 16 July, available at http://www.caijing.com.cn/2008-07-16/100074780.html (accessed 1 October 2009).

Lin, Zhaomu (1998), *1997–1998 Hongguan jingji xingshi fenxi* (Analysis of Macroeconomic Conditions). Beijing: Zhongguo jihua chubanshe.

Ma Guonan (2006), 'Who Pays China's Bank Restructuring Bill?', CEPII Working Paper No. 2006-04.

Ming He (2004), 'Huijin: A SASAC for China's Financial Sector?', *Chatham House Briefing Note*, The Royal Institute of International Affairs, September.

Miracky, William, Davis Dyer, Victoria Barbary, Veljko Fotak and Bill Megginson (2009), *Sovereign Wealth Fund Investment Behaviour*, Monitor Group, July.

Mo, YK (1999), 'A Review of Recent Banking Reform in China', in *Strengthening the Banking System in China: Issues and Experience*, BIS Policy Papers No. 7, October, pp. 90–109.

National Bureau of Statistics (NBS) (2006, 2009), *China Statistical Yearbook*. Beijing: China Statistics Press.

Ouyang Xiaohong and Liu Peng (2009), 'CIC No Longer to Pay Interest to the State', *Economic Observer*, 26 August, available at http://www.eeo.com.cn/ens/homepage/briefs/2009/08/26/149395.shtml (accessed 17 November 2009).

Podpiera, Richard (2006), 'Progress in China's Banking Sector Reform: Has Bank Behaviour Changed?', IMF Working Paper WP/06/01, International Monetary Fund, Washington, DC.

Soon, Christina (2007), 'China Will Keep Buying US Treasuries, Wu Says', *Bloomberg*, 11 March, available at http://www.bloomberg.com/apps/news?pid=20601080&sid=a5waLpE3W.zc&refer=asia (accessed 15 November 2009).

Truman, Edwin (2008), 'The Management of China's International Reserves and Its Sovereign Wealth Funds', paper prepared for the Chinese Academy of Social Sciences Conference Marking the 30th Anniversary of the Reform and Opening-up, Beijing, China, 16–17 December, Peterson Institute for International Economics, available at http://www.petersoninstitute.org/publications/papers/paper.cfm?ResearchID=1074 (accessed 15 November 2009).

USCC (2008), *Report to Congress of the US-China Economic and Security Review Commission*, available at http://www.uscc.gov/annual_report/2008/08_annual_report.php (accessed 9 November 2009).

US Treasury (2007), 'Sovereign Wealth Funds', in *Semiannual Report on International Economic and Exchange Rate Policies*, available at http://www.treas.gov/offices/international-affairs/economic-exchange-rates/pdf/2007_Appendix-3.pdf (accessed 10 November 2009).

US Treasury (2009), 'Daily Treasury Yield Curve Rates', available at http://ustreas.gov/offices/domestic-finance/debt-management/interest-rate/yield_historical_main.shtml (accessed 21 December 2009).

Wu, Friedrich and Arifin Seah (2008), 'The Rise of China Investment Corporation: A New Member of the Sovereign Wealth Club', *World Economics*, 9, pp. 45–68.

Xia Lesheng (1998), 'Dalu guoqiye gaige zhong xiagang wenti zhi yanjiu' (Mainland State-owned Enterprise Reform and Unemployment), *Gongdang wenti yanjiu* (Research on Party Issues), 24, pp. 40–52.

Xinhua (2007a), 'Lou Jiwei: New Deputy Secretary-general of State Council', *Beijing Review*, 7 March, available at http://www.bjreview.com.cn/lianghui/txt/2007-03/07/content_58355.htm (accessed 15 November 2009).

Xinhua (2007b), 'State Forex Investment Company Debuts', 29 September, available at http://www.gov.cn/english/2007-09/29/content_764943.htm (accessed 22 December 2009).

Yu Ning (2008), 'SAFE Searches Out Higher Returns to Compensate for US Dollar Denominated Losses', *Caijing Magazine*, 28 April, available at http://english.caijing.com.cn/2008/100058739.html (accessed 22 December 2009).

Zhang Huanning, Wang Ziwu and Yu Hairong (2009), ' "Re qian" mizong' (Confused Trail of 'Hot Money'), *Caijing*, 23, pp. 94–6.

Zhang Ming (2008), 'China's Sovereign Wealth Fund: Weaknesses and Challenges', Research Center for International Finance Working Paper, No. 0823, China's Academy of Social Sciences.

3
Between Principles and Politics: The Pragmatic Practice of Singapore's Sovereign Wealth Funds

Yvonne C.L. Lee

Introduction

This chapter advances a pragmatic approach towards the governance and regulation of sovereign wealth funds (SWFs), drawn from the practices of Singapore's Temasek Holdings Pte Ltd (Temasek) and Government Investment Corporation of Singapore Pte Ltd (GIC). A starting point of any SWF discussion typically involves an observation of the specific context in which they first received global attention. The US sub-prime crisis that started in 2006 triggered a buying spree of distressed assets and equity portfolios in North America and Western Europe by several sovereign wealth funds[1] from Asia and the Middle East. These SWFs' investments attracted both fascination and flak in the global and domestic realms, notwithstanding the fact that states have, for several decades, engaged in foreign and domestic commercial activities as private investors and held public wealth under several government arms in various other forms such as foreign reserves, pension schemes, state enterprises in home countries and investment vehicles constituted under foreign laws (Hassan 2009, Exhibit 3.11).

Indeed, several recipient countries have raised concerns – the lack of transparency, the possibility of ominous investment strategy and the adverse effect on their domestic economies and national security (Joint Economic Committee Congress of the US 2008).[2] In response, SWFs have reiterated the need to maintain free markets without harmful protectionism or nationalistic measures, and provided assurances of their bona fide intentions, as commercial investors without any political agenda. Such politicisation or de-economisation of SWF investments underscores the diverse interests and concerns of SWF and recipient

47

countries (Broude et al. 2010). Presently, a global or transnational geopolitical impasse has been avoided. This is largely due to the different countries' goal of economic self-preservation. Net gains from capital flows still outweigh the perceived costs and dangers associated with SWF investments.

Given the difficulty in obtaining the requisite consensus among countries, it is unrealistic to posit the creation of a global regime or international organisation, or the adaptation of an existing organisation for the regulation of SWFs. The absence of an international legal framework and a central regulator has resulted in a mixed bag of incremental approaches to the governance or regulation of SWFs. Temasek and GIC, together with other SWFs, have agreed to the broad principles set out in the recently issued Generally Accepted Principles and Practices (GAPP), and key recipient countries have responded by issuing the OECD Declaration on Recipient Policies (OECD Declaration).

This chapter outlines a 'model' of overlapping governance and regulation – the applicable laws and 'good practices' at the global, bilateral and domestic levels, based on the recent public statements and investments in relation to Temasek and GIC. It observes the 'model's' pragmatic balance between principles and political considerations, and the implicit refusal to normatively speak towards the ordering of the domestic politics of a sovereign state. This chapter then concludes by recommending the approach of Temasek and GIC as the starting point for advancing a plausible SWF rule of law.

Singapore's domestic political system in a nutshell

Singapore inherited the Westminster system of government from her British colonial master upon her independence in 1965. The Westminster system is a democratic parliamentary model of government based on a bipartisan system. Key traits of a Westminster system of government include a unicameral legislative chamber freely elected by adult citizens by secret ballot; political pluralism embodied by a real choice between two or more political parties; vesting of executive power in the head of state but largely exercised by a cabinet of ministers headed by a prime minister who is chosen from the party commanding majority support in the elected chamber and answerable to that chamber; a recognised opposition; and a set of constitutional conventions (Bagehot 1963, p. 69; Dale 1993). The ruling party or government is subject to political checks largely through popular elections. However, unlike the British system of government, Singapore's system has evolved into a hybrid with certain unique characteristics. For example, Singapore has an elected president with some oversight powers in relation to certain fiscal matters such as the drawing down of past reserves and public service appointments , a unicameral form of legislature and a written supreme constitution that voids inconsistent primary laws (Tan 1989; Thio 1993; Neo and Lee 2009).

In general, critics have argued that a Westminster parliamentary system that effectively checks and balances the exercise of political power requires an adversarial political culture comprising, inter alia, a viable opposition party, two or more independent media sources, an independent and transparent electoral boundaries' commission, and an active and vocal civil society political party. Political opponents such as Chiam See Tong and J.B. Jeyaretnam cited the lack of by-elections and the introduction of Group Representation Constituencies and gerrymandering as unfair measures, and the political climate of fear, the numbering of ballot papers and constraining free expression and assembly as hindering democratic evolution (*Straits Times* 1999; Thio 2002). The absence or material watering down of such essential traits has resulted in political predominance of the ruling party, the Peoples' Action Party (PAP). Several critics have further observed the numerous defamation lawsuits by certain members of the ruling political party against political opponents such as Chee Soon Juan and J.B. Jeyaratnam, and commented on the significant damages awarded by the Singapore courts to certain members of the ruling political party (Rodan 1996, 2008, 2009).

From 1968 until 1981, PAP controlled all parliamentary seats. After the 2006 general elections, it retained control of 82 out of 84 elected seats in parliament, exceeding the two- thirds parliamentary majority required to amend the Singapore Constitution, and the simple parliamentary majority required to amend legislative Acts or provisions, under Article 5 of the Singapore Constitution. Apart from the absence of a viable opposition, the party whip – a political convention that ensures cohesive party voting, unless lifted – prevents members of the ruling party to vote according to his or her conscience. Furthermore, parliamentary debates and proceedings are specifically subject to procedural requirements such as the time allocated to each member of parliament to stand and speak towards a motion.[3]

The Singapore government has, however, defended its form of government by defining Singapore democracy and culture as 'Asian' and 'communitarian' with an emphasis on 'conciliation' as opposed to 'contention' (Shared Values 1991; *The Straits Times* 1991a; Thio 2002; Sheehy 2004). To address the absence of a viable opposition – ostensibly, a 'parliamentary gap' (Thio 1993, pp. 93–6) – the Singapore Constitution was amended to create new offices such as the non-constituency members of parliament[4] and the nominated members of parliament.[5] These new offices, which significantly reduced the representative nature of the elected legislature, arguably complemented the role of the few opposition members of parliament in discharging their tasks of parliamentary censure and scrutiny.

Critics have observed PAP's alleged avoidance of the institutionalisation of democratic representation and accountability and creation of viable alternatives within an allegedly authoritarian regime (Rodan 2009). Although several nominated members of parliament have materially contributed to the parliamentary debates,[6] they still lack political legitimacy as they are unelected and do not have the power to vote in parliament on substantive motions such as constitutional amendment(s), supply and money bills, vote of no confidence and removal of the President from office (Article 39(2) of the Singapore Constitution).

Recent developments such as the robust debates in and out of parliament concerning issues such as the development of the integrated resorts (casinos) (2005–06), the retention of the law prohibiting homosexual sex (2007), the losses sustained by Singapore's GIC and Temasek during the global recession (2006–09) and the constitutional amendment relating to net investment return (2009) reflect the rise of a vocal section of civil society in Singapore. For example, the proliferation of private blogs,[7] including those hosted by the Singapore government[8] on the Internet, constitutes a new dimension of political participation and a novel means to hold the Singapore government accountable particularly for Acts and policies that are not subject to legal limits or are not justiciable in the Singapore courts.

The pragmatic approach of Singapore's GIC and Temasek

Notwithstanding the absence of an overarching framework of norms and process for the regulation of SWFs and their investments, an optimal level of consultation, cooperation and coordination is necessary to manage investment and capital flows between countries and maintain global financial stability. A pragmatic balance between nationalism and market globalisation must be achieved. This section considers and recommends the structure and practices of Singapore's GIC and Temasek, as a starting point for the governance or regulation of other SWFs.

The origins and objectives of GIC and Temasek

This chapter treats Temasek as an SWF on the basis of its government shareholding and investment strategy. Notwithstanding Temasek's perception of itself as an 'atypical' SWF that does not receive new funds or directions from its shareholder (Dhanabalan 2008), as discussed below, Temasek has made significant attempts to support the Santiago Principles.

GIC and Temasek are private companies incorporated under Singapore's Companies Act (Cap. 50) in 1981 and 1974, respectively.[9] Although both are wholly owned by the Singapore government, the Singapore government has repeatedly affirmed its general oversight as a shareholder who does not 'influence' or 'coordinate' their investments, but 'does look at the risks in totality to ensure that firstly, they are within its overall risk threshold and that, secondly, GIC and Temasek are likely to be able to provide Government with good long-term returns on their overall portfolios' (Perry 2007).

GIC and Temasek differ in some ways. First, they have different sources of funding. While GIC does not own assets and only manages foreign reserves on behalf of the Singapore government, Temasek owns and manages its own assets after initial seeding in 1974 and some transfers of assets from the government in the 1990s. As exempt private companies, both entities do not need to publicly disclose their audited accounts or financial information. Consequently, GIC's website and two (unaudited) annual reports do not disclose information such as its specific fund and investment sizes. In contrast, Temasek, in its annual reviews, discloses its annual returns, value of the whole portfolio on a one-year, two-year, three-year, five-year, ten-year, thirty-year basis, both by market value as well as shareholder funds, full income statements and balance sheets audited by external auditors in accordance with Singapore Standard on Auditing SSA 800 – The Independent Auditor's Report on Special Purpose Audit Engagements (Temasek Review 2009).

GIC's chairman, Minister Mentor Lee Kuan Yew, has articulated two reasons for GIC's reduced transparency – the avoidance of populist pressures and prevention of anticipation of its moves by others (*The Straits Times* 2008a). Indeed, prior to GIC's first annual report released in 2008, GIC was largely opaque with some glimpses of its investment strategy disclosed in the requisite reporting filings in the relevant foreign jurisdiction. For example, in October 1993, GIC's disclosure of its US investment stakes in Schedule 13D – forms which investors must file when they acquire 5 per cent or more of the public company's equity securities in the USA – revealed its strategy of buying depressed stock. GIC had then purchased stakeholdings in eight companies that were all trading significantly below their recent highs, including Magnetek, Tyco Toys Inc. and Gottschalks Inc. It repeated the pattern over the next eight months, buying depressed stocks such as Masland Corp., Life Partners Group Inc. and Structural Dynamics Research Corp. (*The Straits Times* 1996a).

Second, their current investment strategies are different to some extent. GIC focuses on foreign investment whereas Temasek makes foreign and domestic investments. Minister Mentor Lee Kuan Yew, who is also GIC's chairman, confirmed the lower risk approach of GIC: 'Temasek will take higher risk for higher returns. GIC, we treat it more as a pension fund and we are prepared to forego the higher returns because we don't want to take those high risks' (*The Straits Times* 2008b).[10] In the past, GIC invested in both domestic and foreign companies. For example, in 1998, GIC spent A$20 million (S$21.7 million) to double its stake in Australian-listed property developer Ipoh Ltd from 18.8 per cent (Baker 1998). Some of its investments were also speculative to some extent. For example, while GIC made some successful investments such as its sale of some 1.16 million shares in Margaretten Financial Corp. (the Perth Amboy, New Jersey, mortgage company) at US$25 each up from its acquisition price of US$16.28 (1996), it missed out on some opportunities such as the pre-mature sale of 603 200 shares in Technology Solutions, the Chicago-based computer consultant at US$10.05 to US$12.24 (July 1995) compared with the May 1996 trading price of US$29.50 a share (*The Straits Times* 1996b). Some of its local investments such as its acquisition of Singapore Aircraft Leasing Enterprise, the aircraft leasing unit for Singapore Airlines in 1997, were strategic. GIC and Temasek then lent 'weight to the company's aspiration to be among the world's top three aircraft leasing companies by the turn of the century' by injecting US$62.5 million (S$98.4 million) each for 14.5 per cent stakes (Chan 1997).

To reflect Temasek's current investment strategy, its Charter, first issued in 2002, has just been revised. The revised Charter 2009 're-affirms the role of Temasek as a commercial investment company to create and deliver sustainable long-term returns', and 'focus as an active investor and as an active shareholder of successful enterprises' (Temasek News Releases 2009). Prior to 2002, Temasek's investments were less speculative and largely situated in Singapore. Most of its investment holdings were in companies that owned or provided critical resources or services. The references to the government's need to own or control such companies have been omitted from its Charter 2009. As explained by Temasek's chairman, Mr Dhanabalan:

> [The] 2002 Charter was released at a time when there were discussions about whether many Singapore companies faced competition from government-linked companies. In that context, there was a need to clarify which companies were important for the government to hold stakes in; and which companies may not be necessary for the government to hold on to. The companies that we have in our portfolio have gone well beyond Singapore. They have become regional, international and the question whether the government and Temasek should hold companies in Singapore is no longer one that invites much discussion.
>
> (Temasek News Releases 2009)

The 'blind-spot' investment experiences

Singapore SWFs have underestimated certain financial and non-financial risks associated with foreign investments. Such risks are, however, an integral part of investing in assets that can yield a higher return. An example of a sustained financial loss concerns its investment in Australian education provider, ABC Learning (ABC). ABC, of which Temasek is a major shareholder, went into receivership late 2008. A non-profit organisation paid a token A$1 (S$1.09) each for several childcare centres (Teh 2009). Temasek first invested A$401.5 million for a 12 per cent stake at A$7.30 per share in ABC in May 2007. ABC's other major shareholders then included Lazard Asset Management and Morgan Stanley Private Equity. Temasek raised its stake to 14.7 per cent as the ABC stock plunged in early 2008, but this was pared down to 12.7 per cent after ABC's equity placement in June 2008 (Frith 2008).

Other 'blind spots', including geopolitical factors such as nationalism and domestic politics of sectarian interests, which shape recipient countries' perception of and response to SWF investments, are difficult to ascertain. In relation to SWF investments, the common thread running through the reactions of recipient countries is the nationalistic concerns stemming from declining economic factors and pre-existing domestic politics of sectarian interests. These 'blind spots' must be incorporated into any calculation of the 'hurdle rates' for SWF investments, in addition to the initial cost benefit analysis. The subsections below outline the events constituting the 'blind spots' and show the financial and political impact on Singapore's SWFs and their investments.

Banking (US): Citigroup and Merrill Lynch

In the wake of the recent sub-prime mortgage losses, Citigroup and Merrill Lynch turned to external investors to replenish their eroded capital. Some of these investors were GIC, Abu Dhabi Investment Authority, Kuwait Investment Authority and Alwaleed bin Talal, Korean Investment Corp., Mizuho Financial Group and Temasek (Onaran 2008). In January 2008, GIC participated in Citigroup's private offering of convertible preferred securities through an investment of US$6.88 billion. The perpetual convertible securities provided a fixed annual dividend of 7 per cent and allowed GIC to hold them for as long as it chose to do so, subject to certain conditions (Ng 2008).

In December 2008, Temasek invested US$4.4 billion in Merrill Lynch common stock pursuant to a private placement arrangement of US$6.2 billion of newly issued common stock between Merrill Lynch, Temasek and Davis Selected Advisors, with the option to purchase an additional US$600 million of Merrill Lynch common stock in December 2008. Temasek's ownership position then represented less than 10 per cent of Merrill Lynch's outstanding common stock in accordance with US regulatory limits. The chairman and CEO of Merrill Lynch confirmed the transaction with 'savvy investors' having 'proven track records of achieving strong investment returns' not only strengthening the bank's financial position, but also affording 'significant benefits' given Temasek's sizeable investments across Asia, particularly in Singapore, which enhanced the bank's 'ability to drive new growth opportunities around the world' (Merrill Lynch Press Release 2008).

As the sub-prime crisis worsened in 2008, Merrill Lynch raised US$15.3 billion from capital markets including share sales to Temasek. In September 2008, Temasek obtained US regulatory approval and raised its stakes in Merrill Lynch from 9.4 per cent to 13.7 per cent (Reuters 2008).[11] Temasek, however, paid only US$900 million for the additional stake, as US$2.5 billion was offset against the total price of US$3.4 billion (Merrill Lynch Term Sheet 2008). Temasek's earlier investment had embodied a requirement that if Merrill Lynch raised more capital within 12 months at a price lower than the US$48 that Temasek paid, it would be compensated for the difference.

At the outset, various voices warned that the investments undermined the economic and national security interests of the USA, and called for heightened scrutiny and restriction of SWF investments, despite the fact that Singapore's SWFs were invited by Citigroup and Merrill Lynch to participate in the capital raising exercises, had no rights of control and did not desire any role in the governance of these companies (Byrne 2006; Hearing before Senate Committee on Banking, Housing and Urban Affairs 2008; Staff of Joint Committee on Taxation 2008). It appears that the real concerns of the USA relate to what it views to be unacceptable profits by foreign SWF states at its economic expense. This reflected the reversal of the US prescription of a neoliberal market philosophy for its own foreign investments, particularly in developing countries. Indeed, the initial neoliberal development policy framework was constructed by powerful financial institutions such as the World Bank, the IMF and the US Treasury. Its main components which favoured the developed countries were fiscal discipline, tax reform, liberalisation of interest rates, trade and foreign investments, a comprehensive exchange rate and deregulation (Serra and Stiglitz 2008). To allay such fears, lead representatives from Singapore's SWFs visited the USA and met with the relevant authorities. Consequently, the Singapore SWFs joined the other SWFs in formulating and issuing the Santiago Principles.

As of October 2009, Temasek has sold its stakeholding in Bank of America (which had acquired Merrill Lynch) (Citigroup Press Release 2009). GIC converted its Citigroup into common stock in February 2009 and raised its equity ownership of Citigroup to an estimated 11.1 per cent without any injection of funds. It then sold half of its Citigroup stake in September 2009, reaping a profit of US$1.6 billion (S$2.3 billion) (Chan 2009).

Telecommunications (Thailand): Shin Corp.

In January 2006, Temasek, together with its partners, Siam Commercial Bank Pcl (SCB) and a group of Thai investors, through Kularb Kaew Pcl (KKP), purchased an initial 49.6 per cent stake in Shin Corp., Thailand's telecommunications-listed company for US$1.9 billion, from the then popularly elected Thai Prime Minister Thaksin and his family (Lee 2006; Temasek Press Speech 2006). The purchase triggered a mandatory offer for the remaining stake. Consequently, a 96 per cent stake was purchased by the Temasek-led consortium for US$3.8 billion.

Ostensibly, Temasek and its partners had complied with all laws and regulations of Thailand. Domestic political unrest regarding the alleged corruption and enrichment of the rich at the expense of the poor was unfortunately overlooked.

First, the Thai regulators have for more than a decade loosely construed the laws relating to foreign ownership limits. Thai law firms and investment banks have accordingly advised foreign companies operating in Thailand to erect multi-tiered structures such that while the Thais appear to have majority ownership control, management control remains in the hands of the foreign investors (Bowornwathana 2004). Second, there was a change in telecommunication laws to raise the limit on foreign ownership from 25 per cent to 49 per cent shortly before Temasek's initial purchase. On 23 January 2006, the Thai Telecommunication Act 2006 became effective, raising the limit on foreign holdings in telecom companies to 49 per cent. The Act replaced the Telecom Business Law, which took effect in November 2001, and put the foreign investment cap at 25 per cent (Tan 2006). This development attracted popular suspicion about the involvement of political and government figures and personal interests.

Third, Thaksin and his family was not required to pay capital gains tax on the sale price, under Thai tax laws.

Temasek's investment quickly became embroiled in an ongoing political and social disquiet against Thaksin, who had political and military enemies. Charges of corruption and market manipulation were made against Thaksin (*Financial Times* 2006; *The Straits Times* 2006b) resulting in nationalistic sentiments against a sell-out of vital national assets (Lopez 2006). Further to a military coup, Thaksin was removed as prime minister on 19 September 2006. Subsequently, Temasek diluted its stake in Shin Corp. Its stakeholding is now reflected as 42 per cent (Temasek Review – Major Portfolio Companies 2009).

Telecommunications (Indonesia): PT Indosat and Telekomsel

Temasek had indirectly owned a 40.8 per cent stake in Indosat through its wholly owned subsidiary, Singapore Technologies Telemedia Pte (STT). Temasek also owned a 35 per cent stake in Telekomsel through its subsidiary (54 per cent), Singapore Telecommunications Ltd (SingTel). In December 2006, a union representing workers from Indonesia's state-run enterprises filed a complaint against Temasek, claiming the company was fixing call rates through its stakes in two of the largest telecommunications companies in Indonesia, PT Indosat (Indosat) and Telekomunikasi Selular (Telekomsel). The union dropped its claim without furnishing any reason the following year. However, Indonesia's anti-competition watchdog, Commission for the Supervision of Business Competition (KPPU), continued its probe and ruled that Temasek had contravened anti-trust laws.[12]

Temasek responded that it owned no shares in Indosat and Telkomsel, and played no role in their business decisions and operations. It asserted that it was impossible to 'engage in any monopolistic or anti-competitive practices in the Indonesian mobile telecommunications market' given the fact that both Telkomsel and Indosat are regulated businesses operating within the guidelines of the Indonesian Telecommunications Regulatory Authority or Badan Regulasi Telekomunikasi Indonesia (BRTI) (Temasek News Releases 2008). Temasek's appeal against the KPPU decision was, however, rejected by both the Central Jakarta District Court and Indonesia's Supreme Court (Channel News Asia 2008). Temasek has since sold its 40.8 per cent stake in Indosat to Qatar Telecom QSC for US$1.8 billion (Bloomberg Online 2008).

The 'patchwork' of overlapping governance and regulation

Currently, there is no overarching cross-border legal framework establishing the rights and obligations of SWFs. This is unsurprising, given the absence of any international financial architecture of legally binding and enforceable rules, and adjudicative and authoritative tribunal or court. There is, however, a complex matrix of actors ranging from standard-setting bodies such as the Basel Committee and International Organisation of Securities Commissions, to international economic organisations such as the IMF, International Bank for Reconstruction and Development and World Trade Organisation, and regional organisations such as the European Union and the Organisation of American States. The rule-setting and enforcement mechanisms of such actors depend on the agreement of the member states. The nation-state remains the primary standard setting and enforcement agency (Weber and Douglas 2007 p. 427).

SWFs and their investments are regulated by overlapping domestic laws of home and recipient countries, applicable bilateral investment agreements and voluntary codes of conduct and good practices. There is no overarching multilateral treaty framework. Indeed, the difficulty in procuring global consensus for the regulation of foreign direct and indirect (for example, portfolio) investments is underscored by the failure to complete the negotiations relating to the Multilateral Agreement on Investment (MAI) which were launched by the OECD governments in 1995 (OECD Multilateral Agreement on Investments 1998). Existing multilateral treaties such as the General Agreement on Trade and Tariffs (GATT), General Agreement on Trade and Services (GATS) and Agreement on Trade-related Investment Measures (TRIMS), which relate to trade in goods, services and investment measures involving trade in goods respectively, do not directly address the issues posed by SWF investments. Some protection is afforded to foreign investments under customary international law which only prohibits certain types of expropriation by host states such as discriminatory takings or takings without compensation (Sornarajah 2004). Foreign assets and use thereof may be subject to taxation or trade restrictions (Brownlie 2003 p. 509). SWFs continue to shape their investment strategies in light of the constantly changing economic climate. The global recession during the first half of 2009 caused many SWFs to postpone certain investments, sell investments with materially diminished expected returns, and focus on emerging markets or non-financial industries (*Gulf Daily News* 2009). With the recovering global economy buttressed by the performance of emerging markets – specifically China and India, and the financial and property markets of Hong Kong – the SWFs have adopted a more diverse approach that focuses on several different jurisdictions and non-portfolio investments such as property and infrastructure.

A model of governance and regulation

Given the unpredictability of domestic and nationalistic politics in recipient states, the diverse interests of SWFs and their accountability towards their respective domestic constituencies, a viable starting point towards achieving some consensus for the governance of SWF investments is the pragmatic balance between principles and politics maintained by Singapore's SWFs. Their approach comprises governance at the global level, and a mixture of governance and regulation at the bilateral and domestic levels. For the purposes of this chapter, the terms 'governance' and 'regulation' refer to voluntary and non-binding practices, and legally binding and enforceable laws, respectively.

Global level: governance by Santiago Principles and OECD Declaration

SWF countries have rejected recipient countries' promotion of Norway's SWF as the universal model for best accountability and transparency standards. Most, if not all, SWFs including Singapore's GIC and Temasek, however, support the 'good' practices and principles set out in the OECD Declaration and Santiago Principles. In October 2008, responding to the heightened fears articulated by some recipient countries, 22 countries established an International Working Group of Sovereign Wealth Funds (IWG) (IWG Press Release 2008b) and issued 24 voluntary principles concerning SWFs' governance, accountability and investment conduct (Santiago Principles 2008). The Santiago Principles advocate

> a transparent and sound governance structure that provides for adequate operational controls, risk management and accountability;

ensure compliance with applicable regulatory and disclosure requirements in the countries in which SWFs invest; ensure SWFs invest on
the basis of economic and financial risk and return-related considerations; and help maintain a stable global financial system and free
flow of capital and investment.

(IWG Press Release 2008b)

Recipient countries have welcomed these Santiago Principles. The
OECD, which had given its input to the making of the Santiago
Principles, affirmed the content of such principles in its Declaration
on Sovereign Wealth Funds and Recipient Country Policies, General
Investment Policy, Guidelines for Recipient Country Investment Policies
relating to National Security and Freedom of Investment Process: Pre-
serving the Foundations of Global Prosperity and Development (OECD
Declaration 2008).

These non-binding norms are, however, subject to several criticisms.
First, they are not legally binding and enforceable. Second, they embody
vague concepts. The Santiago Principles, for example, stipulate the
option to choose from either 'recognised international or national auditing standards' (GAPP 12) and 'relevant financial information regarding
the SWF should be publicly disclosed' (GAPP 17). Third, they are subject to domestic laws. For example, each Santiago Principle is 'subject to
home country laws, regulations, requirements and obligations'.

The OECD Declaration also accords primacy to domestic laws and
concerns. It calls upon recipient countries not to 'erect protectionist
barriers to foreign investment' and 'discriminate among investors in
like circumstances', and to consider 'additional investment restrictions'
only 'when policies of general application to both foreign and domestic
investors are inadequate to address legitimate national security concerns'. The meaning and application of concepts such as 'protectionist',
'discriminate' and 'legitimate national security concerns' remain highly
contested. Finally, while a voluntary forum, the International Forum
of Sovereign Wealth Funds, has been established pursuant to the Kuwait
Declaration (IFSWF 2009), a forum that comprises mainly SWF countries
and not key recipient countries, it is merely consultative and facilitative
without any mechanism for adjudication or enforcement.

The potential for SWF and recipient countries to reach a common
understanding based on these principles should, however, be recognised. Both groups acknowledge the adverse implications of rising
protectionism and maintain their support for market liberalisation,
specifically, the freedom of investment and benefits of free flows of

capital. The Santiago Principles and OECD Declaration can act as a catalyst of comity for SWF and recipient countries, by crystallising common and 'good practices' concerning fiscal norms of propriety, profits and prudence, corporate governance processes boosting accountability and transparency and macroeconomic objectives of growth and development and financial stability. Countries are then at liberty to create specific aspects of 'good practices' by entering into specific bilateral or regional agreements or 'hardening' their respective domestic laws.

Indeed, the OECD Declaration and Santiago Principles have influenced the behaviour of Singapore's SWFs. Shortly after the IWG was formed to create the Santiago Principles, GIC issued its first report on its investment strategies and policies (GIC Report 2008). It has recently issued its second report (GIC Report 2009). Temasek has also adopted a more transparent stance, namely the public (Temasek FAQs). It currently has the highest score according to one scoreboard (The Linaburg-Maduell Transparency Index 2009) compared with its tenth position in the second quarter of 2008 (The Linaburg-Maduell Transparency Index 2008). In comparison, GIC has a lower score of 6/10 (The Linaburg-Maduell Transparency Index 2009).

Bilateral level: bilateral agreements

Singapore has entered into several bilateral investment treaties and free trade agreements, collectively referred to as 'bilateral agreements' (Singapore Government 2009). These bilateral agreements potentially afford some protection for SWFs and their investments by conferring the most favoured nation status, national treatment and fair and equitable treatment (Hsu 2009). They adopt open-ended definitions of 'trade' or 'investment'.[13] It has, however, been argued that the principle of national treatment may not apply to SWFs. For a violation of such principle, it must be shown that the discrimination was in a situation where there were 'like circumstances'.

Clearly, SWFs with their deep pockets and government associations are not like the other investors (Sornarajah 2009). Recipient countries are also able to protect their interests under bilateral agreements. For example, they may carve out restrictions or limitations falling within 'legitimate public welfare objectives' such as 'public health, safety and the environment' from the provisions relating to 'indirect expropriation' of rights in investments (US–Singapore Free Trade Agreement 2003; US Model BIT 2004). A recipient country may specifically adopt measures for 'prudential reasons' or 'protection of investors, depositors, policy holders' in the financial services industry.[14]

Domestic level: constitutional and legislative laws, voluntary practices

Singapore's SWFs, like those of other SWFs, are constrained by several domestic factors such as wealth management benchmarks (Johnson-Calari and Rietveld 2007) and the corporate rule of law – procedural norms of accountability, transparency and disclosure.

Domestic laws of recipient countries. First, as discussed earlier, Singapore's SWFs must comply with the investment laws of recipient countries.

Public law oversight in Singapore. Singapore's SWFs as companies stipulated in the Fifth Schedule of the Constitution of the Republic of Singapore are subject to public law oversight. The appointment and/or removal of members of the board of directors require(s) the assent of the President; the financial statements and proposed budgets must be submitted to the President for his approval. However, the President's fiscal oversight is limited. He is not involved in the daily monitoring and supervision of their activities. His powers are reactionary, as he does not initiate his own fiscal policies (Lee 2007).

The performance of Singapore's SWFs is also subject to parliamentary scrutiny. The Singapore government has provided public explanations concerning their recent portfolio losses, and their renewed investment strategies. For example, Senior Minister of State for Finance Lim Hwee Hua explained: 'The Government's mandate for GIC is to achieve a reasonable rate of return above global inflation, over a long-term horizon. In the last 20 years to March 2008, the average annual rate of return of the portfolio was 5.8% in Singapore dollar terms. This was 4.5% above global inflation' (Lim 2009). In respect of Temasek's sale of its stakeholding in the Bank of America (which had acquired Merrill Lynch), the Singapore government has clarified that Temasek, as a long-term investor, would regularly reassess the risks and potential returns on its investments, and rebalance its holdings to enhance the long-term value of its portfolio (Shanmugaratnam 2009a).

Another example relates to the resignation of former BHP Billiton CEO Charles Goodyear, who was initially slated to take over from Ho Ching as Temasek's CEO. The reasons for his exit were subject to speculation by both foreign and local press. Officially, Goodyear confirmed that a divergence in strategy was behind his shock departure from Temasek (Burton 2009; *The Straits Times* 2009). In response to a question raised in parliament, the Minister for Finance denied that Goodyear received a 'golden handshake' for his departure, and affirmed that the decision was mutual and amicable and Goodyear was bound by the usual legal obligations concerning Temasek's proprietary information (Shanmugaratnam 2009b).

Private law oversight in Singapore

Although Singapore's SWFs as exempt private companies are not required to disclose their financial accounts, both have voluntarily adopted corporate governance frameworks and some 'best practices' as discussed earlier. Each SWF is, for example, managed by separate and independent professional officers. The Singapore government has emphasised that it neither influences nor second-guesses any Temasek's investment decisions, and Temasek is accountable to it as shareholder for delivering a good rate of return on its overall investment portfolio (Lim 2007; Olsen 2007; Shanmugartnam 2008).

GIC has created risk, remuneration and investment committees to advise its board of directors (GIC About Us). Temasek has implemented a risk management information system to support the decision-making of its board of directors and senior management (Temasek About Us), and constituted international and advisory panels as part of its engagement with external market actors (Temasek Review Advisory and International Panels). Both GIC and Temasek voluntarily issue annual reports and upload updated information on their respective websites from time to time. Several critics have noted, however, the absence of specific key accounting policies.[15]

Conclusion

The recent voluntary measures undertaken by Singapore's SWFs are laudable developments, given the complex balancing act between maintaining official secrecy of government funds and ensuring political accountability to the domestic constituencies. Their pragmatic approach, while facilitating harmonious capital flows between countries, does not purport to speak to the substantive ordering of the domestic affairs or systems of another state by imposing their own economic, social and political values of 'good'. It is therefore a viable model for other SWFs to adapt and adopt in accordance to their respective special and distinct legal and socio-political culture and systems. Indeed, it serves as a good starting point of 'consultation, cooperation and coordination' towards the eventual mirroring of common standards in the respective domestic laws and practices of the different SWFs and recipient countries.

Appendix

Table 3.1 A snapshot of Singapore's SWFs' characteristics

Characteristic	Singapore's SWFS	
	GIC (as of 31 March 2009)	**Temasek (as of 31 March 2009)**
Shareholder	The Government of Singapore – Minister for Finance	
Nature of entity	Exempt private company (incorporated under the Companies Act, Cap. 50), and a government company (pursuant to the Fifth Schedule of the Constitution of the Republic of Singapore)	
Source of fund	GIC does not own the funds. It manages the government's foreign reserves.	Temasek owns and manages its assets on a commercial basis. 1. 1974: Temasek was seeded with an initial portfolio of 35 companies worth S$354 million or US$134 million. 2. Additional assets transferred to Temasek in the early 1990s when the government liberalised provision of basic telecommunication, power and port services.
Size of fund	> US$100 billion	S$130 billion or US$86 billion, down from S$185 billion (a year earlier) and up from S$90 billion five years ago. Book value declined from S$144 billion the year before to S$118 billion, primarily due to a drop in marked to market fair value of available-for-sale investments.
Investment strategy	GIC mandate is to enhance the international purchasing power of Singapore's reserves, via an investment process comprising three levels of decision:	As a long-term investor, to create and deliver sustainable long-term returns for stakeholders. Directed by the board and management, Temasek owns and manages its assets on a commercial basis.

Table 3.1   (Continued)

Characteristic	Singapore's SWFS	
	GIC (as of 31 March 2009)	Temasek (as of 31 March 2009)
	1. Long-term allocation of funds for the various asset classes based on the clients' investment objectives, time horizon and risk tolerance, and the return and risk expectations of each asset class. 2. Management on how the policy mix should be implemented. 3. Portfolio construction or decisions by portfolio managers. These decisions include currency management; country, industry and sector allocation; yield curve management and security selection. Some factors: Reasonable rate of return above global inflation for total portfolio, or absolute return targets. Managing risk by ensuring operating bands for asset classes to contain volatility stay within the risk parameters specified by the government.	Temasek is 'not involved in the day-to-day operations or commercial decisions of our portfolio companies; we engage them as a shareholder to promote robust governance and foster a strong culture of excellence and integrity, as well as to build sustainable competitive advantages, and maximise long-term shareholder returns. We remain open to increase, reduce or maintain our holdings, based on our value test and market opportunities, regularly reviewing our portfolio to rebalance our risk-return stance.'
Shareholder/ ownership rights	Shareholder/ownership rights in the investments, including voting, will be exercised, as appropriate, to protect the financial/commercial interests of the investments.	
Use of external managers	Use of external managers: (1) Investing in funds managed by external fund management institutions, real estate, private equity, bond, index and hedge funds. (2) Issuance of discretionary mandates to external fund managers.	
Performance bench- mark	Real rate of return: 2.6%.	Total shareholder return: >16% Corporate ratings: (1) AAA Standard & Poor; (2) Aaa Moody.

Geographical distribution of asset portfolios	45% (Americas: USA and others); 29% (Europe); 24% (Asia); 2% (Australasia).	22% (OECD Economies excluding Korea); 31% (Singapore); 27% (North Asia: China, Taiwan, Korea); 9% (ASEAN excluding Singapore); 7% (South Asia: India, Pakistan); 4% (Latin America & Others).
Financial disclosures	First Annual Report (2007–08). Second Annual Report (2008–09).	Temasek Review issued on an annual basis since 2004.
Corporate governance (internal)	1. Formal Board of Directors as advised by the Investment Committee, Risk Committee and Remuneration Committee. 2. Senior Management. GIC's wholly owned subsidiaries: GIC Asset Management, GIC Real Estate and GIC Special Investments.	1. Formal Board of Directors. 2. Senior management.
Oversight regimes	Public and private law oversight	

Source: Adapted from contents available at the websites of GIC and Temasek at http://www. gic.com.sg and http://www.temasek.com.sg, respectively, particularly GIC's second annual report of 2008–09 and Temasek Review 2009 at http://www.gic.com.sg/PDF/GIC_Report_ 2009.pdf and http://review.temasek.com.sg/institution, respectively.

Notes

1. There is no universal definition of an SWF, although the prevailing dominant definition appears to be that contained in the Generally Accepted Principles and Practices. The first known SWF was established by Kuwait in 1953. The 'SWF' term was coined by Andrew Rozanov (2005), *Who Holds the Wealth of Nations, State Street Global Advisors*, August, available at http://www.ssga.com/library/esps/Who_Holds_Wealth_of_Nations_ Andrew_Rozanov_8.15.05REVCCRI1145995576.

2. For differing levels of strategic investments and transparency perceived by US commentators and politicians, see Standard Chartered and Oxford Analytica (2008), 'Chart 1: The Largest Sovereign Wealth Funds Overview of Investment Approach and Transparency', in *The Rise of Sovereign Wealth Funds: Impacts on U.S. Foreign Policy and Economic Interests (US Committee on Foreign Affairs House of Representatives)*, Serial No. 110–190, 21 May, http://foreignaffairs.house.gov/110/42480.pdf, p. 13 where it sets out four broad quadrants with strategic-conventional investment approach and low-high level of transparency as the *x* axis and *y* axis, respectively: (1) strategic investment approach with below mid-point level of transparency – UAE

(Dubai) – DIC, UAE (Dubai) – Istithmar, Qatar, China; (2) conventional investment approach with below mid-point level of transparency – UAE (Abdu Dhabi) – ADIA, Brunei, Oman, Kuwait, Taiwan, Venezuela – NDF and Algeria; (3) strategic investment approach with above mid-point level of transparency – Singapore GIC, Malaysia, Singapore – Temasek; (4) conventional investment approach with above mid-point level of transparency – USA (Alaska, Chile, Canada (Alberta) and Norway. According to the chart, South Korea, Kazakhstan and Russia SWFs are characterised by mid-point level of transparency with below mid-point conventional investment approach.

3. Singapore Parliament Standing Orders. Rules of debate in parliament, Sections 47–54, and Questions to Ministers and other members, Sections 19–22, both available at http://www.parliament.gov.sg/Publications/SOmerge per cent20with per cent20SO per cent20notes.pdf.
4. Article 39(1)(b), pursuant to Constitution of the Republic of Singapore (Amendment) Act 16 1984.
5. Article 39(1)(c), Article 44(1) and Fourth Schedule, pursuant to Constitution of the Republic of Singapore (Amendment) Act 11 1990.
6. See, for example, Singapore Parliamentary Debates relating to the development of integrated resorts (casinos) (2005–06), the retention of the law prohibiting homosexual sex (2007) and the constitutional amendment relating to net investment returns (2009).
7. For example, http://www.theonlinecitizen.com and www.temasekreview.com.
8. REACH at http://www.reach.gov.sg and STOMP at http://www.stomp.com.sg. Although REACH hosts numerous forum discussions that cover many current topics and attract diverse and in-depth contributions, it has been criticised by some commentators as being 'state controlled'. See, for example, Garry Rodan (2009), 'Human Rights, Singaporean Style', *Far Eastern Economic Review*, 4 December, available at http://www.feer.com/essays/2009/december51/human-rights-singaporean-style.
9. For a summary of key facts, see Appendix, 'A snapshot of Singapore's SWFs' characteristics'.
10. Temasek said that it is not affected by an agreement by Singapore, Abu Dhabi and the United States on principles to increase the transparency of sovereign wealth funds. 'Temasek is not a sovereign wealth fund' its spokesman Mark Lee said in a telephone interview. Temasek has to 'sell assets to raise cash for new investments and doesn't require the government to give approvals' (*The Straits Times* 2008b).
11. Temasek, however, converted its 13.7 per cent stake (219.7 million shares) in Merrill Lynch into 189 million shares of Bank of America. Bank of America has acquired Merrill Lynch. Temasek has recently sold its entire stakeholding in Bank of America.
12. 'The Ban on Monopolistic Practices and Unfair Business Competition', *Law of the Republic of Indonesia*, No. 5/1999, at Article 27(a).
13. Article 1, US Model BIT (2004, available at http://www.state.gov/documents/organization/117601.pdf. For a similar and arguably broader definition, see the German model treaty at http://www.fes-globalization.org/dog_publications/Appendix per cent201%20German%20Model%20Treaty.pdf.
14. Article 10.10(1) of USSFTA.

15. The Temasek Review 2000 was audited using Singapore Standard of Account-
    ing (SSA 800). See http://review.temasek.com.sg/performance/statement-by-
    independent-auditors. Generally, the Temasek Reviews are brief, without the
    specific key accounting policies, pay and incentive schemes, and paint only
    a 'broad-brush' picture of its balance sheet, income statement and cash
    flow. See http://www.temasekholdings.com.sg/pdf/TR2007%20FAQs.pdf for
    Temasek Holdings' brief clarification.

References

Bagehot, Walter (1963), *The English Constitution*. London: The Fontana
Library.

Baker, Russell (1998), 'GIC Doubles Stake in Aussie Property Firm Ipoh to 18.8 Per
Cent', *Business Times (Singapore)*, 26 February.

Bloomberg Online (2008), 'Qatar Telecom to Pay S\$2.4 Billion for Indosat Stake',
Bloomberg Online, 7 June, available at http://www.bloomberg.com/apps/news?
sid=aQ9BG.Aj.KP0&pid=20601087.

Bowornwathana, Bidhya (2004), 'Thaksin's Model of Government Reform: Prime
Ministerialisation Through "A Country is My Company" Approach', *Asian
Journal of Political Science*, 12(1), pp. 135–53.

Broude, Tomer, Marc L. Busch and Amy Porges (eds) (forthcoming 2010), *The
Politics of International Economic Law*. Cambridge, UK: Cambridge University
Press.

Brownlie, Ian (2003), *Public International Law*. Oxford: Oxford University Press.

Burton, John (2009), 'Temasek Says Goodyear Will Not be Chief', *Financial Times*,
21 July.

Byrne, Matthew R. (2006), 'Protecting National Security and Promoting Foreign
Investment: Maintaining the Exxon-Florio Balance', *Ohio State Law Journal*,
67(4), pp. 849–910.

Calari, Jennifer Johnson and Rietveld Malan (eds) (2007), *Sovereign Wealth
Management*. United Kingdom: Central Banking Publications.

Chan, Fiona (2009), 'GIC Profits From Citi Stake', *The Straits Times (Singapore)*,
23 September.

Chan, Wee Chuan (1997), 'GIC and Temasek Buy into SIA's Aircraft Leasing Unit',
The Straits Times (Singapore), 11 November.

Channel News Asia (2008), 'Indonesia's Supreme Court Turns Down Appeal by
Temasek Holdings', 12 September, available at http://www.channelnewsasia.
com/stories/singaporebusinessnews/view/375403/1/.html.

Citigroup Press Release (2009), 'Citi to Exchange Preferred Securities for
Common, Increasing Tangible Common Equity to as Much as \$81 Billion',
27 February, available at http://www.citigroup.com/citi/press/2009/090227a.htm.

Companies Act, Singapore (Cap. 50 rev. edn 2006), available at http://www.acra.
gov.sg/Legislation/Companies_Act.htm.

Companies (Exempt Private Companies) (Consolidation) Notification (Cap. 50),
available at http://www.acra.gov.sg/Legislation/Companies_Act.htm.

Dale, William (1993), 'The Making and Remaking of Commonwealth Constitu-
tions', *International and Comparative Law Quarterly*, 42, pp. 67–83.

Dhanabalan, S. (2008), Chairman of Temasek, 'Role of Sovereign Funds in Today's Globalization', speech at The Indus Entrepreneurs event, 21 August, available at http://www.temasekholdings.com.sg/media_centre_news_speeches_210808.htm.

Financial Times (2006), 'Singapore May See Worst Fallout from Thai Coup', 20 September.

Frith, Bryan (2008), 'Australian Education Trust Distances Itself from ABC', *The Australian*, 28 August, available at http://www.theaustralian.news.com.au/story/0,25197,24252285-16941,00.html.

GATT, GATS, TRIMS World Trade Organisation, http://www.wto.org/english/docs_e/legal_e/legal_e.htm#agreements.

'GIC About Us', http://www.gic.com.sg/aboutus_check.htm.

GIC News Release (2009), 'GIC Converts its Convertible Preferred Notes in Citigroup to Common Shares', 27 February, available at http://www.gic.com.sg/newsroom_newsreleases_270209.htm.

GIC Press Release (2008), 'GIC Invests USD 6.88 Billion in Citigroup', 15 January.

GIC Report (2008), http://www.gic.com.sg/PDF/GICreport0708_Full.pdf (accessed 4 June 2010).

GIC Report (2009), http://www.gic.com.sg/PDF/GIC_Report_2009.pdf (accessed 4 June 2010).

GIC website, http://www.gic.com.sg (accessed 4 June 2010).

Gulf Daily News (2009), 'Qatar Fund Puts Off Investments', 13 March.

Hall, Ben (2008), 'Sarkozy Puts €20bn Barrier Around Industry', *Financial Times*, 20 November.

Hassan, Adnan (2009), *A Practical Guide to Sovereign Wealth Funds*. London: Euromoney Institutional Investor Plc, pp. 24–7.

Hearing before Senate Committee on Banking, Housing and Urban Affairs (2008), Turmoil in US Credit Markets: Examining the US Regulatory Framework for Assessing Sovereign Investments, 10th Congress.

Hsu, Locknie (2009), 'SWFs, Recent US Legislative Changes, and Treaty Obligations', *Journal of World Trade*, 43(3) pp. 458–69.

IFSWF (2009), The International Forum of Sovereign Wealth Funds (IFSWF) was set up pursuant to the 'Kuwait Declaration', 6 April, available at http://www.iwg-swf.org/mis/kuwaitdec.htm. See also IFSWF, http://www.ifswf.org/index.htm.

IWG Press Release (2008a), 'International Working Group of Sovereign Wealth Funds Presents the "Santiago Principles" to the International Monetary and Financial Committee, Press Release No. 08/06, 11 October, available at http://www.iwg-swf.org/pr/swfpr0806.htm.

IWG Press Release (2008b), 'International Working Group of Sovereign Wealth Funds is Established to Facilitate Work on Voluntary Principles', Press Release No. 08/01, 1 May, available at http://www.iwg-swf.org/pr/swfpr0801.htm.

Joint Economic Committee Congress of the US (2008), 'Do Sovereign Wealth Funds Make the U.S. Economy Stronger or Pose National Security Risks?', S. Hrg., pp. 110–499.

Lee, Bryan (2006), 'Temasek Partners Complete Shin Corp Takeover', *The Straits Times (Singapore)*, 15 March.

Lee, Yvonne C.L. (2007), 'Under Lock And Key: The Evolving Role of the Elected President as a Fiscal Guardian', *Singapore Journal of Legal Studies*, pp. 290–322.

Lim, Hwee Hua (2007), *Singapore Parliamentary Debates*, 82, March.

Lim, Hwee Hua (2009), *Singapore Parliamentary Debates*, 85, April.

Lopez, Leslie (2006), 'Shin Corp Deal Fallout Spooks Foreign Investors in Thailand', *The Straits Times (Singapore)*, 8 November.

Merrill Lynch Press Release (2008), 'Merrill Lynch Enhances its Capital Position by Raising up to $6.2 Billion from Investors, Temasek Holdings and Davis Selected Advisors', 24 December.

Merrill Lynch Term Sheet (2008), 24 December, available at http://www.ml.com/media/92240.pdf.

Neo, Jaclyn Ling-Chien and Yvonne C.L. Lee (2009), 'Constitutional Supremacy: Still a Little Dicey', in Li-ann Thio and Kevin Y.L. Tan (eds), *Evolution of a Revolution – Forty Years of the Singapore Constitution*. Oxford, United Kingdom: Routledge-Cavendish.

Ng, Grace (2008), 'GIC Pumps S$9.8b into Troubled Citigroup', *The Straits Times (Singapore)*, 16 January.

OECD Declaration (2008), OECD Investment Committee, October, available at http://www.oecd.org/dataoecd/0/23/41456730.pdf (accessed 4 June 2010).

OECD Multilateral Agreement on Investments (1998), http://www.oecd.org/daf/mai/intro.htm (accessed 4 June 2010).

Olsen, Eunice Elizabeth (2007), *Singapore Parliamentary Debates*, 82, 7 March.

Onaran, Yalman (2008), 'Citigroup, Merrill Receive $21 Billion from Investors', *Bloomberg Online*, 15 January, available at http://www.bloomberg.com/apps/news?pid=20601103&sid=aevafxG9n_ls (accessed 15 June 2009).

Perry, Margaret (2007), 'Temasek and GIC are Two Distinct Institutions: MM Lee', *Channel News Asia (Singapore)*, 25 April, available at http://www.channelnewsasia.com/stories/singaporebusinessnews/view/272292/1/.html (accessed 4 June 2010).

Reuters (2008), 'Temasek Raises Stake in Merrill Lynch', Reuters, 30 September.

Reuters (2009), 'Temasek's Merrill Investment Reduced by More than $2 Bln', Reuters, 8 January.

Rodan, Garry (1996), 'Elections Without Representation: The Singapore Experience Under the PAP', in R.H. Taylor (ed), *The Politics of Elections in Southeast Asia*. Cambridge, UK: Cambridge University Press.

Rodan, Garry (2008), 'Singapore Maneuvers in Response to Chee', *Far Eastern Economic Review*, 171(1), pp. 39–41.

Rodan, Garry (2009), 'New Modes of Political Participation and Singapore's Nominated Members of Parliament', *Government and Opposition*, 44(4), pp.438–62.

Santiago Principles, (2008), available at http://www.iwg-swf.org/pubs/eng/santiagoprinciples.pdf (4 June 2010).

Serra, Narcis and Joseph E. Stiglitz (2008), *The Washington Consensus Reconsidered*. Oxford: Oxford University Press.

Shanmugaratnam, Tharman (2008), *Singapore Parliamentary Debates*, 84, 21 January.

Shanmugaratnam, Tharman (2009a), *Singapore Parliamentary Debates*, 86, 28 May.

Shanmugaratnam, Tharman (2009b), *Singapore Parliamentary Debates*, CEO-Designate of Temasek Holdings (Resignation).

'Shared Values' (1991), Singapore: Singapore National Printers.

Sheehy, Benedict (2004), 'Singapore "Shared Values" and Law: Non East Versus West Constitutional Hermeneutic', *Hong Kong Law Journal*, 34(1), pp. 67–82.

Singapore Government (2009), Free Trade Agreements, at http://www.fta.gov.sg/sg_fta.asp.

Singapore Parliament, http://www.parliament.gov.sg/AboutUs/Org-PartyWhip. htm (accessed 4 June 2010).

Sornarajah, M. (2004), *The International Law on Foreign Investment*. Cambridge, United Kingdom: Cambridge University Press.

Sornarajah, M. (2009), 'Sovereign Wealth Funds and the Existing Structure of Regulation of Investments', paper presented at Sovereign Wealth Funds – Governance and Regulation, Asian Society of International Law, National University of Singapore, Sigapore, 9–11 September.

Staff of Joint Committee on Taxation (2008), 110th Congress, 'Economic and U.S. Income Tax Issues Raised by Sovereign Wealth Funds Investment in the United States', JCX-49-08, available at http://www.house.gov/jct/x-49-08.pdf (accessed 4 June 2010).

Tan, Angela (2006), 'Temasek's Stake in Thai bank Under Scrutiny', *Business Times (Singapore)*, 6 April.

Tan, Kevin Y.L. (1989), 'The Evolution of Singapore's Modern Constitution: Developments from 1946 to the Present Day', *Singapore Academy of Law Journal*, 1, pp. 17–23.

Teh, Shi Ning (2009), 'ABC Learning Centres Go for A$1 Each: Failed Australian Childcare Facility Operator's Assets Being Hived Off', *Business Times (Singapore)*, May, available at http://www.asiaone.com/News/Education/Story/A1Story20090507-139890.html (accessed 4 June 2010).

'Temasek About Us', http://www.temasekholdings.com.sg/about_us_corporate_governace.htm (accessed 4 June 2010).

Temasek Annual Review (2009), *Major Portfolio Companies*, available at http://review.temasek.com.sg/portfolio/major-portfolio-companies?page=2 (accessed 4 June 2010).

Temasek FAQs, http://www.temasekholdings.com.sg/media_centre.htm (accessed 4 June 2010).

Temasek News Releases (2008), http://www.temasekholdings.com.sg/media_centre_news_releases_kppu_09may.htm (accessed 4 June 2010).

Temasek News Releases (2009), http://www.temasekholdings.com.sg/media_centre_news_releases_250809.htm (accessed 4 June 2010).

Temasek Press Speech (2006), 'Temasek-SCB Led Investor Group Acquires Shinawatra and Damapong Families' Stakes in Shin Corp', 3 January, available at http://www.temasekholdings.com.sg/news_room/press_speeches/23_01_2006.htm (accessed 4 June 2010).

Temasek Review (2009), http://review.temasek.com.sg/performance/statement-by-independent-auditors (accessed 4 June 2010).

Temasek Review Advisory and International Panels, http://review.temasek.com.sg/engagement/temasek-advisory-panel and http://review.temasek.com.sg/engagement/temasek-international-panel (accessed 4 June 2010).

Temasek's website, http://www.temasekholdings.com.sg (accessed 4 June 2010).

The Linaburg-Maduell Transparency Index (2008), http://www.swfinstitute.org/news/augeight.php (accessed 4 June 2010).

The Linaburg-Maduell Transparency Index (2009), Developed by Carl Linaburg and Michael Maduell, http://www.swfinstitute.org/research/ transparencyindex.php, (accessed 4 June 2010) 3rd quarter.

The Straits Times (1991a), 'Shared Values Should Help Us Develop a Singapore Identity', *The Straits Times (Singapore)*, 6 January.

The Straits Times (1991b), 'BG Lee: Why We Stress Communicatarian Values', *The Straits Times (Singapore)*, 15 January.

The Straits Times (1996a), 'GIC's US Investments Give a Glimpse of its Strategy', *The Straits Times (Singapore)*, 11–12 May.

The Straits Times (1996b), 'Filings on US Stock Buys Give Glimpse of GIC's Investments', *The Straits Times (Singapore)*, 11 May.

The Straits Times (1999), 'Opposition Says PAP Hinder Democracy', *The Straits Times (Singapore)*, 7 September.

The Straits Times (2006), 'Temasek "May have Overstepped Ownership Laws" in Shin Deal', *The Straits Times (Singapore)*, 3 October, and 'Thai Probe Turns up Heat on Temasek's Shin Deal', *The Straits Times (Singapore)*, 2 October.

The Straits Times (2008a), 'MM: Good Reasons for GIC Not to be "Too Transparent"', *The Straits Times (Singapore)*, 1 May, available at http://www.asiaone.com/ News/The%2BStraits%2BTimes/Story/A1Story20080128-46891.html (accessed 4 June 2010).

The Straits Times (2008b), 'Temasek Says it is Not a Sovereign Wealth Fund', *The Straits Times (Singapore)*, 22 March.

The Straits Times (2009), 'Yes, Exit was Over Strategy: Goodyear', *The Straits Times (Singapore)*, 25 September.

Thio, Li-ann (2002), 'The right to political participation in Singapore: Tailor-making a Westminster-modelled constitution to fit the imperatives of "Asian" Democracy', *Singapore Journal of International & Comparative Law* 6(1), pp. 181–243.

Thio, Li-ann (1993), 'The Post-colonial Constitutional Evolution of the Singapore Legislature: A Case Study', *Singapore Journal of Legal Studies*, pp. 80–122.

US Model BIT (2004), Issued by the US Department of State, Annex B, paragraph 4(b), available at http://www.state.gov/documents/organization/38710.pdf (accessed 4 June 2010).

US–Singapore Free Trade Agreement (2003), 'Exchange of Letters on Expropriation', 6 July, in relation to US–Singapore Free Trade Agreement.

Weber, Rolf H. and Arner W. Douglas (2007), 'Toward a New Design for International Financial Regulation', *University of Pennsylvania Journal of International Law*, 29(2), pp. 391–454.

4
Kuwait Investment Authority – An Assessment

Gawdat Bahgat

In the early part of the 2000s, the world witnessed a two-fold dramatic redistribution of global wealth. First, the skyrocketing of oil prices (up until July 2008) meant that oil-producing nations accumulated massive revenues. Similarly, emerging markets, particularly China, continued its impressive economic growth. Meanwhile, developed countries, such as the USA and those in Europe, built up substantial current account deficits. Stated differently, there had been a massive inflow of capital from the latter to the former. Consequently, oil producers and emerging markets became major creditors to the world and to industrialised countries in particular. Second, a substantial share of this new wealth is owned and managed by governments, not by the private sector. This emerging and growing framework is at sharp variance with today's general perception of a market-based global economy and financial system in which decision-making is largely in the hands of private agents, principally pursuing commercial interests.

Sovereign wealth funds (SWFs) are a clear embodiment of these fundamental changes in the global financial system. These government-owned investment funds are 'commonly funded by the transfer of foreign exchange assets that are invested long-term overseas' (Allen and Caruana 2008, p. 16). SWFs can be divided into two categories, based on the source of the foreign exchange assets: commodity funds established through commodity exports and non-commodity funds typically established through transfers of assets from official foreign exchange reserves. This chapter focuses on the former, particularly on oil funds.

Countries that rely on oil and other non-renewable resources for a substantial share of their revenue face two key problems: the revenue stream is uncertain and volatile because of the fluctuation in prices, and the supply of the resource is exhaustible. Kuwait, like many

Table 4.1   Oil prices (US dollars per barrel)

Year	Price	Year	Price	Year	Price
1972	1.90	1985	27.53	1998	12.21
1973	2.83	1986	13.10	1999	17.25
1974	10.41	1987	16.95	2000	26.20
1975	10.70	1988	13.27	2001	22.81
1976	11.63	1989	15.62	2002	23.74
1977	12.38	1990	20.45	2003	26.78
1978	13.03	1991	16.63	2004	33.64
1979	29.75	1992	17.17	2005	49.35
1980	35.69	1993	14.93	2006	61.50
1981	34.32	1994	14.74	2007	68.19
1982	31.80	1995	16.10	2008	94.34
1983	28.78	1996	18.52		
1984	28.06	1997	18.23		

Source: British Petroleum, BP Statistical Review of World Energy (2009), London, p. 16.

other oil-exporting countries, has not succeeded in reducing its heavy dependence on oil revenues. Officials from the International Monetary Fund (IMF) continue to call on Kuwait to reduce this dependence and invest in developing the non-oil sectors (International Monetary Fund 2009a). Table 4.1 illustrates the volatility of oil prices since the early 1970s.

Unlike solar, wind and other renewable energy forms, oil (and other fossil fuels) is a finite resource. This fact suggests that global production will peak one day and eventually the world will run out of oil. This is known in oil literature as Peak Oil Theory. Its roots go back to Marion King Hubbert, a Shell geologist, who in 1956 correctly predicted that US production would peak between 1965 and 1970 (Hubbert 1962). His model maintains that the production rate of a finite resource follows a largely symmetrical bell-shaped curve. This theory has since ignited an intense debate regarding the availability of enough supplies to meet global demand and the future of oil in general. Peter Odell agrees that production does indeed go up, and then down and that the downside usually falls off gradually, 'following a depletion pattern modeled fairly accurately by production that is a fixed percentage of what remain (i.e. exponential decline)' (Odell 2000, p. 132).

Most of the world's oil executives, government ministers, analysts and consultants reject the Peak Oil Theory on both technological and economic grounds. They argue that technological advances and market laws have always expanded the life span of the world's endowment of proven oil reserves. Despite this sense of optimism, the bottom line is that oil is a finite fuel.

To address these challenges, oil-exporting countries have created special funds. Generally, these funds serve either as stabilisation or saving vehicles. Stabilisation funds aim to reduce the impact of volatile revenue on the fiscal system and public policy, while saving funds seek to create a store of wealth for future generations. In most countries, oil funds pursue these two objectives simultaneously.

SWFs are not new. A few of them have existed for decades. The accumulation of massive oil revenues, due to skyrocketing oil prices in the early part of the 2000s, has brought attention to these government-controlled investment vehicles. Indeed, in 2006 oil-exporting countries became the world's largest source of global capital flows, surpassing Asia for the first time since the 1970s (Farrell and Lund 2008). Little wonder in recent years there has been a substantial increase in the number and assets of oil funds.

Kuwait was the first oil-producing country to establish such a SWF. By the late 2000s, the Kuwait Investment Authority (KIA) was the world's fourth-largest SWF, surpassed only by those of Abu Dhabi, Norway and Singapore, respectively. Given the massive financial assets held by the KIA, decisions made by its managers have significant impact on socio-economic developments in Kuwait and on recipient countries where the fund invests its assets. This chapter seeks to examine the history, governance and investment portfolio of the KIA. I argue that, despite fundamental drawbacks, the fund has proven crucial in supporting the country's economic and political system.

The creation of the world's first sovereign fund

The evolution of the Kuwaiti economy and its heavy dependence on oil revenues have prompted the country's leaders to create the world's first SWF in 1953, eight years before Kuwait's independence. Historically, Kuwait has had a free market economy based on trade and pearl diving activities before the discovery and export of oil in the middle of the twentieth century. Some of the principle features which characterised the growth of the economy were initiative, perseverance and openness to the outside world, which were all seen as essential elements in an economy based on external trade. This foundation resulted in the evolution and growth of the merchant class, which formed the backbone of economic activity.

Before the discovery of oil, the lack of rain and fresh water for farming forced the people of Kuwait to look seaward for an economic means of support. Boatbuilding flourished, and Kuwaiti craft were known throughout coastal Arabia for their quality. In addition, pearling was a large-scale activity until the rise of the cultured pearl industry in Japan in the 1920s and 1930s. The good harbour in Kuwait Bay stimulated other maritime activity and led to the development of a merchant class in Kuwait city. During the eighteenth and nineteenth centuries, the city rivalled Basra in Iraq as a centre for the trade between India and parts of the Middle East. The legacy of seafaring and trading gave the Kuwaiti people a maritime outlook and an aptitude for trade that distinguished them from other people in the region. Conditions had begun to change by the time oil was found.

In 1938 oil was first discovered in Kuwait by Kuwait Oil Company (KOC), a London-based joint venture of the Anglo-Persian Oil company (now British Petroleum) and Gulf Oil (now Chevron Corporation), under a concession granted by the then Emir of Kuwait, Sheikh Ahmad al-Jaber al-Sabah. KOC had been formed in 1934 following more than a decade of concession negotiations. Discovery of oil in commercial quantities was made in 1938. World War II slowed the development of oil fields, but at the end of the war the infrastructure was completed and commercial export of crude oil began in June 1946 (Kuwait Petroleum Corporation 2009). By 1953, Kuwait was the main producer in the Persian Gulf region, a position held until 1965 (McLachlan 1980).

Following the discovery of oil and its export, the role of the state as the provider of basic services – including health care, education and public utilities – was considerably expanded to meet the needs of a rapidly growing population. In the 1960s, the state expanded its role in the economy to form partnerships with the private sector to establish certain large-scale industrial enterprises for which there was a pressing need. The rise in oil prices in the mid-1970s and the subsequent increase in oil revenues led to a fundamental restructure of the oil industry and an expansion of the role of the state in all economic activities. Indeed, it is generally recognised that the government is the motor driving the Kuwaiti economy. The government has the capital because it collects the oil revenues; it redistributes that capital through its budget, its capital expenditures and its purchasing power; it decides who will profit and by how much through its spending and regulatory policies (Gause 1994).

The Supreme Petroleum Council was formed in 1974 and the Ministry of Oil was established the following year to oversee the country's oil interests. By 1976, the industry was fully nationalised and in January 1980 the government established the Kuwait Petroleum Corporation (KPC), which became the country's national integrated oil company. Currently the KPC is one of the largest oil companies in the world with extensive overseas operations including refineries and large downstream distribution networks.

Table 4.2 Oil revenues 1978–2008

Year	Nominal revenues (US$ billion)	Real revenues (2000US$ billion)	Nominal per capita revenues (US$)	Real per capita revenues (2000US$)
1978	10.4	22.5	8555	18 481
1979	18.6	37.1	14 394	28 677
1980	18.7	34.4	13 678	25 174
1981	13.5	22.7	9432	15 906
1982	8.4	13.3	5637	8903
1983	11.1	14.9	6253	9487
1984	10.8	15.6	6527	9563
1985	9.7	12.3	4994	7098
1986	5.1	8.8	3517	4894
1987	5.9	12.7	4970	6721
1988	5.9	9.1	3538	4627
1989	7	13.3	5111	6434
1990	10.7	8.2	2936	3593
1991	9.8	1	965	1123
1992	9.4	6.8	4094	4687
1993	7.7	11	6588	7384
1994	7.5	11.5	6737	7390
1995	8.3	12.8	7358	7914
1996	10.2	15.1	8462	8929
1997	9.1	12.9	7036	7307
1998	6	8.3	4418	4538
1999	7.7	10.7	5534	5595
2000	13.2	18.1	9244	9154
2001	15	14.5	7367	7132
2002	15	14.2	7073	6722
2003	19.1	17.8	8763	8158
2004	26.3	23.8	11 642	10 532
2005	40.4	35.4	17 286	15 134
2006	51	43.3	21 085	17 906
2007	55.3	45.7	22 050	18 212
2008	80.6	65.3	31 095	25 170

Source: Energy Information Administration, OPEC Revenues Fact Sheet, available at http://www.eia.doe.gov/emeu/cabs/OPEC_Revenues/Factsheet.html (accessed 2 April 2009).

In the 1970s, the Kuwaiti government believed that oil in the ground was worth more to future generations than holding such paper claims as securities and corporate shares that were subject to price inflation, exchange-rate risks and sequestration. Accordingly, a policy of conservation and reduced output was implemented. Sustained low oil prices from the mid-1980s to the late 1990s, however, had reversed this policy. The fluctuation of oil prices since the mid-1970s has led to drastic rises and falls in oil revenues as Table 4.2 illustrates.

These dramatic swings in oil revenues and the realisation that oil is a finite source, which belongs to current and future Kuwaiti generations, are the driving force for the founding of the country's sovereign fund. Bader al-Sa'ad, managing director of KIA, sums up the underlying reason for creating his country's SWF, 'We must deploy the money in a way to keep Kuwait going when the oil is gone. We don't have the cheap labor of China or the services of Switzerland or the efficiency of Singapore' (Sender 2007, p. A10).

Structure and governance

Sheikh Abdullah al-Salem al-Sabah, the ruler of Kuwait from 1950–65, decided in 1953 to establish the Kuwait Investment Board (KIB) with the aim of investing the surplus oil revenue in order to provide a fund for the future and reduce reliance on a single finite resource. The Kuwait Investment Office in London (KIO) was set up to pursue these objectives. Preparing for independence from the UK, the Kuwaiti government established the General Reserve Fund (GRF) in 1960. The GRF is the main treasurer for the government and receives all revenues (including all oil revenues) from which all state budgetary expenditures are paid. The GRF also holds all government assets, including Kuwait's participation in public enterprises such as the Kuwait Fund for Arab Economic Development and Kuwait Petroleum Corporation, as well as Kuwait's participation in multilateral and international organisations such as the World Bank, IMF and Arab Fund.

In 1976 Jaber al-Ahmed al-Jaber al-Sabah, Deputy Emir of Kuwait and Crown Prince, issued Law No.106, under which the Future Generations Fund (FGF) was established. Article 2 of the law stated: 'A special account shall be opened for creating a reserve that would act as an alternative to oil wealth. An amount of 50 per cent of the available State's General Reserve Fund is to be added to this account.' Article 1 stated: 'An amount of 10 per cent shall be allocated from the state's general revenues every year.' Finally, Law No.106 stipulated that the Ministry of Finance shall employ these funds into investments, and the profits accruing from them shall go into this account (Kuwait Investment Authority 2009a).

Finally, in 1982 Jaber al-Ahmed al-Sabah, Emir of Kuwait issued Law No. 47, establishing the Public Investment Authority, now known as the Kuwait Investment Authority. Law No. 47 stated that the objective of the KIA is to 'undertake the management of the GRF, the monies allocated to the FGF, as well as such other monies that the Minister of Finance may entrust the KIA with its management' (Article 2). The KIA's mission is to achieve a long-term investment return on the financial reserves, providing an alternative to oil reserves (Kuwait Investment Authority 2008a). In 1986, the KIA's revenues from investments exceeded revenue from exporting oil (Kuwait Investment Authority 2008b).

The KIA is managed by a Board of Directors composed of the Minister of Finance as chairman, the Minister of Oil, the under-secretary of the Ministry of Finance and the governor of the Central Bank, as well as five other members from the private sector (Article 3). The Board of Directors meets at least four times a year. The Kuwaiti government does not consider any of the assets managed by the KIA as international reserve of the state (Kuwait Investment Authority 2009b).

Transparency

Transparency is an abstract term that can be defined in terms of (a) clarity of roles and responsibilities; (b) public availability of information; (c) open budget preparation, execution and reporting; and (d) assurances of integrity (International Monetary Fund 2009). Three areas of transparency can be distinguished: governance structure (that is, who owns and manages the funds and what are the procedures for auditing and supervision?); investment objectives (that is, what are the goals and the time horizon to pursue them?); and investment strategy and implementation (that is, what is the size of the fund, asset composition, risk limits and returns?). Most SWFs do not disclose such information (Skancke 2008).

The degree of transparency of the KIA cannot be understood in isolation from the broader socio-economic and political system in Kuwait. Many Kuwaitis are proud that, in 1962, their country was the first Gulf state to adopt a parliamentary democracy and a constitution. For many years, the Kuwaiti press was among the most open in the Gulf region and the broader Middle East. Furthermore, the Kuwaiti General Assembly (parliament) has enjoyed real power in supervising public policy. This parliamentary power was clearly demonstrated in 2006 when a succession crisis erupted and the parliament members voted Sheikh Sa'ad al-Abdullah al-Sabah, the then Emir, out of office on health grounds.

Despite these signs of openness, Kuwaiti democracy suffers from serious flaws and still has a long way to go. The al-Sabah dynasty has ruled Kuwait for more than two and half centuries. The founder of the dynasty, who also gave it his name, was Sabah bin Jabir, the first ruler of Kuwait (1752–56). He was a member of the Utub tribe, a branch of the much larger Anaiza tribal confederation, to which the al-Saud of Saudi Arabia belongs. Towards the end of the seventeenth century, the Utub migrated from central Arabia following a devastating famine. After considerable wandering, they finally settled in Kuwait, which was largely uninhabited, with the agreement of the tribes controlling the area. Sabah bin Jabir was responsible for the establishment of Kuwait town and for promoting its role as a major trade centre on the trade route from India to the eastern Mediterranean and Europe.

From those early days to the present, the al-Sabah has ruled Kuwait. They have grown into a very large family. The exact number of al-Sabah is difficult to assess, though they are known to be over a thousand (Zahlan 1989). Their power is almost synonymous with that of the state. Indeed, it is often heard in Kuwaiti circles that Kuwait is the al-Sabah and the al-Sabah is Kuwait.

In August 1961, Emir Abdullah ordered the election of a 20-member constituent assembly to draft the country's first permanent constitution. This group completed its work within a year, and in November 1962, the Emir promulgated the final document. Freedom of opinion, the press, religion and demonstrations are mandated in accordance with the dictates of law. Kuwait is described as a hereditary emirate with an independent judiciary, an elected national assembly and a ministerial system.

The National Assembly held four elections in 1963, 1967, 1971 and 1975 – before being suspended in 1976. The assembly reopened following elections in 1981. Elections were again held in 1985, but then the body was dissolved in July 1986. In both cases of closure, the Emir responded to increasingly sharp opposition attacks on members of the ruling family and, especially in 1986, to what was seen as an increasingly threatening regional environment. Following the liberation of Kuwait from Iraqi occupation, the country held an election in October 1992 (Crystal and al-Shayeji 1998).

Political parties do not exist and the ultimate power still rests at the hands of the royal family. The growing intensity of the confrontation between the parliament and the government in recent years has prompted the Emir to frequently dissolve the parliament and call for elections. Since the 1991 Gulf War, parliamentary elections were held seven times (1992, 1996, 1999, 2003, 2006, 2008 and 2009). This limited but growing democratisation of public life is echoed in the practice of accountability and transparency of the KIA.

According to Article 8 of Law No. 47 of 1982, members of the Board of Directors, the employees of the KIA or any of those participating in any form in its activities may not disclose data or information about their work or the position of the invested assets, without a written permission from the chairman of the Board of Directors. Article 9 stipulates that 'Whoever divulges any of the secrets of the work of the KIA or data or information of which he became aware shall be punished with imprisonment for a period not exceeding three years' (Kuwait Investment Authority 2009c).

On the other hand, the KIA's activities are reviewed by both external and internal auditors. The Board of Directors appoints an external auditor, who reviews the FGF and GRF as well as the funds managed by the KIA. The KIA has an independent audit department that reports to the chairman of the Board. In addition, the State Audit Bureau has on-site personnel to monitor KIA's activities on an ongoing basis. Finally, the KIA makes annual closed-door presentations on the full details of all funds under its management, including its strategic asset allocation, benchmarks and rates of return, to the Council of Ministers and to the National Assembly (Kuwait Investment Authority 2009d).

The KIA, like many other big financial institutions all over the world, is not immune to corruption. Limited transparency and public accountability have further contributed to occasional mismanagements of the KIA's investments. Furthermore, as a study by the IMF concludes, if the SWF is not well integrated with the budget, it can 'complicate fiscal management and lead to an inefficient allocation of the government's total resources' (Davis et al. 2001, p. 8).

One of the most publicised cases of corruption and gross mismanagement involved a Spanish company called Torras Hostench. It started as a troubled paper company and quickly grew into one of Spain's largest industrial conglomerates, with holdings in chemicals, fertiliser, real estate, food and paper. The group was the largest in Spain not owned either by the government or a bank. Kuwaiti authorities contend that in the late 1980s and early 1990s Torras management conspired to steal at least US$500 million through the use of various shell companies, fictitious loans, fraud and embezzlement. Additionally, US$5 billion was squandered through egregious mismanagement. Sheikh Fahd Muhammad al-Sabah, a former chairman of the KIO, Fouad Khaled Jaffar, former general manager of the investment office, and De La Rosa, director of Torras, were all involved in this affair (Cohen 1993).

Investment portfolio

Like many other SWFs, the KIA does not disclose information on its assets, rates of return and allocations of its investments. However, in the last few years some data became available. In 2007, the Kuwaiti Finance Minister Bader Mishari al-Humaidhi announced that the KIA's assets reached US$213 billion, the largest in the country's history. These assets were divided between the FGF (US$174 billion) and the GRF (US$39 billion) (*Arab Times* 2007). Other sources give similar estimates. JP Morgan puts KIA's assets at US$250 billion (JP Morgan 2009), McKinsey Global Institute at US$200 billion (McKinsey Global Institute 2008) and the *Financial Times* at US$270 billion (Sender 2008).

Investment guidelines prohibit the KIA from investing in the following: (a) share ownership in companies whose principal business involves gambling, liquor or adult entertainment; (b) private placements and venture capitalisation; and (c) investing in single issuer/issues in excess of 5 per cent of the portfolio at the time of the purchase (Kuwait Investment Authority 2009f).

By their nature, SWFs are expected to invest in more diversified portfolios and riskier assets than traditional reserve holdings (Allen and Caruana 2008). In the early 2000s, however, the KIA pursued a conservative investment strategy aimed at preserving capital. Accordingly, the bulk of the KIA's assets were invested in the US Treasury. With a new management since the mid-2000s, the KIA has moved away from safe but low-return bonds and started to invest in alternative assets, such as private equity, real estate, hedge funds and commodities.

In the mid-2000s, the then new managing director of the KIA, Bader al-Sa'ad, hired Mercer Investment Consulting to review the fund's strategic asset allocation (Sender 2007). The consulting firm compared the KIA's cautious investing practices with those of the Yale and Harvard endowments, regarded as pioneers of institutional investing. The endowments, which have some of the same flexibility as the KIA to take a long-term approach, had achieved strong returns by investing in, for example, emerging-market stocks, real estate, hedge funds and private-equity funds. Mercer recommended that KIA decrease its allocations to traditional asset classes (such as public listed equities and bonds) and increase its allocation to non-traditional and uncorrelated asset classes (such as alternative investments, private equities and real estate). Mercer also recommended that KIA explore markets other than the traditional and developed economies of the USA, Western Europe and Japan (Kuwait Investment Authority 2009e).

Based on Mercer's recommendations, the KIA has pursued a more aggressive investment strategy aimed at diversifying its portfolio. The KIA has been particularly interested in investing in global financial institutions, including the Citigroup and Merrill Lynch. Like other SWFs from the Gulf region, the KIA has targeted Islamic finance. It purchased stakes in Islamic financial institutions and the securities they issued (Ziemba 2008). The biggest Islamic banks are in the Persian Gulf, including Dubai Islamic Bank, Kuwait Finance House and Saudi Arabia's al-Rajhi Bank. Malaysia and London are growing as major centres of Islamic banking as well. The KIA has also purchased properties, particularly in London and New York.

Other major investments were allocated to Daimler AG, the owner of Mercedes-Benz and British Petroleum (BP). Since 1974, the KIA was the largest shareholder in German auto manufacturer. In early 2009, Daimler AG sold new shares of stock worth about 1.95 billion euros ($2.65 billion) to Aabar, an investment company wholly owned by the Abu Dhabi government. Following the capital increase, the stake of Kuwait decreased to 6.9 per cent from its previous level of 7.6 per cent (Rauwald 2009).

In the late 1980s, the British government, led by Margaret Thatcher, decided to privatise some of the country's major corporations. Taking advantage of this investment opportunity, the KIA acquired 20 per cent of BP's shares, becoming the largest shareholders. Upon review, the UK Monopoly and Mergers Commission decided that the KIA might exercise influence over BP and constrain it from acting competitively. The KIA responded by reducing its shareholding to 9.9 per cent over a 12-month period (Behrendt 2008).

This aggressive investment strategy is reflected in the KIA's asset allocation. At the end of 2007, 60 per cent of the fund's assets were invested in equity, 25 per cent in bonds and 15 per cent in alternatives (Setser and Ziemba 2008). In recent years, the returns on these investments have been speculative: 11.4 per cent (2005), 13.2 per cent (2006) and 13.3 per cent (2007) (Thornton and Reed 2008).

In addition to these changes in the KIA portfolio, the fund has sought to diversify its investments across various geographic locations. Ideally, the KIA's investments in any given region are roughly proportional to that region's share of worldwide production. However, due to historical and strategic strong ties with Europe and the USA, KIA's holdings in these two markets are significantly higher. This geographical allocation has witnessed fundamental changes in recent years. The KIA management has expressed strong interest in investing in emerging markets in Asia. The goal is to reduce the portion of the portfolio invested in the USA and Europe to less than 70 per cent from about 90 per cent in 2007. The drive behind this shift is commercial. As Bader al-Sa'ad, managing director of the KIA, asked, 'Why invest in 2 per cent growth economies when you can invest in 8 per cent growth economies' (Sender 2007, p. A10)? The magnitude of the economic crisis in Europe and the USA in the second half of the 2000s has further reinforced this approach.

In 2008, Mustapha al-Shamali, Kuwait's Finance Minister, announced his country's intention to 'double or triple its investment in Japan' (Sender 2008). In recent years the KIA has steadily increased its investment in Asia. So far, China has been the main beneficiary. The Kuwaiti fund has a major stake in the Industrial and Commercial Bank of China. It has also invested in real estate in several Chinese cities. This move to increase investments in emerging markets at the expense of the USA has been further facilitated and reinforced by a major change in Kuwait's currency policy. Other Gulf Cooperation Council members (Bahrain, Oman, Qatar, Saudi Arabia and the United Arab Emirates) peg their currencies at a fixed rate to the dollar. Kuwait, on the other hand, stopped pegging its dinar to the dollar in June 2007 and moved to an exchange rate linked to an undisclosed basket of currencies (Wigglesworth 2009).

The global economic crisis has dealt a heavy blow to financial markets all over the world. Oil-producing nations and their SWFs have had to deal with at least two consequences of this crisis – substantial loses of the value of their investments and a sharp reduction in oil prices. In response to the global economic downturn, the KIA had to adjust its investment portfolio in a number of ways. First, the fund has reduced the volume of its investments in several markets. For example, Dow Chemical, the USA's largest chemicals group, reached a joint-venture agreement with Kuwait's Petroleum Corporation for a 50 per cent stake in its commodity chemical business. This US$17.4 billion deal was supposed to be partly funded by the KIA. In December 2008, just days before the agreement was due to come into effect, the KPC and KIA withdrew (Van Duyn 2008).

Second, many Kuwaitis and the parliament have called for the government to spend more of its wealth at home to stabilise the country's economy. In January 2009, the KIA pumped US$418 million into Gulf Bank, Kuwait's fourth largest traded lender, after it suffered heavy derivatives-trading losses (Critchlow 2009). The KIA also invested US$5.2 billion as part of a government fund to stabilise the stock market (England 2009). Third, despite this scaling back of investments overseas and focus on the local economy, the KIA managers have been aware that the global economic crisis offers some investment opportunities and have sought to take advantage of such 'bargains' (Cha 2008).

The KIA – an assessment

The proliferation of SWFs and the expansion of their size in recent years raise an important question – what benefits do sovereign funds bring to their home countries and to the receiving markets? The limited number of cases, the fact that many of them were created just in the last decade, and the unavailability of adequate data on their assets, strategies and governance make it hard to reach a conclusive conclusion.

The KIA, the world's oldest SWF, has been investing the country's oil revenues since 1953. Some important lessons can be drawn from this long history. First, the KIA has been proven crucial not only to Kuwait's economic wellbeing, but to its survival. The fundamental logic behind creating oil funds, including the KIA, is to save oil revenues for a 'rainy day'. On 2 August 1990, when Iraq invaded and occupied Kuwait, this rainy day arrived. During the course of the occupation and the liberation, more than 700 oil wells were set on fire and the government and hundreds of thousands of Kuwaitis were placed in exile. On the eve of the invasion the KIA's assets were estimated at US$100 billion. The British authorities, like all the other governments in the world, blocked Kuwaiti accounts so that Saddam Hussein could not get hold of them (Seznec 2008). The KIO in London served as a central bank for Kuwait during the occupation and organised the transfer of funds throughout the world and to the exiled Kuwaiti government in Saudi Arabia (Kuwait Investment Authority 2008c). An estimated US$80 billion was drawn down from the KIA to pay for the war to liberate Kuwait and the subsequent reconstruction efforts (*Middle East Economic Digest* 2004).

Second, at least three dynamics are likely to shape KIA's, and other oil funds' activities in the foreseeable future – fluctuation in oil prices, scale of domestic spending and recipient countries' policies on foreign investment, particularly from SWFs. Third, KIA's stakes in Daimler and BP, among others, suggest that the fund has a good track record as a passive and long-term investment vehicle. There is no evidence that the KIA has sought political leverage; rather, commercial interests appear to be the main driver for the KIA's activities.

Fourth, the KIA officials have taken an active role in the ongoing dialogue between SWFs, the IMF, Organisation for Economic Cooperation and Development (OECD) and other international financial institutions to reach a consensus on the most appropriate way to regulate SWFs' investments. For example, the KIA was a member in the International Working Group, which adopted the Generally Accepted Principles and Practices, known also as 'Santiago Principles', in October 2008. KIA officials voiced their concerns against any discrimination or restrictions by recipient nations against SWFs. They warned that the 'unfounded fear' of SWFs might lead to the rise of protectionism and complicate the free flow of trade and investment (Al-Sa'ad 2009). KIA officials also argue that across-border investments bind creditor and recipient nations together and reinforce bonds of mutual dependence among countries, thereby increasing the costs of international conflict.

References

Al-Sa'ad, Bader (2009), Keynote Speech at the First Luxembourg Foreign Trade Conference, 9 April 2008, available at http://www.kia.gov (accessed 21 March 2009).

Allen, Mark and Jaime Caruana (2008), *Sovereign Wealth Funds – A Work Agenda*. Washington, DC: International Monetary Fund, July.

Arab Times (2007), 'Kuwaiti Assets Top $200 billion: Al-Humaidhi: KIA Funds Grow to $213 Billion', 31 March.

Behrendt, Sven (2008), 'When Money Talks: Arab Sovereign Wealth Funds in the Global Public Policy Discourse', Carnegie Endowment, available at http://www.carnegieendowment.org (accessed 12 October 2008).

Cha, Ariana (2008), 'Foreign Wealth Funds Defend U.S. Investments', *Washington Post*, 27 March.

Cohen, Roger (1993), 'Missing Millions – Kuwait's Bad Bet – A Special Report: Big Wallets and Little Supervision', *New York Times*, 28 September.

Critchlow, Andrew (2009), 'Big Mideast Funds Scale Back Investments', *Wall Street Journal*, 27 January.

Crystal, Jill and Abdullah al-Shayeji (1998). 'The Pro-Democratic Agenda in Kuwait: Structures and Context', in Bahgat Korany, Rex Brynen and Paul Noble (eds), *Political Liberalization and Democratization in the Arab World*. Boulder, CO: Lynne Rienner Publisher, pp. 101–25.

Davis, Jeffrey, Rolando Ossowski, James Daniel and Steve Barnett (2001), 'Stabilization and Saving Funds for Nonrenewable Resources: Experience and Fiscal

Policy Implications', International Monetary Fund, Occasional Paper No. 205, Washington, DC.

England, Andrew (2009), 'Sovereign Wealth Funds Lose Their Gloss', *Financial Times*, 28 January.

Farrell, Diana and Susan Lund (2008), 'The World's New Financial Power Brokers', *McKinsey Quarterly*, 12(1), January.

Gause, Gregory F. (1994), *Oil Monarchies: Domestic and Security Challenges in the Arab Gulf States*. New York: Council on Foreign Relations Press.

Hubbert, Marion K. (1962), *Energy Resources*. Washington, DC: National Academy of Science, pp. 16–38.

International Monetary Fund (2009a), 'Guide on Resource Revenue Transparency', available at http://imf.org/external/pubs/ft/grrt/eng/060705.pdf (accessed 28 February 2009).

International Monetary Fund (2009b), 'IMF Executive Board Concludes 2009 Article IV Consultation with Kuwait', available at http://www.imf.org/external/np/sec/pn/2009/pn0956.htm (accessed 13 May 2009).

JP Morgan (2009), 'Sovereign Wealth Funds: A Bottom-up Primer', available at http://www.econ.puc-rio.br/mgarcia/Seminario/textos_preliminares/SWF22May08.pdf (accessed 15 March 2009).

Kuwait Petroleum Corporation (2008a), 'History of Oil', available at http://www.kpc.com/kw/www/h_default.htm (accessed 1 April 2009).

Kuwait Investment Authority (2008b), 'Mission and Principles', available at http://www.kia.gov.kw/NR/exeres/028BE69B-028BE69B-0BBE-449E-8FB3-0A6AD8E62639.htm (accessed 27 January 2008).

Kuwait Investment Authority (2008c), 'Kuwait Investment Office in London', available at http://www.Kia.gov.Kw/NR/exeres/73CF85E2-0C5A-4060-B94B-54E2D9EDA231.htm (accessed 31 May 2008).

Kuwait Investment Authority (2009a), 'Overview of Funds', available at http://www.kia/gov/kw/En/About_KIA/Overview_of_funds/pages/default.aspx (accessed 18 March 2009).

Kuwait Investment Authority (2009b), 'International Reserves of Kuwait', available at http://www.Kia.gov.Kw/En/About_KIA/International_Reserves/Pages/default.aspx (accessed 18 March 2009).

Kuwait Investment Authority (2009c), 'Transparency and Disclosure of Information', available at http://www.Kia.gov.Kw/En/About_KIA/Transparency/Pages/default.aspx (accessed 18 March 2009).

Kuwait Investment Authority (2009d), 'Governance at KIA', available at http://www.kia.gov.Kw/En/About_KIA/Governance/Pages/default.aspx (accessed 18 March 2009).

Kuwait Investment Authority (2009e), 'New Developments', available at http://www.Kia.gov/Kw/En/About_KIA/New_Developments/Pages/default.aspx (accessed 18 March 2009).

Kuwait Investment Authority (2009f), 'Portfolio Management', available at http://www.Kia.gov/Kw/En/Marketable_Securities/Portfolio_Management/Pages/default.aspx (accessed 21 March 2009).

McKinsey Global Institute (2008), 'The Coming Oil Windfall in the Gulf', available at http://www.mckinsey.com/mgi (accessed 20 January 2008).

McLachlan, Keith (1980), 'Oil in the Persian Gulf', in Alvin J. Cottrell (ed), *The Persian Gulf States: A General Survey*. Baltimore, MD: Johns Hopkins University Press, pp. 195–224.

Middle East Economic Digest (2004), 'New direction: With an Estimated $85,000 Million of Assets Under Management, the Kuwait Investment Authority is One of the Largest Institutional Investors in the World', 28 May.

Odell, Peter (2000), 'The Global Energy Market in the Long Term: The Continuing Dominance of Affordable Non-renewable Resources', *Energy Exploration and Exploitation*, 18(2–3), pp. 131–206.

Rauwald, Christoph (2009), 'Abu Dhabi Firm Buys 9.1% of Daimler – Parent of Mercedes Secures $2.65 Billion of Private Funds at a Time When Rivals Seek Government Aid', *Wall Street Journal*, 23 March.

Sender, Henny (2007), 'Deep Well: How a Gulf Petro-state Invests its Oil Riches; Kuwait's Mr. Al-Sa'ad Likes Asian Real Estate but is Cool to Treasury', *Wall Street Journal*, 24 August.

Sender, Henny (2008), 'Kuwait to Lift Japan Exposure', *Financial Times*, 3 August.

Setser, Brad and Rachel Ziemba (2008), 'Understanding the New Financial SuperpowerThe Management of GCC Official Foreign Assets', available at http://www.cfr.org (accessed 6 June 2008).

Seznec, Jean-Francois (2008), 'The Gulf Sovereign Wealth Funds: Myths and Reality', *Middle East Policy*, 15(2), pp. 97–111.

Shancke, Martin (2008), 'Foreign Government Investment in the U.S. Economy and Financial Sector', Hearing before the Subcommittee on Domestic and International Monetary Policy, Committee on Financial Service, US House of Representatives, available at http://financialservices.house.gov/hearing110/skancke030508.pdf (accessed 5 March 2008).

Thornton, Emily and Stanley Reed (2008), 'Who's Afraid of Mideast Money?', *Business Week*, 10 January, p. 24.

Van Duyn, Aline (2008), 'Kuwait Cancels Dow Chemical Deal', *Financial Times*, 28 December.

Wigglesworth, Robin (2009), 'Gulf Countries Extend Currency Union Deadline', *Financial Times*, 25 March.

Zahlan, Rosemarie Said (1989), *The Making of the Modern Gulf States: Kuwait, Bahrain, Qatar, the United Arab Emirates and Oman*. London: Unwin Hyman.

Ziemba, Rachel (2008), 'What are GCC Funds Buying? A Look at Their Investment Strategies', *RGE Monitor*, available at http://www.rgemonitor.com/redir.php?sid=1&cid=259853 (accessed 19 October 2008).

5
Sovereign Wealth Funds in the United Arab Emirates

Joseph A. Kéchichian

The phantom of sovereign wealth funds (SWFs) looms ominously over the United Arab Emirates (UAE) because it allegedly controls a significant portion of all such global funds. Simply stated, it is mistakenly assumed that the UAE is one of those countries that holds 'foreign assets far in excess of anything needed to respond to financial contingencies' and, consequently, because Emirati leaders may 'feel pressure to deploy them strategically or at least to earn higher returns than those available in US Treasury bills or their foreign equivalents' (Summers 2007, p. 10).

Naturally, there is much more than a natural apprehension about the motives and capacities of UAE officials as they invest SWF-holdings, since the Emirates is an oil-producing state. Presumably how Arabs invest these funds, especially if they are done outside of carefully vetted Western mechanisms, raise eyebrows among leading industrialised powers. Many fear that SWF-holdings grant undue influence to relatively small or even insignificant economic entities – which the UAE is not though it is perceived as such by the powerful as well as the envious – perhaps even to undermine global economic interests as defined by the Organisation for Economic Cooperation and Development (OECD) countries.

The gravest perceived danger, again from a narrow OECD perspective, is to see UAE SWFs bypassing intermediary asset managers. In short, SWFs are excellent when invested through established endowments and pension funds, but ghastly when they bypass institutional pools of capital. In the words of Mohamed El-Erian, a former International Monetary Fund (IMF) official, as well as a well-known former manager of Harvard University's US$35 billion endowment, and now the co-CEO of

PIMCO, one of the largest investment management companies in the world:

> I suspect that the broadening of the SWF phenomenon will be deemed a 'success' at both the national and international levels if it is underpinned by governance and organisational structures that result in high-adjusted investment returns. On the national level, this would preserve and enhance wealth for the current and future generations. On the international level, it would respond decisively to concerns that SWFs could undermine the functioning of global capitalism through politically induced investments and commercially questionable activities.
>
> (El-Erian 2008, pp. 137–8)

How could leading OECD powers, which can no longer count on cheap overseas labour and commodities to pay for their insatiable consumer appetites, channel SWFs to serve them? The answer seems to be relatively easy, as El-Erian notes. Because major changes are underway in the workings of global capital markets that require emerging countries to act as growth vehicles, the high risk assumed by most will render their financial resources, SWFs, fair game, which is akin to declaring that demand is demand and the emerging markets is where some large part of any portfolio must be if it is to flourish. The only flaw in this logic is that one cannot really be impressed by a predatory focus to go after other peoples' cash to solve one's own problems. Again, in El-Erian's own inimitable words:

> the debate on sovereign wealth funds (SWFs) ... is being heavily influenced by incomplete analysis, ill-defined concepts of national security and reciprocity, and monster-like characterisations of motives pertaining to political, military, and mercantilist issues. ... With time, SWFs will shift from being important sources of temporary and permanent capital for alternative funds managers to being more important competitors. As such, SWF scrutiny will likely increase and broaden.
>
> (El-Erian 2008, p. 241)

Consequently, whatever apprehensions exist must be understood to be fuelled by fundamentally different conceptions about the role of government investments and, in the case of the UAE, questioning the very conservative model whose long-term priorities differ sharply from those in any OECD state. Given such a major dichotomy, why did several Emirates within the UAE decide to create these investment funds, and do they truly operate differently from other institutional or private financial ventures?

To better answer these two basic questions, an effort is made to assess the SWFs under the control of the Emirate of Abu Dhabi, the largest of the seven Shaykhdoms nestled within the federal state of the UAE. Given space limitations, the chapter does not provide a complete assessment of the myriad private family funds held by some of the wealthiest Emiratis in Abu Dhabi, nor does it cover SWFs in Dubai, Sharjah, Ras al-Khaimah, Ajman, Umm al-Qiwain and Fujairah. These are undetermined both in terms of their numbers as well as total values, with several private SWFs under the control of respective Shaykhdoms suspected to be substantial, though impossible to quantify.

There are eight major SWFs in Abu Dhabi, including the motherload Abu Dhabi Investment Authority (ADIA), certainly the largest and best-known SWF. While ADIA is dominant and will likely occupy that position, additional non-negligible SWFs include: the Abu Dhabi Fund for Development (ADFD), the Abu Dhabi Investment Company (ADIC), the International Petroleum Investment Company (IPIC), the Abu Dhabi Retirement Pensions and Benefits Fund (ADRPBF), Mubadala Development Corporation (MDC), the Abu Dhabi National Energy Company (ADNEC) and the Abu Dhabi Investment Council (ADICO). All eight were created and funded to serve the Shaykhdom of Abu Dhabi and all received seed funds derived from the rich Emirate's significant petroleum income. The government of Abu Dhabi directly or indirectly controls each one of these SWFs even if their respective boards include foreign managers. Equally important, within that government, the Al Nahyan ruling family exercisesimmense powers, which means that fundamental decisions are often reached at the highest levels. This is unlikely to change for the foreseeable future (Kéchichian 2008, pp. 279–348). Moreover, the perception that these financial instruments are sources of threat is probably wrong, because the UAE SWFs have been politically innocuous. In fact, UAE SWFs have proven to be useful, both in currency stabilisation, investment ties throughout the Muslim world, preparing for future pensions obligations, advancing the vertical integration in oil production (as well as downstream) and, of course, in building up rent-derived investments overseas to meet the needs of the next generation, the so-called post-oil citizens. Consequently, it would be logical to assume that SWFs will remain a trait of future UAE strategic initiatives, especially because of likely oil price increases.

Eight major Abu Dhabi SWFs

Although UAE SWFs are a small percentage of transnational investment flows on the global scale, they play a critical role in the *rentier*
state system, along with the intrinsic bargains associated with them.
Before addressing these critical questions, and while most of the funds
reveal only rudimentary information about themselves, it is important
to examine the eight Abu Dhabi SWFs, to better assess their value to the
Shaykhdom, the UAE and the international financial environment.

Abu Dhabi Investment Authority

Originally established in 1971, ADIA was meant to function as an
emergency fund for the government, when oil prices were relatively
low, expenditures skyrocketing and budgets wildly fluctuating. At first,
its mission was to invest windfall revenues from price shocks, which
flooded the region with cash reserves in the aftermath of dramatic price
adjustments after the 1973–74 oil crisis. When oil prices fell sharply
in the 1980s and 1990s, Abu Dhabi relied on ADIA's deep pockets to
meet budgetary requirements, though the fund's mission evolved significantly as the century came to a close. Today, ADIA's mission is to 'secure
and maintain the current and future prosperity of the Emirate of Abu
Dhabi, through the prudent management of the Emirate's investment
assets'. Consequently, ADIA evolved into a premier global institutional
investor and, for the past three decades, has built a solid reputation
across global financial markets as a trusted and responsible investor as
well as a leading provider of capital.

With oil income soaring during the past few years, the ebb and flow of
net earnings became a one-way torrent, which transformed ADIA into
the world's largest SWF, with estimates of its assets ranging between
US$500 and US$900 billion. Though not all of Abu Dhabi's earnings
are safely invested in ADIA, the Emirate's estimated US$350 million
daily income in 2008 allow for a lucrative and envied nest egg. Though
the Emirate's non-oil resources are diversified, Abu Dhabi remains in
the enviable position of generating more than 75 per cent of revenues
from oil exports, a phenomenon unlikely to change for the foreseeable
future.[1]

Two leading observers of SWF funds in the Gulf region estimated that
ADIA assets stood at around US$150 billion in 2001 that permitted the
fund to secure index-based returns on a portfolio with a heavy allocation towards equities and emerging markets (Setser and Ziemba 2009,
p. 21). Given that ADIA reportedly had high returns on its portfolio

in 2005–07, the authors' estimate probably understated returns and assets under management, though both observers concluded that recent losses should not be overstated. They believed that estimates for ADIA encompassed the foreign holdings of the Abu Dhabi Investment Council (ADICO), which was created in 2007 and received all of ADIA's regional and domestic holdings (see below), although this could not be verified independently. ADIA, ADICO and other funds were mandated to diversify the Emirate's investments both to help invest the deluge and, more likely, to protect investments by spreading them across the board. In the event, ADIA's large allocation to equities, especially those in Europe and emerging markets, contributed to its high returns in 2005–07.[2] There was little controversy on the significant returns on ADIA's equity investments, which were the largest source of its asset growth from 2003 to mid-2007, even if losses since mid-2008 may have offset the oil windfall. Setser and Ziemba estimated that assets under management of ADIA and ADICO fell by about US$140 billion in 2008 (2009, p. 22).

Notwithstanding such losses, ADIA's success stemmed from its tight governance, with a literal 'Who's Who' of the Al Nahyan ruling family in tight control of the fund. As the chart (Figure 5.1) illustrates, the ADIA 'Board of Directors' includes Shaykh Khalifa bin Zayed Al Nahyan (Ruler of Abu Dhabi and President of the UAE), along with his brothers, Shaykh Sultan bin Zayed (personal representative of the President), Shaykh Muhammad bin Zayed (heir apparent of the Emirate of Abu Dhabi), Shaykh Ahmed bin Zayed (the fund's managing director),[3] Shaykh Mansur bin Zayed (Minister of Presidential Affairs) and Shaykh Muhammad bin Khalifa bin Zayed (second son of the President and son-in-law of the personal representative). This is, without a doubt, a most formidable representation of the Al Nahyan ruling family, whose fiduciary responsibilities towards the Emirate cannot be doubted. The board also includes Muhammad Habrush Al Suwaydi, Dr Jua`an Salim Al Dhaheri, Hamad Muhammad Al Hurr Al Suwaydi and Sa`id Mubarak Rashid Al Hajiri, further enhancing its legitimacy given the expertise of the last named in financial matters and diversified global financial connections. Naturally, as the chart depicts, all of these men are senior government officials appointed by Ruler's Decree, assisted by a collection of talented individuals from the UAE and from around the world to assist the managing director run ADIA. Though difficult to confirm, but in line with similar outfits throughout the UAE, ADIA's Abu Dhabi head office is staffed with individuals hailing from more than 40 countries, which portrays a rich diversity and fosters high standards of leadership, integrity and professionalism.

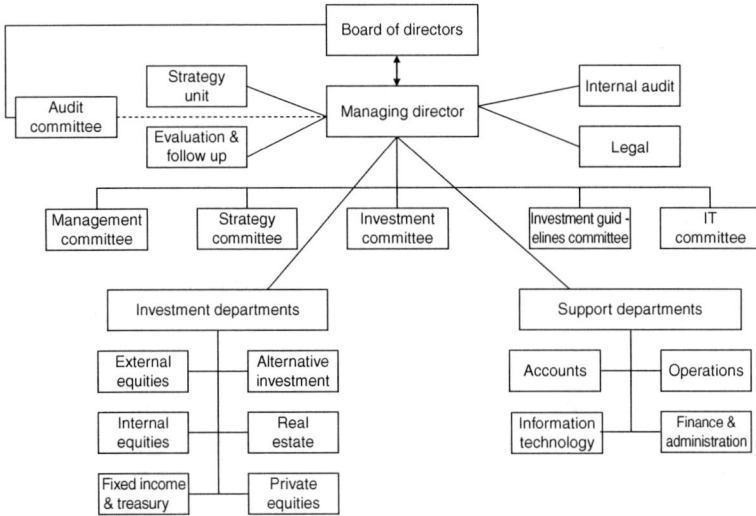

Figure 5.1   Organisational structure of Abu Dhabi Investment Authority

Indeed, ADIA manages a substantial global portfolio of holdings across sectors, geographies and asset classes, including publicly listed equities, fixed income, real estate and private equities. The goal was and remains to secure sustained long-term financial returns and, in the words of President Shaykh Khalifah bin Zayed Al Nahyan,

> to depend on long-term investments because we believe that our investments are part of our commitment to future generations, which may not have the same resources available now. That is especially true if one takes into consideration that oil resources are depleting and global demand on energy is on the rise.
>
> (bin Zayed 2008)

How ADIA addresses this objective, to fulfil its commitment to developing local UAE talent and securing a wide range of opportunities while withstanding an increased visibility on the global stage that prompted scrutiny from other countries, are the key concerns that face the fund's leaders.

Certainly, money will continue to flow into ADIA accounts but other contenders are poised to claim a share of the Emirate's resources, though ADIA will probably continue to occupy the position of *primus inter pares* among the eight UAW SWFs.

Abu Dhabi Fund for Development

The late ruler of Abu Dhabi, Shaykh Zayed bin Sultan Al Nahyan, was a visionary leader though he and the Emirate of Abu Dhabi benefited from generous financial aid flowing from Kuwait throughout the 1950s and 1960s. This traditional form of aid practised by many tribes on the Arabian Peninsula was not lost on Zayed who vowed to emulate the Kuwaiti model after he acceded to rulership in 1966. Towards that end, and even before the UAE gained its independence from Britain on 1 December 1971, Zayed established the Abu Dhabi Fund for Development in July 1971. ADFD's mission was to assist developing countries, focusing on Arab, Muslim and friendly emergent nations that faced financial difficulties, infrastructure challenges or other development problems. Over the years, the Fund provided substantial assistance in the form of loans, grants or contributions to capital projects (Demir 1979, pp. 25–39).[4]

Zayed's torch passed to Khalifah as the fund remained a model institution in providing development assistance that alleviates global poverty. Today, ADFD continues a unique benevolent march, whose policies to extend economic support at the regional and international levels seek to achieve the type of development goals that seldom trickled down. Naturally, developing countries benefit from the fund, but it is investing financial resources to earn the highest possible returns that preoccupy ADFD leaders the most.

Critics point out that ADFD provides economic assistance to Arab, African, Asian and other countries to support their economic development aid while ignoring equally needed candidates. Focusing on Arab and Muslim countries may be inherently discriminatory but loans and grants must enhance Abu Dhabi leaders' core values, which give preference to Arab and Muslim societies. Still, it would be a mistake to assume that ADFD discriminates against non-Arab and non-Muslim recipients, with additional assistance going to needy countries beyond the fund's traditional zone of interest. In recent years, ADFD's strategy focused on the following pillars:

1. Providing economic assistance to developing countries.
2. Promoting a distinguished image of the Abu Dhabi Emirate and its government through development projects.
3. Enhancing capabilities by supporting programmes that increase the possibilities of achieving the sought development in these countries.
4. Encouraging relations and local partnerships with developing countries.
5. Qualifying and developing national human resources in recipient countries.

Since its foundation, and during the past 37 years, ADFD's total disbursements reached approximately US$10 billion (around 23 billion UAE Dirhams) to 267 development projects in 52 developing countries around the world.[5] In addition to its myriad activities, ADFD also manages several specialised loans and grants on behalf of the Abu Dhabi government, 'as it plays an essential role in designing, executing, supervising and assessing the projects financed by the government'. The total amount of aid granted by the Abu Dhabi government and managed by ADFD may have reached US$4 billion (10 billion UAE Dirhams), although these are 'guesstimates' at best.

The ADFD portfolio includes a variety of cases that illustrate the type of investment preferred by fund managers.

Al Dhabi Development Company LLC

Established in October 2007, Al Dhabi is a holding company which is fully owned by the ADFD and has two subsidiary companies: Al Dhabi Property Company, which owns and manages several presidential villas, and the Al Dhabi Agriculture Company.

UAE-Bangladesh Investment Company 'UBICO' (Bangladesh)

UBICO was established in 1986, a joint partnership between ADFD (60 per cent) and the government of Bangladesh (40 per cent). UBICO invested in a 'Textile and Clothes Factory' situated 20 kilometres south of Dacca with a workforce of about 600.

Company of Studies and Development for Sousse Nord (Tunisia)

Set up in 1973, the company works on the promotion and development of all tourist activities in North Sousse situated 60 kilometres south of the Tunisian capital, and stands as a model of effective tourist development projects in North Africa. The venture includes apartments, villas, hotels, a tourist seaport, a golf club as well as other entertainment facilities. The ADFD owns 32.3 per cent of its paid-up capital with the participation of the Tunisian Development Bank.

Raysut Cement Company (Sultanate of Oman)

The company was founded in 1981 with two production lines, Portland cement (the most basic ingredient of concrete, mortar, stucco and most non-specialty grout) and Pozzolan, which derives from Pozzolana, a siliceous and aluminous material that is poured underwater with very strong properties. Since 1996, the company has embarked on an extension plan intended to upgrade its cement production capacity from 288 000 to 788 000 metric tons per year, which is primarily intended for use in oil wells. ADFD owns 10 per cent of this company.

Societe Rebab (Morocco)

Rebab was established in 1984. Its shares are listed in the Moroccan stock exchange and ADFD owns 82.82 per cent of the total share capital. In turn, Rebab invests in three major companies that include hotels, mining, the banking sector and in materials trading.

DELMA for Tourist Investments (Morocco)

DELMA Company owns the five-star Casablanca-Sheraton, which is situated in the heart of the famed city. Inaugurated in April 1988, the Sheraton facility includes 302 rooms and several restaurants that cater to the city's large business community. ADFD owns 33.71 per cent of DELMA.

Union Maroc Emirat de Peches UMEP (Morocco)

Based in Aghadir, UMEP started operations in late 1989 with six trawlers well equipped for fishing in the high seas, each boasting a 350-tonnes capacity. The trawlers, equipped with the best fish-detecting technologies, cater to Japanese and West European markets. Due to its operational and financial success, the company is planning to expand its business in the future. ADFD owns 40 per cent of the company.

Emirates-Moroccan PALMARE Company (Morocco)

Established in February 1987, the company owns a four-star tourist village that includes 328 rooms, restaurants, cafes and several recreational facilities inside Marrakech city. PALMARE accommodates mostly Western European tourists. The sprawling facility is managed by the Tamaris Company, which is part of the ACCOR Group, through a limited-term leasing contract. ADFD owns 17 per cent of the company.

CIMAR Cement Company (Morocco)

Although established in 1972, the company could not produce Portland cement before 1976. Its factories, with the primary production capacity of 550 000 metric tons /year, are situated 45 kilometres from Marrakech.

In 1995, the company embarked on an expansion plan, which enabled it to increase annual production capacity to 1.3 million metric tons/year. It is now considered one of the largest cement producers in Morocco, and covers about 15 per cent of local market needs. ADFD owns 5.38 per cent of CIMAR.

Abu Dhabi Tourist Investment Company ADTIC

Established in 1988, the company owns and operates three five-star hotels in Egypt, two in Sharm al-Sheikh and another in Hurgada. In addition, the company owns the majority of the capital share of The Arab Egypt Company for Hotels, which is developing a five-star tourist village near Sharm al-Sheikh. ADFD owns 84.28 per cent of ADTIC. It may be interesting to note that ADFD's activities in Egypt focus on the hospitality sector, with major shares in the Sphinx Sofitel Hotel, located opposite the Giza Pyramids, the Hurgada Sofitel inaugurated in April 1995 and the Sharm al-Sheikh Sofitel inaugurated in November 1996, all of which are managed by the French group ACCOR.[6]

As these sample investment projects illustrate, ADFD poured its resources into moneymaking schemes throughout leading Arab and Muslim societies, with a special emphasis on employment opportunities. Exponential increases, through carefully vetted trickle-down preferences, meant that the impact of investments went beyond the mere income-generating portfolios but also included effective work programmes that lifted the downtrodden from the abyss of poverty. It fulfilled Shaykh Zayed's vision that to those who have been given much, much will be required, a catechism that fulfilled his Muslim faith's injunctions.

Abu Dhabi Investment Company

The Abu Dhabi Investment Company was founded in 1977 by decree of the late Shaykh Zayed bin Sultan as the first UAE investment company in the capital. ADIC is a Joint Stock Company that specialises in providing investment and corporate finance in addition to advisory services. It is jointly owned by ADIA and the National Bank of Abu Dhabi and invests primarily in private equity, real estate, asset management and infrastructure. In 2007, the company was given a fresh mandate, to attract and manage third-party funds. While ADIC continued to invest government assets, its strategy was described by one leading group as 'Invest AD', which was also the brand name adopted in mid-2009 (Walid 2009).

ADIC offers its investment expertise to institutional investors in the UAE and beyond, with clients benefiting from the Abu Dhabi-based company's access to select opportunities in the Middle East and North Africa (MENA). Undoubtedly, this is the unquantifiable advantage of ADIC managers – access to key decision-makers who may have an intrinsic interest in facilitating the success of a particular investment, as well as an intimate knowledge of local conditions. While this may be interpreted as insider trading, the access and knowledge are largely proprietary, which is extremely difficult under normal circumstances and nearly impossible at other times. Consequently, Invest AD is closely aligned with the long-term diversification and growth objectives of Abu Dhabi authorities as clearly expressed in the government's long-term strategy, the Abu Dhabi 2030 Vision.

International Petroleum Investment Company

The International Petroleum Investment Company (IPIC) was formed by the Abu Dhabi government in 1984, tasked with an ambitious mandate to invest in hydrocarbons industries throughout the world. Because Abu Dhabi is keen to maintain a leading presence on the global hydrocarbons scene, a leading member of the ruling Al Nahyan family, Shaykh Mansur bin Zayed, was appointed Chairman and is reputedly aware of the company's progress.

In 2009, IPIC's investment portfolio is estimated to be worth more than US$14 billion, with major stakes in 14 world leading hydrocarbons companies. Through careful consideration and investment, IPIC has continued to grow exponentially to maximise value for its primary shareholder, the government of Abu Dhabi. The first IPIC outlay was made in 1988, when the company acquired a substantial minority in the Spanish refiner/marketer CEPSA. Following this successful tie-up, 'IPIC's partners have been chosen based on their ability to add shareholder value through technology, operational excellence, and participation in growth markets, while delivering synergies with the existing portfolio'.[7] This track record should allow IPIC to embrace new ventures with high levels of return.

Abu Dhabi Retirement Pensions and Benefits Fund

The Abu Dhabi Retirement Pensions and Benefits Fund (ADRPBF) is an important entity of the Abu Dhabi government and was founded in 2000 to manage contributions, pensions and end-of-service benefits for

UAE nationals working for, or retired from, government service. Importantly, coverage is also provided to individuals indirectly employed by the Emirate, either on the current payroll or potential future employees, including private sector workers who may not be on the Emirate's payroll but whose services towards the Shaykhdom are widely recognised. A good illustration of such employees included retirees from banks that were entirely owned by Abu Dhabi but whose private statuses left this workforce in limbo.

The fund's 'vision is to be one of the top five providers of retirement pensions and benefits services in the world' and, in striving for this goal, focuses on continuously improving customer service. Guided by the spirit of the words of the late ruler, Shaykh Zayed, the fund motto is: 'Men, not money, are our real wealth' (Zayed 2005).

Unlike ADIA or ADFD, ADRPBF collects pension contributions from eligible UAE nationals, their employers, as well as steady contributions from the government of Abu Dhabi. Consequently, total financial assets are invested to ensure hefty returns that can pay future pensions and benefits to every eligible Abu Dhabian entitled to receive them. Part of the fund's mandate is to advise Abu Dhabi officials on strategy and policies for social insurance and retirement provision to help ensure that the fund achieves its aims. Beyond Abu Dhabi and, perhaps, other UAE Emirates, ADRPBF plans to become one of the top five providers of retirement pensions and benefits services in the world. Chances are excellent that the fund may gain a foothold in several Gulf countries before long, introducing innovative mechanisms to provide retirement services to Gulf nationals who have served in their respective governments, all within Gulf Cooperation Council (GCC) regulations that permit such crossovers.[8]

Mubadala Development Corporation

Mubadala Development Corporation (MDC), a Public Joint Stock Company headquartered in Abu Dhabi, was established in 2002 and now boasts a portfolio estimated at US$15 billion. Though its focus is on developing and managing an extensive and economically diverse portfolio of commercial initiatives, MDC's seed resources are derived from the Emirate's oil income, anchored on long-term capital-intensive investments that would deliver strong financial returns. The corporation's sole shareholder is the government of the Emirate of Abu Dhabi, under the leadership of one of Abu Dhabi's most dynamic officials, Khaldoon Khalifah Al Mubarak. Its preferred investment portfolios concentrate on aerospace, energy and industry, health care, information and communications technology, infrastructure, real estate and hospitality services and, according to its 2009 annual report, invested both locally as well as overseas (Mubadala 2009).[9]

It remains a mystery why MDC was created when ADIA or a number of other funds were functioning except in the sense that it allowed certain members of the ruling Al Nahyan family members to control a more specific share of the Emirate's assets. This is not necessarily a sinister scenario along the lines of conspiracy theorists who insist that MDC's very existence was an illustration of financial disputes at the highest levels of the Abu Dhabi government, although such an eventuality cannot be ruled out. Suffice it to say that MDC's board is significantly different from ADIA's and is led by Chairman Shaykh Muhammad bin Zayed, the Emirate's Heir Apparent, not Shaykh Khalifah bin Zayed, the ruler and President of the UAE. Other than Shaykh Muhammad, no other sons of Shaykh Zayed serve on its board, although Al Nahyan cadet branch members do.

Unlike other Abu Dhabi funds, MDC published its first annual report in April 2009, providing detailed insights on its portfolios, incomes and expenses. One of the first projects financed by MDC was to develop clean-burning natural gas to meet the Emirate's growing demand for electricity and water. This was the Dolphin Energy project, which was in effect an integrated upstream development with a processing plant, compression facilities, subsea pipelines and distribution network that involved 364 kilometres of pipeline, laid to transport natural gas from Qatar to customers in Abu Dhabi, Dubai, the Northern Emirates as well as Oman. Dolphin Energy, which is 51 per cent owned by MDC (with the balance of ownership evenly split between the French Total S.A. and the American Occidental Petroleum Corporation), started operation in 2007, and introduced the company regionally and worldwide, with financial commitments that were covered by a conventional bank facility of US$1.36 billion. In time, this note was refinanced through a combination of Islamic and conventional financing instruments, which totalled US$3.45 billion.

If the Dolphin project operated in familiar grounds, MDC quickly emancipated its investments, to create clusters in a variety of other industries, including aerospace. In fact, the company was keenly interested in developing a composite aero-structure plant in Abu Dhabi, the first of its kind in the region, which marks a significant step forward in the creation of a robust aerospace hub within the Emirate. The ultimate purpose of the hub will be to 'manufacture' technology intensive aero-structure composite components and assemblies. Alenia Aeronautica, a subsidiary of leading Italian aerospace conglomerate Finmeccanica, is one of the companies that will provide technology, technical assistance and specialised training, as well as the transfer of composite aero-structure manufacturing work to the new composites plant (Mubadala 2009).

A sustainable industrial ecosystem has also been created through projects such as Emirates Aluminium Company Limited (EMAL). Established in 2007, EMAL is a strategic joint venture between Dubal (Dubai Aluminium) and MDC, and is responsible for owning, constructing and operating a 1.5 million tonne/annum primary aluminum smelter at Al Taweelah in Abu Dhabi. Phase One will have a nominal production capacity of approximately 718 000 tonne/annum, and when completed it is expected to be the largest greenfield aluminium smelter in the world. Environmental controls will ensure that the plant can operate without damage to the surrounding flora and fauna (Mubadala 2009).

Notable investments in 2007 and 2008 included an 8.1 per cent stake in computer chip maker AMD for US$622 million, as well as a US$1.35 billion investment in the private equity giant Carlyle Group, which gave Abu Dhabi a 7.5 per cent stake in the well-connected firm. MDC also committed a further US$500 million to a Carlyle investment fund.

On 31 December 2008, MDC investments included the following (partial list):

1. Abu Dhabi Finance PSC 20 per cent.
2. Abu Dhabi Future Energy Company PSC 100 per cent.
3. Abu Dhabi Knee & Sports Medicine Centre LLC 100 per cent.
4. Abu Dhabi Molecular Imaging Centre LLC 100 per cent.
5. Abu Dhabi Ship Building PJSC 40 per cent.
6. Advanced Micro Devices, Inc. 8.1 per cent.
7. Al Hikma Development Company PSC 100 per cent.
8. Al Maabar International Investments LLC 20 per cent.
9. Al Maqsad Development Company PSC 100 per cent.
10. Al Taif Technical Services PSC 100 per cent.
11. Al Waha Capital PJSC 14.7 per cent.
12. ALDAR Properties PJSC 19.06 per cent.
13. Al Yah Satellite Communications Company PSC (Yahsat) 100 per cent.
14. Cleveland Clinic Abu Dhabi LLC 100 per cent.
15. Dolphin Energy Limited 51 per cent.

16. Emerging Markets Telecommunications Company (Etisalat Nigeria) 30 per cent.
17. Emirates Aluminium Company Limited 50 per cent.
18. Emirates Integrated Telecommunications Company PJSC (du) 19.72 per cent.
19. Emirates Ship Investment Company LLC 32.9 per cent.
20. Ferrari S.p.A. 5 per cent.
21. Guinea Alumina Corporation Limited 8.33 per cent.
22. Horizon International Flight Academy LLC 100 per cent.
23. Imperial College London Diabetes Centre 100 per cent.
24. Injazat Data Systems LLC 60 per cent.
25. Iskandar (Holdings) Company Ltd. 22.2 per cent.
26. John Buck International Properties LLC 51 per cent.
27. Khadamat Facilities Management Company LLC 51 per cent.
28. KOR Hotel Group 50 per cent.
29. LeasePlan Emirates Fleet Management LLC 51 per cent.
30. LeasePlan Corporation NV 25 per cent.
31. London Array Limited 20 per cent.
32. Manhal Development Company PSC 100 per cent.
33. Masdar Clean Tech Fund, L.P. 40 per cent.
34. Mubadala Capital and Real Estate LLC 51 per cent.
35. Mubadala Petroleum Services Company LLC 100 per cent.
36. National Central Cooling Company PJSC (Tabreed) 15.79 per cent.
37. National Reference Laboratory 100 per cent.
38. Pearl Energy Limited 100 per cent.
39. Petrofac Emirates LLC 51 per cent.
40. PF Emirates Interior LLC 51 per cent.
41. Piaggio Aero Industries S.p.A. 31.5 per cent.
42. PSN Emirates LLC 51 per cent.
43. Spyker Cars N.V. 22.8 per cent.
44. SR Technics 36 per cent.
45. The Carlyle Group 7.50 per cent.
46. The John Buck Company 24.9 per cent.
47. Torresol Energy Investments SA 40 per cent (Mubadala 2009).

Inasmuch as many of these companies recorded dramatic financial swings in 2007 and 2008, MDC reported that its total losses in 2008 stood at 11.8 billion Dirhams (US$3.21 billion) compared to a profit of 1.3 billion Dirhams (US$350 million) in 2007 (Mubadala 2009). The mere fact that the Fund acknowledged losses was also new although many of its investments were long term and would probably weather periodic downturns.

These examples confirm that Abu Dhabi, perhaps unlike its sister emirates, has a 'peculiar devotion to manufacturing'. In fact, 'much of its oil wealth is being used to start industries from scratch: in cars and aerospace, components and chips', which certainly means that Abu Dhabi's SWFs' potential earnings will increase even more in the future (Financial Times 2009). In the *Financial Times'* incomparable description of this emphasis – 'this may look quixotic, yet invariably these stakes come with local training and manufacturing commitments', which will reverse underlying Arab defeatism, best explained by the Syrian philosopher Sadek al-Azm who wrote a famous critique of the mindset some 40 years ago. Al-Azm then declared that 'Arabs … have become removed from the social and economic processes that make innovation and scientific breakthroughs possible' (Financial Times 2009). Abu Dhabi's acquisitions, whether a stake in Daimler Benz, or General Electric, Rolls-Royce, EADS and Advanced Micro Devices, strongly imply a desire to create long-term sustainable economies that will enjoy consumerism without being simply satisfied with its narrow benefits.

Abu Dhabi National Energy Company

Created in 2006, the Abu Dhabi National Energy Company – known as TAQA for its Arabic acronym – sought to become a blue-chip energy business, eager to transform itself into a US$40–60 billion group by 2020, to 'both look and act like a Fortune 500 company'.[10] This vision meant that managers would need to run the company profitably and, if TAQA is to ever become like a Fortune 500 business, its gross revenues must be sustainable.

TAQA was founded through an initial public offering [IPO] issued on the Abu Dhabi Stock Market (ADSM that is now known as the Abu Dhabi Securities Exchange (ADX)). Original investors owned shares in the previously state-owned assets of the Abu Dhabi Water and Electricity Authority (ADWEA), akin to a transfer from one state entity to another, although the new IPO was heavily over-subscribed. Both public and private investors reaped strong rewards from the fast-growing company, fully backed by the government, which poured in a significant percentage of its seed funds. In 2009, TAQA assets exceeded US$23.4 billion, with operations in 13 markets around the world. Among its more noteworthy financial milestones were:

1. Six Independent Water and Power Producers (IWPPs) in the UAE, with operations that handled 85 per cent of water and electricity in Abu Dhabi, 11 000 megawatts of installed power, and a 591 million gallons/day desalination capacity.

2. In November 2006, TAQA issued the largest ever international bond offer at US$3.5 billion, along with a long bond at US$1.5 billion, as well as a prime euro benchmark at €750 million, all of which demonstrated the international value of the company.

TAQA was awarded the 'Emerging Market Deal of the Year' and 'Middle East Corporate Bond of the Year' by *EuroWeek* in 2006, which further illustrated its acclaim.[11]

Abu Dhabi Investment Council

The Abu Dhabi Investment Council is an investment arm of the government of Abu Dhabi that started operations in April 2007 to invest part of the government's surplus financial resources. ADICO received an unspecified dividend from Abu Dhabi's surplus oil revenue, estimated at 30 per cent, which is quite different from the funding formula for MDC. The latter's internal mechanisms are somewhat unknown, though assumed to be qualified to receive funds on an as-needed basis, similar in nature as well as substance to comparable Abu Dhabi funds. IPIC, for example, which is a joint venture of ADIA, ADNOC (the national oil company) and TAQA, a subsidiary of the partly privatised Abu Dhabi power company, also receive some private funding.

What is interesting about ADICO is its open culture and quick decision-making process that allows its managers to earn a solid reputation. In the event, ADICO is empowered to broaden Abu Dhabi's economic base and facilitate the international development of local companies. Towards that end, managers opted for an investment strategy that sought to achieve superior risk-adjusted returns across the entire capital structure, while preserving capital. In Abu Dhabi some of ADICO's investments include:

1. National Bank of Abu Dhabi
2. Abu Dhabi Commercial Bank
3. Union National Bank
4. Al Hilal Bank
5. Abu Dhabi National Insurance Company
6. Abu Dhabi Aviation Company
7. Abu Dhabi Investment Company (ADIC).

ADICO is led by Khalifah Muhammad Al Kindi, and has a powerhouse board, which includes the following Al Nahyan family members: Shaykh

Sultan bin Zayed, the President's representative, Shaykh Muhammad bin Zayed, the Heir Apparent, Shaykh Mansur bin Zayed and Shaykh Hamad bin Zayed. In addition, Muhammad Habroush Al Suwaydi, Khalifah Muhammad Al Kindi and Yunes Haji Khoury complete the board roster. Needless to say, the presence of these men ensures that ADICO was both well funded and free to fall back on Abu Dhabi's near limitless resources to fill its coffers.

Protect and preserve SWFs

To better address the USA's serious economic woes, Thomas Friedman recently opined in the *New York Times* that 'the cheapest and surest way to stimulate our economy' was immigration and, towards that end, quoted Shekhar Gupta, the editor of *The Indian Express* newspaper with a ready solution: 'All you need to do is grant visas to two million Indians, Chinese and Koreans' (Friedman 2009, p. A31). The Indian editor allegedly offered to 'buy up all the subprime homes [so-called toxic assets]... [and] work 18 hours a day to pay for them. We will immediately improve your savings rate – no Indian bank today has more than 2% non-performing loans because not paying your mortgage is considered shameful here. And we will start new companies to create our own jobs and jobs for more Americans.'

If Friedman wanted to bring in Indians to the USA as a source of cheap labour, Mohamed El-Erian proposed something equally sinister in *When Markets Collide*: to strip less developed countries (LDCs), including oil-producing states from their SWFs (El-Erian 2008). While major investors focused on dramatic changes in the structure and flow of global capital markets, many perceived SWFs, especially from cash-rich countries such as the UAE, as ideal credit sources to tap at will. El-Erian, for example, harboured an optimistic take on the world, concluding that virtue was better than vice even if the latter was practised far more often than the former. In fact, emerging markets were growth vehicles for him, and with the growth came high risk – for them – because their financial resources (SWFs) were fair game. Given such perceptions, how could Abu Dhabi protect its SWFs?

As was the case for most major investors, 2008 generated a remarkable reversal of the relative fortunes of the UAE, and Abu Dhabi in particular. If at the end of 2007, the Emirates as a whole held an estimated US$600 billion in foreign assets, of which ADIC/ADIA and the UAE central bank combined for an estimated US$550 billion (higher figures were sometimes advanced if foreign assets of some smaller funds were included along with the substantial private assets of the al-Nahyan, al-Maktoum and other prominent families), the Emirate of Abu Dhabi, consequently, recorded non-negligible losses. Of course, the ascendancy was solid, given that the 2005 to 2007 period recorded significant capital gains on ADIA's portfolio alone, which accounted for more of its growth than oil revenues.

Yet, with less oil than Saudi Arabia, for example, Abu Dhabi intended to build a larger (visible) external portfolio, a more dynamic skyline, all of which garnered the attention of the financial world. Among the other Emirates, Dubai never had a great deal of oil – and never had a comparable stockpile of foreign assets – although its aggressive expansion created a global buzz. Dubai enhanced its international profile but there was much drama in the outlook, with huge external borrowing, which jeopardised its star holdings. Because of Dubai's overextension, and its now near-dependence on Abu Dhabi, the Emirates' net foreign asset position weakened during 2008 and early 2009. The phrase 'Shanghai, Mumbai, Dubai, or goodbye' irritated Abu Dhabi, but as global markets recovered, ADIA's equity heavy portfolio rode its bull market gains.

The UAE in general and Abu Dhabi in particular were not able to generate a large increase in their foreign assets in 2008, in part because some revenues were allocated to servicing debt. In fact, private and parastatal borrowers in the UAE have racked up a US$100 billion external debt bill, with Dubai facing a financing squeeze. Its government and ruling family-sponsored firms posted US$80 billion in debt, with long-term liabilities several times higher, although precise figures are not available. Investment vehicles such as Istithmar Global and DIC have invested overseas, but their external investments were illiquid and probably suffered significant losses during the past few years.

Not every investment was poised for the long term, as the June 2009 IPIC sale of a large part of its £3.25 billion (19.52 billion Dirhams) stake in the British bank – Barclays for a £1.5 billion profit – illustrated. This impressive profit led critics to conclude that UAE SWFs tricked investors into believing that Emiratis held 'a long-term vision', but recent sales for cash highlighted how they backtracked 'to book the profit instead'. That may be the case, but neither Barclays nor any other 'client' was hoodwinked given that SWFs follow rules not of their own making. Rather, they invest and lend, sometimes recording significant losses, as was the case after the 2008–09 global financial meltdown. As one observer correctly concluded: 'In fact, it is simply the art of investing.' As Hesiod, the Greek poet and farmer labelled by some as the first economist, wrote, 'Observe due measure, for right timing is in all things the most important factor.' Savvy Arab investors obviously paid heed to the old adage (McFarlane 2009).

Furthermore, various financial vehicles were funded from other proceeds and, in the case of Dubai, from a multitude of investments, including the domestic property market, where prices fell throughout 2008 and 2009. There was little doubt that 'Dubai Inc.' – defined as entities owned by the government and ruling family – racked more external liabilities than external assets, and far more short-term external debts than liquid external assets. Moreover, Dubai relied on a roughly US$20 billion annual increase in its external debt to cover an ongoing current account deficit: it consequently needed more financing than implied by the amount of its maturing external debt. Abu Dhabi did not quite take on as much debt as Dubai, but its private and quasi-private firms were also significant net borrowers.

As stated above, Abu Dhabi's SWFs focused on a policy of diversification, especially 'into high-tech industries such as renewable energy, aerospace, chemicals and semiconductors', with MDC investing in a mega-project called Masdar that aims to create 'a large renewable energy venture that includes a carbon-neutral city and a clean technology research institute' (Wigglesworth 2009).

Such an approach requires a level of flexibility, which UAE SWFs are eager to demonstrate, as the recent case with the Citigroup illustrated. In mid-December 2009, ADIA filed a claim against Citibank 'seeking to either terminate a deal to buy US$7.5 billion worth of its stock or receive damages of more than US$4 billion'. ADIA's November 2007 bailout, which arrived in the New York-based bank's near-empty coffers to offset huge losses associated with the infamous toxic mortgages fiasco, was supposed to be compensated with equity units that paid a high annual dividend, estimated to reach US$37.24 a share between 15 March 2010 and 15 September 2011. Still, because Citibank was hit hard by the credit crisis and rising loan defaults, its shares tumbled 89 per cent from the US$33 range to less than US$4. According to an Associated Press report, at 'US$37.24 per share, the conversion price would amount to more than ten times Citigroup's closing stock price Tuesday [15 December 2009] of US$3.56', which ushered in the ADIA complaint (Associated Press 2009).

This paradigm illustrated how the financial health of many Emirati companies hinged on their ability to draw on Abu Dhabi's external assets – as the liquid external assets of Dubai, Inc. were likely to be too small to cover Dubai's 2009 financing need. Towards that end, the UAE central bank guaranteed all external liabilities of Emirati banks, a decision that effectively allowed banks in Dubai to draw on the resources of Abu Dhabi. UAE central bank officials, with full Al Nahyan ruling family blessings, agreed to provide funds to the domestic banking system to address its liquidity shortage – though high penalties deferred some banks from availing themselves of the funds.

In fact, Abu Dhabi rushed to Dubai's assistance in February 2009, when the Northern Emirate announced that 'it would issue US$20 billion in long-term bonds, and that the first installment of US$10 billion was fully subscribed by the UAE's central bank' (Cummins 2009, p. A1). Abu Dhabi apparently provided an additional US$10 billion to help Dubai World, the state-owned holding company, avoid defaulting on a US$4.1 billion bond payment that roiled global financial markets during most of November 2009, although it was not clear whether this was part of the original February US$20 billion package, or an additional US$10 billion on top of the first US$20 billion (Anwar 2009). What was clear was that this was the third intervention in 2009, although few knew what the concessions were, if any, made by Dubai. Observers believed that the price to pay would be elevated, with John Sfakianakis, the chief economist of Banque Saudi Fransi-Credit Agricole, in Riyadh, concluding that he 'highly doubt[ed] this kind of money ha[d] no strings attached'. For his part, Fahd Iqbal, the Gulf region strategist for EFG-Hermes, declared that the latest development did not necessarily change the 'longer-term outlook', believing that 'his investment banking firm still had other concerns regarding the "hit in confidence" Dubai had experienced' (BBC 2009, Le Monde 2009).

If additional support is needed in 2010 and beyond, chances are excellent that Abu Dhabi would continue its bailout, simply because it had so few choices. In the event, such assistance would further reduce assets managed by ADIA, which could be problematic for Abu Dhabi. In the past, ADIA has shied away from investments in the Emirates and indeed investments in the region, viewing itself as a pure portfolio manager that sought (not always successfully) to secure the highest risk-adjusted return – not a fund that supported domestic or regional economic development. Other, smaller funds consequently seemed to be more likely to manage any 'Dubai' assets that Abu Dhabi received in exchange for financial support. Consequently, SWFs like MDC should continue to attract resources to support their domestic economic development aims, which could limit overseas expansion – unless the Emirate's leadership changes long-term domestic investment policies.

A final clarification may be necessary in terms of the dramatic changes that *rentier* states experience as they earn unproductively generated external income to distribute to various SWFs. Naturally, *rentier* incomes stand in contrast to returns earned by *allocative* states, and even *extractive* states. *Allocative* states can be autonomous or detached from society and undemocratic, whereas *extractive* states tax and redistribute at will. Whether UAE SWFs may be of the 'late *rentierism*' remains to be determined. 'Late *rentierism*' refers to the second phase or half of a rent-earning period, when waste of wealth and a full state autonomy from society is replaced by policies about post-rent state viability that solidify state capitalism. Naturally, such a preference requires planning against a critical mass of domestic opposition, especially from non-elites/social forces, but the UAE was largely protected from such pressures because of its tribal political make-up (Tetreault 2000, pp. 107–48). Nevertheless, the UAE was poised to adopt post-*rentierism* features before long that would allow it to retain its capitalist preferences, while it moves slowly with political reforms to decompress from its more rigid rules. Abu Dhabi will most likely encourage the appearance of responsible reforms, especially to portray a modernising image to the international community, perhaps by easing on labour questions as well as a further diversification of the economy. Its SWFs will lead the way, to spend oil rents responsibly, manage the economy better and, above all, to plan for post-oil income for future generations.

Conclusion

The overall story of UAE SWFs includes both positive and negative aspects. Through judicious placements, eight government-owned or government-controlled institutions now investing sovereign funds on behalf of Abu Dhabi investors have largely avoided the so-called 'Dutch Disease', including real appreciations of their assets, loss of small quantities of manufacturing exports and reduced international investment positions. Though the leading UAE SWF – ADIA – is opaque, it is well integrated into Abu Dhabi's fiscal system. Abu Dhabi has a very small native population, probably less than 1 million, with oil export revenues hovering around US$50 billion a year (roughly US$50 000 per person), and has accumulated more than US$600 billion in its wealth fund, a figure that probably hovers around US$800 billion when all of the private family funds are added, although this is a 'guesstimate'. Consequently, Abu Dhabians embarked on SWFs to save as well as stay price-competitive, even if political pressures abounded. Distributing income from oil and investment funds equitably, certainly a reasonable assumption given the Emirate's record during the past 30 years, would easily guarantee that all of its citizens – and by default all residents living in the UAE – would enjoy one of the highest standards of living anywhere.

Yet, UAE SWFs have also become part of a wider controversy, because they helped transform Abu Dhabi – once an Arab backwater with little or no 'culture' – into one of the world's richest and most powerful investors, one that commands respect. Given that Abu Dhabi is not just trying to drive up short-term gains but invest to enhance its shares in long-term prosperity, provide nest eggs for retirement, secure long-term supplies of food and energy, promote the development of new industries that create skilled jobs, reduce its dependence on oil and amass endowments entice greedy predators to 'manage' whatever wealth is thus created.

To its credit, after 2008 Abu Dhabi tackled the global liquidity crisis responsibly, keeping its assets, both foreign and domestic, in safe, liquid dollar securities instead of investing in countries that borrowed aggressively or that invested uncompromisingly. The slump in oil prices has equally favoured the UAE because Abu Dhabi controlled domestic spending and investment plans and, according to local observers, required several high-flying Dubai investors to cut back. It seems that Abu Dhabi learned an important risk management lesson, to streamline its revenues with global growth and not invest all of its wealth in assets that were likely to be highly correlated with global growth. The eight SWFs under its control may have lost value in 2008 but as long-term investors eager to stabilise income, backed by significant projected oil income for the foreseeable future, Abu Dhabi was poised to add value to its many portfolios.

Notes

1. Published estimates that ADIA managed almost US$900 billion before the recent market slump may overstate ADIA's true size, although it is impossible to know the whole truth. In fact, ADIA's assets may be closer to the US$500 billion mark (at the beginning of 2008 – an assumption supported by statements from Abu Dhabi officials and the IMF's Middle East division chief, Mohsin Khan). See Kerr (2007).
2. ADIA's holdings of emerging market assets are thought to be as high as 15–20 per cent, with the remainder roughly split between dollar and euro/pound assets. See Sender (2007).
3. Shaykh Ahmad bin Zayid died on March 26, 2010 when the glider he was riding crashed into a lake near the Sidi Mohammad Bin Abdullah Dam near Rabat, in Morocco. See Abdulla Rasheed, 'Obituary: Shaikh Ahmad Bin Zayed

Al Nahyan March 31, 2010', at *http://gulfnews.com/news/gulf/uae/government/obituary-shaikh-ahmad-bin-zayed-al-nahyan-1.605489*.

4. The fund was first known as the 'Abu Dhabi Fund for Arab Economic Development', and had an initial ceiling of US$150 million, which was increased to US$500 million in 1974. Though somewhat dated, one of the best studies on the subject is Demir (1979), especially pp. 25–39.
5. Additional details are available at http://www.adfd.ae/aboutadfd/default. aspx.
6. For additional details on ADFD holdings, see http://www.adfd.ae/equities/eqinvestlist/default.aspx.
7. http://www.ipic.ae/En/Menu/index.aspx?MenuID=3&CatID=6&mnu=Cat.
8. For additional details on the fund, see http://www.pension.gov.ae/About TheFund/default.aspx. GCC regulations allow nationals from the six member state countries, Bahrain, Kuwait, Oman, Qatar, Saudi Arabia and the UAE, to invest throughout the zone. For an analysis on GCC economic affairs, with a concentration on monetary issues, see Rutledge (2009).
9. The Annual Report, the publication of which was something of a surprise, is available on the fund's web page at http://www.mubadala.ae.
10. http://www.taqa.ae/en/vision&mission.html.
11. http://www.taqa.ae/en/investments_acquisitions.html.

References

Anwar, Haris (2009), 'Abu Dhabi Bails Out Dubai World With $10 billion', *Bloomberg Online*, 14 December, available at http://www.bloomberg.com/apps/news?pid=20601087&sid=aqHghOxWdO00.

Associated Press 2009, 'Abu Dhabi Seeks to Terminate Citi Stock Purchase', *The Associated Press*, 15 December, available at http://www.google.com/hostednews/ap/article/ALeqM5gFBkwh-FNHR9oYgOZTP4OP1KF4cAD9CK5 TG80.

BBC News, 'Abu Dhabi Gives Dubai $10bn to Help Pay Debts', available at http://news.bbc.co.uk/go/pr/fr/-/2/hi/business/8411215.stm.

bin Zayed, Shaykh Khalifah (2008), 'Security and Stability in UAE Result From Dignified Life the Country Guarantees Everyone', Interview with Lebanese newspaper, *An Nahar*, 28 June.

Cummins, Chip (2009), 'Dubai Gets $10 Billion Bailout to Ease Debt', *Wall Street Journal*, 23 February.

Demir, Soliman (1979), *Arab Development Funds in the Middle East*. New York: Pergamon Press (published for UNITAR).

El-Erian, Mohamed (2008), *When Markets Collide: Investment Strategies for the Age of Global Economic Change*. New York: McGraw Hill.

Financial Times (2009), 'Abu Dhabi's Goals', *Financial Times*, 23 March, at http://www.ft.com/cms/s/0/6d43eafc-17cf-11de-8c9d-0000779fd2ac.html.

Friedman, Thomas L. (2009), 'The Open-Door Bailout', *New York Times*, 10 February.

http://www.ft.com/cms/s/0/6d43eafc-17cf-11de-8c9d-0000779fd2ac,dwp_uuid=b03d580a-4ff0-11dc-a6b0-0000779fd2ac.html.

Kéchichian, Joseph A. (2008), *Power and Succession in Arab Monarchies*. Boulder, CO: Lynne Rienner Publishers.

Kerr, Simeon (2007), 'Secretive Funds Urged on Disclosure', *Financial Times*, 29 October.

Le Monde 2009, 'Dubaï pourrait payer un prix élevé pour l'aide d'Abou Dhabi', *Le Monde*, 16 December, available at http://www.lemonde.fr/web/depeches/0,14-0,39-41177717@7-46,0.html.

McFarlane, Trevor (2009), 'Are Sovereign Wealth Funds Still Focused on Long Term?', *Gulf News* (Dubai), 19 December.

Mubadala (2009), Annual Report, available at at www.mubadala.ae.

Rutledge, Emilie J. (2009), *Monetary Union in the Gulf: Prospects for a Single Currency in the Arabian Peninsula*. London and New York: Routledge.

Sender, Henny (2007), 'Apollo Talks with Arab Fund: Abu Dhabi Investment Could Preside an IPO, Private Equity's Latest', *Wall Street Journal*, 6 July.

Setser, Brad and Rachel Ziemba, (2009), 'GCC sovereign funds: reversal of fortune', Working Paper published under the auspices of the Center for Geoeconomic Studies, Council on Foreign Relations, New York, January.

Summers, Lawrence (2007), 'Sovereign Funds Shake the Logic of Capitalism', *Financial Times*, 30 July, p. 10.

Tétreault, Mary Ann (2000), 'The Economies of National Autonomy in the UAE', in Joseph A. Kéchichian (ed.), *A Century in Thirty Years: Shaykh Zayed and the United Arab Emirates*. Washington, DC: Middle East Policy Council, pp. 107–48.

Walid, Tamara (2009), 'UAE's invest AD to Launch $400 Million Fund for Acquisitions', Reuters, 22 October, available at http://www.reuters.com/article/idUSLM39055320091022.

Wigglesworth, Robin (2009), 'Emirate Prepares for Post-oil Economy', *Financial Times*, 7 September.

Zayed, Sheikh (2005), 'Sheikh Zayed in quotes', UAE internet, 11 February, available at http://www.uaeinteract.com/docs/Sheikh_Zayed_in_quotes/18411.htm.

6
Russia's SWFs: Controlled by a Domestic Agenda

Stephen Fortescue

Benjamin Cohen, in writing about sovereign wealth funds (SWFs), states that 'a turning point was reached...when China and Russia – two countries with unmistakable geopolitical ambitions – joined the game....Here suddenly were two major powers with pockets deep enough to make a real impact.' As quoted by Cohen, John McConnell, then director of US national intelligence, believed that 'concerns about the financial capabilities of Russia, China, and OPEC countries and the potential use of their market access to exert financial leverage to achieve political ends represents a major national security issue' (Cohen 2009, pp. 719–20).

In this chapter, I examine the SWFs of Russia to determine whether they have been used as just described. I find that they have a relatively small and very conservative presence in the global economy. An analysis of the policy process surrounding the Russian funds helps us understand why they do not play the role so apprehensively referred to in the quotations above.

The story is divided into three stages: the Stabilisation Fund stage, the divided fund stage and the global financial crisis. It was in the first stage, from 2003 to early 2008, that the very limited policy goals of Russia's SWFs were most evident. In the second stage, a slightly more aggressive global investment strategy was introduced. It was this shift, coming at roughly the same time that China set up its fund that produced the reaction as stated above. A new stage began as the global financial crisis rudely intervened. It brought a sudden and strong commitment to spending the assets of the SWFs on domestic crisis management.

The Stabilisation Fund

Russia's first SWF was called the Stabilisation Fund. It first surfaced in the formal policy arena as a discussion document (*kontseptsiia*) prepared by the Ministry of Finance and was presented to cabinet in February 2003. No decision was made, the document being sent back for reworking ('Ot redaktsii' 2003). In May, President Putin called for the creation of such a fund in his annual budget message (Putin 2003). In November–December of that year, the parliament passed legislation amending the Budget Code to allow for its creation ('O vnesenii' 2003). The purpose of the fund was not set out in the legislation. However, in the policy discussion, it was explicitly used to sterilise the large foreign currency inflows entering the country through the sale of oil, in an economy in which inflation was a persistent problem. It was also seen as addressing the 'Dutch Disease' problem of a persistently appreciating ruble (Kudrin 2006). Aleksei Kudrin, the Minister of Finance and chief champion of the Stabilisation Fund, had little interest in what happened to the money that went into it as long as it was kept out of circulation in the domestic economy.

The fund was fed by oil (not gas) export duties and taxes collected once the price exceeded a price set in the budget. The price was initially set at US$20 per barrel. The money could be accessed – as revenue into the budget – only if the price of oil fell below the set level or once R500 billion (US$17.5 billion) had been accumulated. The money flowing into the fund was held in a Treasury account at the Central Bank until it was invested in the foreign sovereign debt of a list of countries to be confirmed by the government. The fund came formally into existence on 1 January 2004. The rules for its operation were set out in a government decree of 23 January 2004 ('Ob utverzhdenii' 2004).

Although money accumulated quickly (on 1 March 2005 it contained R707.5 billion (US$25 billion)) R200 billion over the limit at which inflows could be diverted to the budget) ('Ot redaktsii' 2005), it simply sat in a ruble-denominated account at the Central Bank for some time, while rules and regulations on how it was to be invested and spent were debated. At the end of September 2004, Prime Minister Fradkov signed a decree establishing that the money could be converted into US dollars, euros or pounds sterling, and then invested in the bonds of 14 countries (Austria, Belgium, Finland, France, Germany, Greece, Ireland, Italy, Luxembourg, Netherlands, Portugal, Spain, UK and USA), providing the bond issue had a AAA rating from two of the three major agencies. No more than 15 per cent of the nominal value of any issue could be purchased by the fund. It was to be managed by the Ministry of Finance, although it could transfer some management responsibilities to the Central Bank ('O poriadke' 2004).

Nothing happened, and Kudrin was criticised for allowing the fund to be eaten away by inflation as it sat, uninvested, in a Central Bank ruble account. Initially the ministry defended itself by claiming that exchange rate uncertainties meant that leaving the money in rubles was the safest approach. However, it was then claimed that the real reason for the delay was the so-called 'Noga factor'. Noga, a Swiss firm, had been harassing the Russian government for many years with court cases seeking the arrest of Russian foreign assets in order to obtain repayment of a debt. It was feared that the assets of the Stabilisation Fund would be liable to arrest if the management arrangements were not very carefully designed. It was suggested that a solution to the problem would be to assign the funds to the Central Bank in such a way that the bank would have temporary ownership, and therefore be protected by the international norm that Central Bank reserves could not be subject to arrest in cases brought against sovereign governments. Such an arrangement meant that the fund's monies would probably be treated the same as the bank's foreign exchange reserves, that is, invested very conservatively (Bekker 2006; Netreba 2006a).

In April 2006, when Fradkov signed a new decree ('O poriadke' 2006), signs of the Noga factor could be detected. Although with the same title and containing essentially the same provisions as the 2004 decree, this one made no specific mention of the possible transfer of management powers from the Ministry of Finance to the Central Bank, and the contract to be drawn up between the two was to be a 'bank account contract' (*dogovor bankovskogo scheta*) rather than the previously called for management contract (Bekker 2006). While the Noga factor was presumably a genuine fear, there is little doubt that it also suited Kudrin to use it to reinforce his desire that the Stabilisation Fund be invested in the most conservative manner.

The deadlines set out in the 2006 decree were met and investments were made in the instruments listed, with the first purchase of foreign currency for investment purposes being transacted on 24 July 2006 ('Svedeniia', 2006).[1] By then, however, significant changes had been made to the structure of the fund.

The growth versus stability debate

From the earliest days of the Stabilisation Fund there was dissatisfaction on the part of those who believed that Russia's resource revenues should be put to more active use ('Ot redaktsii' 2003). Particularly by mid-2004, as oil prices rose and the amount of money flowing into the fund went beyond the R500 billion limit more quickly than expected, the pressure increased on the Ministry of Finance and its combatant minister, Aleksei Kudrin, to 'do something' with the money. The criticism consisted of (and sometimes confused) the two issues of how the money should be invested (if at all) and how it should be spent (if at all).

The opposition to Kudrin and the Stabilisation Fund came from two major sources. The so-called 'party of growth' consisted of those who claimed to believe in market mechanisms but who nevertheless believed that the Russian economy had to be weaned away from its dependence on resource rents by spending those rents on infrastructure and 'developmental' projects, particularly in hi-tech and innovation. The key bureaucratic component of the 'party of growth' was the Ministry of Economic Development and Trade (MERT). MERT had always had an edgy relationship with the Ministry of Finance, a combination of policy differences and turf wars. But they had been generally on the same 'reformist' side of the policy fence. The struggle over investment policy, of which the Stabilisation Fund was a part, became so keen as to suggest the two were now on opposite sides of some new fence. MERT was generally of the view that Russia's resource rent need not be invested at all, but simply spent on development and infrastructure (Petrachkova 2006b). The competition between it and the Ministry of Finance was keenly encouraged by Prime Minister Fradkov, as part of a feud he was carrying on with Kudrin (Stanovaia 2006).

Another group of opponents of Kudrin and the Stabilisation Fund also supported the view that resource rent should be spent in the domestic economy. However they had none of the 'reformist' baggage of the party of growth, and their views on where the money should be spent were more oriented towards the traditional industrial and agricultural sectors. Let us call them the 'industrialists'. They could be found among the owners and managers of the 'real' economy, and in the parliament among the communists and nationalist wing of the dominant, pro-Putin party, United Russia. The Ministry of Industry and Energy was more a potential than actual bureaucratic champion.

Both sets of opponents were critical of the Ministry of Finance's view of inflation, the control of which was a fundamental argument in favour of the Stabilisation Fund. For Kudrin the fund was necessary to mop up excess resource-derived liquidity. In the view of his opponents Russian inflation was not caused by excessive money supply but by inadequate domestic capacity to meet demand. Money had to be spent to improve the capacity of the domestic economy to meet demand, whether on 'developmental' infrastructure or to maintain established manufacturing output. This could be done without inflationary consequences (Dmitrieva 2006; Petrachkova 2006a). MERT, in claiming that inflation was predominantly of a non-monetary nature, blamed the liquidity squeeze of 2004 on the introduction of the Stabilisation Fund (Kharchenko 2006).

There was an element in the attacks on the Stabilisation Fund, particularly from the 'industrialists', of the chauvinism that found it unacceptable that Russian money be put to work in foreign economies. In November 2003, during the Duma debate on the law which created the Stabilisation Fund, deputies V.A. Kolomeitsev, of the Communist Party, and A.V. Mitrofanov, of Zhirinovsky's Liberal Democratic Party, each raised the issue of the foreign placement of the fund's assets. Kolomeitsev asked for a 'little amendment' (*popravochka*) that 'the Stabilisation Fund be such that the money went to the stabilisation of our economy and not into foreign financial instruments'; Mitrofanov, not without a degree of prescience, noted the dangers of investing in the USA's 'green pyramid'. The deputy prime minister presenting the legislation, A.D. Zhukov, rather disingenuously responded by noting that the legislation did not require that the fund be invested in foreign instruments, only that it 'may' be. In principle, he claimed, investment in Russia was possible ('O proekte' 2003).

It is true that there was a small degree of semantic ambiguity in the law and the 2004 decree on the management of the fund. That ambiguity was sufficient for Fradkov, in December 2004, to direct MERT and the Ministry of Industry and Energy to draw up proposals for the use of fund money for investment projects. In response MERT proposed an investment fund, funded in the same way as the Stabilisation Fund but to be devoted to domestic projects (Bekker 2005a; Kornysheva and Liashenko 2005). Kudrin resisted the idea at this stage without difficulty, and the semantic ambiguity was removed in a later 2006 decree.

The battle with both opponents was a hard-fought one, of words and bureaucratic gamesmanship. Through 2004, Kudrin was conceding that it might be possible to raid the Stabilisation Fund once it climbed over the R500 billion mark, but only to fill holes in the Pension Fund and to pay down foreign debt (Ivanova 2004). In his July 2004 budget message, Putin confirmed that any surplus over the R500 billion mark was to be spent exclusively on those purposes (Putin 2004). The budget that was signed into law on 23 December contained the appropriate provisions ('O federal'nom biudzhete' 2004, Articles 2 and 3). Through 2005, money was indeed taken from the Stabilisation Fund to pay off foreign debt, with a payment to cover the pension deficit also coming very late in that year ('Svedeniia' 2005, transaction for 22 December 2005). This, however, was not the end of the matter. Fierce debate continued, leading in the end to a radical restructuring of the Stabilisation Fund. The protagonists continued to be Kudrin and the various forces trying to pry out of his clutches more oil revenues for domestic spending purposes. At the end of 2004, Kudrin offered a deal, under which he would raise the price of oil at which payments into the Stabilisation Fund kicked in, thereby leaving a bigger share of oil revenues in the budget. In return, he argued that the limit of R500 billion was too low, and demanded that it be changed to a fixed percentage of GDP (Ivanova 2004). This proposal got nowhere, and it was only in October 2005 that a policy proposal was put forward that would eventually lead to change. Oleg Viugin, the head of the Russian Financial Markets Service, suggested that the fund be divided into two. A firm decision would be made on what level of reserves had to be maintained in order to protect against future oil price movements, and the excess would go into a separate fund purely for pensions. This was a proposal that Kudrin felt able to support (Petrachkova and Bekker 2005).

But it took a further period of furious argument with Fradkov before the proposal could form the basis of a new policy. In March 2006, Fradkov attacked the concept of sterilisation at a meeting of the board of the Ministry of Finance. Kudrin responded that if in 2005 all the money in the Stabilisation Fund had been spent, the growth in the money supply would have been not its actual 38.6 per cent but 70.5 per cent, and annual inflation would have increased not by its actual 12.7 per cent but 18–20 per cent (Netreba 2006b). There was fierce debate over whether Russia needed a developmental industry policy, with Kudrin storming out of a meeting discussing the matter and Fradkov threatening Kudrin with dismissal (Netreba 2006c).

Fradkov then adopted another line of attack. He supported the deputy head of his cabinet office, Mikhail Kopeikin, in his criticism of the fund's conservative investment strategy. Kopeikin aggressively pushed the idea that Stabilisation Fund money should be invested in foreign shares (Butrin 2006a). Before agreeing to such an adventurous approach, Kudrin wanted the budget process to show clearly the extent to which the Russian economy was dependent on oil and gas revenues. Fradkov agreed to draw up future budgets in such a way that hydrocarbon-derived revenues would be clearly separated. They, including revenues from gas, would all be held in a separate account which would form the basis of a restructured Stabilisation Fund. This meant that a greatly increased amount of money would be paid into the fund. Fradkov made it clear that he wanted something in return for the support he had given Kudrin on the hydrocarbon budget, and so the Ministry of Finance gave ground on how the fund would be invested (Netreba 2006b).

The divided fund

It was widely reported that Fradkov signed the decree setting out the procedures for the investment of the Stabilisation Fund's holdings in April 2006 on the understanding that the Ministry of Finance would draw up legislation allowing for the more aggressive investment of some proportion of the money (Bekker 2006; Netreba and Shishkin 2006). After Deputy Prime Minister Aleksandr Zhukov announced on 22 May that the government was considering dividing the Stabilisation Fund into a Reserve Fund and what he called a Future Generations Fund, Kudrin declared that he had no intention of setting up such a structure in the foreseeable future (Bekker and Ragozina 2006). However, on 30 May 2006 in his yearly budget message Putin announced that a Future Generations Fund would be created, in the following terms:

> The policy of accumulating 'windfall' (*'kon"iunkturnye'*) budget receipts in a Stabilisation Fund must be continued. The assets of the Stabilisation Fund above the base level must be used exclusively to replace external sources of funding of the budget deficit and/or the early repayment of external sovereign debt.

> At the same time there must be a firm distinction made between the assets set aside in the Stabilisation Fund for the purpose of minimising the negative consequences of a fall in oil prices (the reserve component), and the resources accumulated above this level ('the fund for future generations'). The size of the reserve component should be set as a percentage of GDP.

> (Putin 2006)

He did not specify how or where the funds might invest their monies. Putin's economic advisor, Arkadii Dvorkovich, expanded on the declaration: the new Reserve Fund would consist of something less than 10 per cent of GDP, and at least part of the Future Generations Fund would be invested in Russia (Butrin 2006b).

In December 2006, Kudrin sent a discussion document on the new structure to cabinet, in which it was acknowledged that the Reserve

Fund should make-up something between 7 per cent and 10 per cent of GDP (at the time the Stabilisation Fund held 8 per cent of GDP). It included the riskier investment of the Future Generations Fund, although there was no mention of domestic investments (Bekker and Petrachkova 2006).

In March 2007, Putin utilised that year's budget message to repeat essentially what he had said the previous year (Putin 2007a). A week or two later the cabinet's budget commission approved the basic parameters of the 2008–10 budget (a three-year budget cycle had just been adopted). The new fund structure was by now taking on clearer shape. In addressing the commission, Kudrin called for the Reserve Fund to be set at 10 per cent of GDP, against the less than 10 per cent previously mentioned. An amount, specified in the budget, would be taken out of the Reserve Fund and transferred directly to the budget. What remained would be invested the same way as the Stabilisation Fund. What was now called the National Welfare Fund (NWF), made up of hydrocarbon revenues received that were more than the 10 per cent of GDP in the Reserve Fund, would be invested more aggressively in pursuit of a return of between 6.5 per cent to 7 per cent. He suggested that if the need arose it should also be used as a reserve; that is, spent to meet budgetary needs. He noted that with the budget transfer being taken out of the Reserve Fund, the NWF was likely to be quite small (Netreba 2007).

On 26 April 2007, Putin returned to the new divided fund in his state of the union address. He repeated what he had said in his last two budget messages, but with a suggestion that the NWF should provide a pension reserve and start-up capital for 'development institutions' (*instituty razvitiia*), above all the Development Bank (the state-owned Vneshekonombank, which was to become a major player in Russia's crisis management, in another guise), the Investment Fund and the Russian Venture Company. He proposed an initial amount of R300 billion (US$12 billion) (Putin 2007). Legislation was signed into law the same day, amending the Budget Code to create the two new funds ('O vnesenii' 2007, Article 5). No details were included on how the money should be invested or spent. The new funds were to be set up by 1 February 2008.

The 'developmental' payment called for by Putin was made out of the Stabilisation Fund before the new funds were set up. On 28 November 2007, R300 billion was transferred to Vneshekonombank and the new state corporation 'Russian Nanotechnology' ('Ostatki').[2] As we will see below, provision for such payments was not included in the arrangements for the new funds.

Despite calls for a fully diversified and aggressively managed fund, with Putin himself, in May 2007, raising the question of whether the fund should be invested domestically (Panov et al. 2007), the Ministry of Finance continued for the rest of the year to delay matters, talking of the need for careful consideration of the matter (Granik et al. 2007).

When on 29 December 2007 a government decree on the management of the Reserve Fund, replacing that of 2006, was issued ('O poriadke' 2007), the range of permissible instruments for investment had been widened, although again there was no provision for domestic investments nor for investments in corporate shares and bonds. Investments, still only in US dollars, euros and pounds sterling, could now be made in treasury bonds (the same 14 countries mentioned earlier), the bonds of 'foreign state agencies and central banks' (of the same 14 countries) and of international agencies, as well as being placed on deposit in foreign banks and credit organisations. The permissible ranges were: Treasuries, 50–100 per cent; state agencies and central banks, 0–30 per cent; international agencies, 0–15 per cent; and deposits, 0–30 per cent. Foreign state agencies were defined as those 'set up to carry out such functions as offering government services, the management of state property and providing credit to specific sectors of the economy. The identified organisations (legal entities) must be subordinated to the organs of state power of the foreign states in which they are created.' The international agencies in which investments could be made were listed in the rules (*Trebovaniia*) accompanying the decree. They were primarily regional development banks, including the European Bank for Reconstruction and Development (EBRD), as well as the International Finance Corporation (IFC) and International Bank for Reconstruction and Development (IBRD).[3] The decree left it to the Ministry of Finance to draw up the list of foreign state agencies, with the agreement of the Central Bank. The list appeared in the form of a Ministry of Finance decree on 16 January 2008 ('Ob utverzhdenii' 2008a). Fifteen were listed, from Spain, Austria, Germany, Netherlands, UK, USA and France. They included Fannie Mae, Freddie Mac and Federal Home Loan Bank (FHLB).

The arrangements for the NWF were set out in a government decree of 19 January 2008 ('O poriadke' 2008). They were essentially the same as for the Reserve Fund. However, two decrees from the Ministry of Finance a few days later, while listing the same institutions as for the Reserve Fund, changed the proportions of investments allowed for each category of instrument significantly to: Treasuries 80 per cent, state agencies 15 per cent, international agencies 5 per cent and deposits 0 per cent

('Ob utverzhdenii' 2008b; 'Ob utverzhdenii' 2008c). This was hardly aggressive investing.

The authorities immediately took advantage of the new possibilities. The Ministry of Finance announced in February 2008 that money from the NWF would be invested in the bonds of the US mortgage agencies, Fannie Mae, Freddie Mac and FHLB. The investment apparently reached US$100 billion at its peak. Dvorkovich, the President's economics advisor, had stated in an interview with AFP just before the announcement was made and not long after the SWFs of Singapore, Kuwait and South Korea had invested US$21 billion in Citigroup and Merril Lynch that, at a time when Russia was not officially affected by the global economic crisis, it would expand its investments abroad and help 'stabilise the situation in other countries with our money' (Lazarro 2008; 'Russia Wealth Fund' 2008; 'Russian State Investments' 2008). It seems just as likely that the Ministry of Finance was looking for good yields as interest rates dropped. Kudrin later claimed a US$1 billion profit on the investment ('Rossiia vlozhila' 2008).

While Kudrin had not unprofitably allowed a more aggressive investment strategy, he was still fighting hard over how NWF money should be spent as it became available. The usual claims were being made on the money, but the most powerful political force, Vladimir Putin, had his own priorities. To shore up his political popularity he wanted to raise pensions, and his previously stated desire that the NWF be used to plug holes in the Pension Fund was reinforced (Kuvshinova et al. 2008). There was no sign of a continuation of the provision of money for domestic 'developmental' purposes, such as the payment of R300 billion to Vneshekonombank and Russian Nanotechnology the year before.

Although Kudrin had seemingly given ground, in the end the outcome was similar to the proposal made by his ally, Oleg Viugin, back in October 2005, a proposal that Kudrin had supported at the time. He had agreed to the slightly riskier investment of some proportion of resource revenues and had rather cunningly given a token amount to the party of growth out of the Stabilisation Fund just before it was closed. But beyond that, he had successfully resisted all the pressure to either invest or spend fund assets domestically other than on the fiscally acceptable Pension Fund. He had also gained access, for stabilisation and reserve purposes, to all hydrocarbon revenues, not just the 'excess' oil revenues that had gone into the Stabilisation Fund. He had also retained full management control of the funds, with some cooperation with the friendly Central Bank, despite the expectations of some that a separate management entity be established. It was an impressive performance, the basis of which will be analysed in more depth in the conclusion.

The crisis

Meanwhile, global storm clouds were about to change the situation dramatically. As the global financial crisis intensified there was drama over the investment in the US mortgage agencies, particularly as some critics seemed to have trouble distinguishing between bonds and shares ('U.S. Mortage Giants' 2008). Nevertheless the investment was wound down. In February 2009, the Ministry of Finance amended its January 2008 decree to remove foreign state agencies as an investment option for the Reserve Fund, although apparently there was no equivalent action regarding the NWF ('O vnesenii' 2009a).

Both funds quickly came to be used for what had always been seen as one of their main purposes, shoring up the economy during periods of falling oil prices. Three initial approaches were funded from the NWF: buying the shares of Russian blue chips to support the share market (R350 billion) ('O vnesenii' 2008a; 'Krizis zavalivaiut' 2008); providing loans to companies that were unable to meet debt payments and margin calls, particularly on loans to foreign banks (R450 billion allocated, although only a small proportion was taken up) ('O dopolnitel'nykh' 2008; Pis'mennaia 2009); and providing subordinated credits to Russian banks, in order to improve liquidity conditions in the general economy (up to R257 billion as of 1 July 2009) ('Osnovnye polozheniia' 2009; 'O vnesenii' 2009b).

As fierce as Kudrin had been in salting away as much money as safely as possible in Russia's various funds, he had no qualms about spending it when the time came. In addition to the emergency allocations from the NWF, there were large transfers from the Reserve Fund directly to the budget to fund a large budget deficit. On 10 March 2009, Putin issued an instruction (*rasporiazhenie*) that in the first half of 2009 R1.604 trillion (US$45.8 billion) be taken from the Reserve Fund 'for financial support for the balancing of the federal budget' (Pravitel'stvo 2009). Soon after, the government's anti-crisis programme for 2009 called for an increase in government expenditure using R2.76 trillion from the Reserve Fund (*Programma* 2009). A further R1.5 trillion was allocated for the second half of 2009. That, it was predicted, would leave R1.7–1.8 trillion in the fund at the end of the year (Butrin 2009). Parliament passed the requisite amendment to the Budget Code (Visloguzov 2009).

A picture of the use of the funds can be gained from the transaction records published on the Ministry of Finance website. These show greatly reduced payments into both funds in 2009, small amounts converted into foreign currency for investment and continuing transfers to the budget. As of 1 October 2009 the Reserve Fund contained R2.298 trillion (US$76.37 billion) and the NWF R2.764 trillion (US$91.86 billion). (The Reserve Fund's peak in dollar terms had been US$142.6 billion in September 2008, although in ruble terms it had been R4.870 trillion in March 2009. The latest figure represents the NWF's peak in dollar terms, although in ruble terms its peak, at R2.996 trillion, had also been in March 2009, 'Sovokupnyi ob"em'). As policymakers have perceived the worst of the crisis-management period to be over, the NWF has been redirected to its primary purpose, of providing a reserve for the Pension Fund.

While Kudrin appeared happy to play the unfamiliar role of spending money, he certainly did not give up his more familiar role of pushing hard for cuts in expenditure, especially including investment programmes (Netreba 2009; 'Vyskazyvaniia' 2009). Putin supported his old ally (Netreba and Shapovalov 2009). At the height of the crisis, at a meeting on budget policy in February 2009, President Medvedev, although clearly prepared to run down reserves to maintain social spending, also stressed that the future was uncertain and something had to be left in reserve (Medvedev 2009a). Both Putin and Medvedev continued to stress the importance of covering future pension requirements (Medvedev 2009b; Putin 2009).

Time – rapidly approaching time – will tell us whether the crisis will, despite the warnings of Putin and Medvedev, fully deplete the Reserve and even NWF, with Russia's sovereign welfare fund having been no more than a brief blip in history. Whatever the outcome in that regard, what do we learn from the story?

Conclusion

The first and clearest lesson is that the Russian funds have never been aggressive purchasers of foreign assets, whether state or privately owned. No Russian fund has ever bought a foreign share. The Russian funds were generally invested in treasury bonds, although there was the brief period in 2008 when they invested in state-backed agencies such as Fannie Mae and Freddie Mac. If there was any 'political' element in these investments, it was the suggestion that Russia was helping out the developed world in a time of difficulty. But the investment was just as likely to have been commercially driven. Although there was some sense that the disinvestment out of the US mortgage agencies was driven by a panicky and not fully informed domestic reaction to the state of US markets, Kudrin was probably glad to take his profits, at a time when crisis-management demands on the funds were about to surge. The sums involved, in both Treasuries and state-backed agencies, have been significant, but not of a size to make or break Western economies or even individual agencies.

Russia has other forms of involvement in global economic affairs, some of which might well be seen as threatening: oil and gas sales in the 'near abroad' and Western Europe, the use of trade barriers as a foreign policy weapon, the sale of arms and sensitive technologies. The author sees the outward foreign direct investment (FDI) of Russian firms, whether state or privately owned, as relatively benign; nevertheless it is a phenomenon worth examining, not least because some might see in it threatening qualities (Fortescue 2008). Nevertheless, there has been little about the Russian use of its SWFs to induce fear abroad.

Why is this so? Why has a country that has in other ways shown a strong desire to assert itself as a resurgent 'Great Power' not used its resource revenues for that purpose? Or, to take a different angle, why did a country with clear developmental and sectoral support pressures lock its money away – until a full-blown crisis intervened – in safe, low-yield foreign investments? The simple answer would be that Kudrin has been able consistently to win the policy debate and the bureaucratic politics that go with it. That answer begs two questions: why did Kudrin pursue a policy of conservative investment abroad, and how did he win, against strong and persistent opposition?

The simplest answer to the first question is that Kudrin pursued a conservative policy because he is a typically cautious Minister of Finance, with a primary interest in controlling inflation. But additional to that, he operates in a country in which there is no strong lobby for aggressive investment abroad. There are probably two reasons for this. First, Russia does not have the foreign resource security issues that some other countries have, most dramatically China. Russia is more than self-sufficient in virtually all resources. Second, it has the strong industrial lobbies that come from being a nation with a fully industrialised past. The desire of non-industrialised nations with resource wealth to use that wealth to fund industrialisation has always been strong, even if it is one that has been considerably dampened in recent times by a history of failure and changes in the international intellectual and policy climate. A country that is already industrialised, but which sees its industry disintegrating around it, is even more likely to want to use resource wealth to rectify the situation.

This means that even Putin, a leader strongly committed to projecting Russia's image as a 'Great Power' and not shy in using economic levers as part of that policy, has not used foreign financial investments for that purpose. He would find it difficult to dress up investing Russia's resource revenues in Western economies as an assertion of Russia's might as far as the Russian nationalist constituency is concerned, even if foreign audiences might see it in those terms.

The strength of the domestic lobby has had one consequence for the nature of the investment of Russia's SWFs. One strongly suspects that Kudrin's temperament and policy orientation would not be conducive to aggressive investment. But the political cost of possible losses on foreign markets, by providing strong grounds for attack by domestic lobbies, has reinforced his conservative inclinations. There is no political kudos to be gained from successful investment abroad; there is a major downside political risk if foreign investments turn sour.

How is it that Kudrin has been able to resist the pressure from the domestic lobbies? The story shows that he has been tactically clever throughout. What is more important, however, is that he has generally had the support of Putin. Why has that been? They are old St Petersburg colleagues who apparently enjoy a good personal relationship. Kudrin is no 'soft liberal', as he demonstrated by his support for the harsh treatment meted out to businessman Mikhail Khodorkovsky, once one of the richest men in the world, who was found guilty of fraud and sentenced to nine years in prison in 2005. Khodorkovsky's shareholding in the Russian petroleum company Yukos collapsed and subsequently the government froze shares in the company.

In policy terms, Putin is receptive to Kudrin's warnings on the dangers of inflation. Putin's popular support is based on his guarantees of stability and a basic level of prosperity, things that are destroyed by inflation. That was well demonstrated by the runaway inflation of the early 1990s, a period from which Putin wants, above all, to distance himself. His strong commitment to using the NWF as a reserve for the Pension Fund, which is also as much a political as economic commitment, is a further reflection of this basic policy orientation.

While Putin has a politically based commitment to controlling inflation, one might nevertheless expect him to be receptive to the domestic lobbies. He has personal and past employment links with many contemporary 'industrialists', particularly those of a KGB background that he has brought into industrial management. He is unable to ignore their demands and pays them off on occasion. The Yukos affair could be interpreted in those terms, and more recently Putin's former KGB colleague Sergei Chemezov has been handed a bewilderingly sprawling industrial empire, one which is now attracting a significant proportion of the crisis-management funds being taken out of Russia's SWFs. But Putin is far too cautious a politician to give these allies too much. The Yukos affair did not have the broader consequences in terms of further dispossessions that many expected; Chemezov is now under considerable pressure to perform.

Putin has strong policy, political and factional reasons to support Kudrin, and that fact is evident in the story of Russia's SWFs. What of a post-crisis future? If resource revenues were to start rolling in again at a level that required new consideration of what to do with them, would the policy outcome be the same? There are those who question whether revenues will ever roll in again at that rate. Kudrin's forecasts have always suggested that the Stabilisation Fund would be a relatively brief phenomenon, even before the crisis was on the horizon. The Russian economy would develop its domestic capacity to absorb foreign currency inflows without inflation, and imports would increase to the degree that the current account balance would even out, putting less 'Dutch Disease' pressure on the ruble ('Stabfondu' 2006). There are those who pessimistically doubt Russia's capacity to maintain oil and gas output as deposits deplete and new ones are ever more remote and capital intensive.[4] But if the money were to start rolling in, the policy outcome would probably be the same, with the control of inflation and therefore the primacy of sterilisation being the main policy drivers. The political dangers, of making losses while a rabid domestic lobby looks on, mean that foreign investments would continue to be conservative. And if the anti-inflationary forces were not able to hold the line, the money would be 'invested' aggressively in the domestic economy, not abroad.

Notes

1. The Ministry of Finance website reports when monies are paid into a SWF, when they are converted into foreign currency for investment abroad and when they are converted back to rubles for disbursement to various domestic recipients. Specific investments are not reported.
2. This transaction, as recorded on the Ministry of Finance website, cites a ministry decree, No. 718 of 28 November 2007, that appears not to have been published. It is unclear, therefore, on what legal basis it was made.

3. In November 2008 the IMF was added to the list, and by 1 September 2009 Russia had used Reserve Fund money to purchase SDR991.94 million ('O vnesenii' 2008b; 'Informatsionnoe soobshchenie' 2009).

4. It should be noted that such predictions have been made for something like 40 years (Oxenstierna 2009, pp. 27–30).

References

Normative documents and statistical reporting relating to Russian SWFs listed here without a URL can be found on the Ministry of Finance website, http://www.minfin.ru. All articles from the newspapers *Vedomosti* and *Kommersant* are taken from their online editions and are available through their archives at http://www.vedomosti.ru and www.kommersant.ru.

Bekker, Aleksandr (2005a), 'Nikakikh investitsii', *Vedomosti*, 28 March.

Bekker, Aleksandr (2005b), 'Sredstvo ot Noga', *Vedomosti*, 28 December.

Bekker, Aleksandr (2006), 'Ispugalis' Noga', *Vedomosti*, 25 April.

Bekker, Aleksandr and Aleksandra Petrachkova (2006), 'Stabfond razdvaivaetsia', *Vedomosti*, 6 December.

Bekker, Aleksandr and Elena Ragozina (2006), 'Stabfond raspechatan', *Vedomosti*, 26 May.

Butrin, Dmitrii (2006a), 'Apparat pravitel'stva nashel $2 mlrd v bumagakh', *Kommersant*, 13 March.

Butrin, Dmitrii (2006b), 'Biudzhet poshel na tretii srok', *Kommersant*, 31 May.

Butrin, Dmitrii (2009), 'Rezervnaia monopoliia', *Kommersant*, 2 July.

Cohen, Benjamin (2009), 'Sovereign Wealth Funds and National Security: the Great Tradeoff', *International Affairs*, 85(4), pp. 713–31.

Dmitrieva, Oksana (2006), 'Lozhnye tseli i lozhnye sredstva', *Kommersant*, 4 May.

Fortescue, Stephen (2008), 'Outward FDI by Russian Minerals Firms', paper presented to a conference of Research Committee 38, International Political Science Association, Hobart, April.

Granik, Irina (2009), 'Men'she sotsializma, a demokratii dostatochno', *Kommersant*, 6 May.

Granik, Irina, Aleksei Shapovalov, Dmitrii Butrin and Maksim Shishkin (2007), 'Andrei Vavilov vyshel na stabfond', *Kommersant*, 16 November.

'Informatsionnoe soobshchenie ob ispol'zovanii neftegazovykh dokhodov federal'nogo biudzheta' (2009), Ministry of Finance, 1 September.

Ivanova, Svetlana (2004), 'Nikakoi infrastruktury', *Vedomosti*, 2 November.

Kharchenko, Al'vina (2006), 'MERT dokazal nemonetarnuiu prirodu infliatsii', *Kommersant*, 4 April.

Kornysheva, Alena and Galina Liashenko (2005), 'German Gref vykhodit na fondovyi rynok', *Kommersant*, 9 March.

'Krizis zavalivaiut den'gami' (2008), *Kommersant*, 17 October.

Kudrin, Aleksei (2006), 'Aleksei Kudrin: tratit' stabfond – znachit razrushat' ekonomiku', *Kommersant*, 30 March.

Kuvshinova, Ol'ga, Boris Grozovskii and Filipp Sterkin (2008), 'Trillion terzanii', *Vedomosti*, 11 April.

Lazzaro, Joseph (2008), 'Russia to Invest in Fannie Mae, Freddie Mac Bonds', *BloggingStocks*, 21 February, available at http://www.bloggingstocks.com/2008/02/21/russia-to-invest-in-fannie-mae-freddie-mac-bonds/.

Medvedev, D. (2009a), 'Vstupitel'noe slovo na soveshchanii po ekonomicheskim voprosam', 9 February, available at http://news.kremlin.ru/transcripts/3099/.

Medvedev, D.(2009b), 'Biudzhetnoe poslanie Prezidenta Rossiiskoi Federatsii o biudzhetnoi politike v 2010–2012 godakh', 25 May, available at http://www.kremlin.ru/acts?date_text=25+%D0%BC%D0%B0%D1%8F+2009&since=&till=.

Netreba, Petr (2006a), 'Minfin priachet stabfond ot sudebnykh pristavov', *Kommersant*, 20 January.

Netreba, Petr (2006b), 'Gosudarstvo potrebovalo effektivnykh gosraskhodov', *Kommersant*, 4 April.

Netreba, Petr (2006c), 'Aleksei Kudrin prizval pravitel'stvo otkazat'sia ot boltovni', *Kommersant*, 16 June.

Netreba, Petr (2007), 'Stabfond popolniat budushchie pokoleniia', *Kommersant*, 22 March.

Netreba, Petr (2009), 'Pravitel'stvu nadoela rol' investora', *Kommersant*, 16 June.

Netreba, Petr and Aleksei Shapovalov (2009), 'Rossii ne perezhit' krizis za god', *Kommersant*, 26 March.

Netreba, Petr and Maksim Shishkin (2006), 'Stabfond peredan TsB i Minfinu na razmeshchenie', *Kommersant*, 25 April.

'O dopolnitel'nykh merakh po podderzhke finansovoi sistemy Rossiiskoi Federatsii' (2008), Federal Law No.173-FZ, 13 October.

'O federal'nom biudzhete na 2005 god' (2004), Federal Law No.173, 23 December.

'O poriadke upravleniia sredstvami Stabilizatsionnogo fonda Rossiiskoi Federatsii' (2004), Government decree No. 508, 30 September.

'O poriadke upravleniia sredstvami Stabilizatsionnogo fonda Rossiiskoi Federatsii' (2006), Government decree No. 229, 21 April.

'O poriadke upravleniia sredstvami Rezervnogo fonda' (2007), Government decree No. 955, 29 December.

'O poriadke upravleniia sredstvami Fonda natsional'nogo blagosostoianiia' (2008), Government decree No.18, 19 January.

'O proekte federal'nogo zakona No. 362803-3, 'O vnesenii dopolnenii v Biudzhetnyi kodeks Rossiiskoi Federatsii v chasti sozdaniia Stabilizatsionnogo fonda Rossiiskoi Federatsii' (2003), *Stenogrammy GD FS RF*, 28 November.

'O vnesenii dopolnenii v Biudzhetnyi kodeks Rossiiskoi Federatsii v chasti sozdaniia Stabilizatsionnogo fonda Rossiiskoi Federatsii' (2003), Federal Law No. 184-FZ, 23 December.

'O vnesenii izmenenii v Biudzhetnyi kodeks Rossiiskoi Federatsii v chasti regulirovaniia biudzhetnogo protsessa i privedenii v sootvetstvie s biudzhetnym zakonodatel'stvom Rossiiskoi Federatsii otdel'nykh zakonodatel'nykh aktov Rossiiskoi Federatsii' (2007), Federal Law No. 63, 26 April.

'O vnesenii izmenenii v postanovlenie Pravitel'stva Rossiiskoi Federatsii ot 19 ianvaria 2008 g. No.18' (2008a), Government decree No.766, 15 October.

'O vnesenii izmenenii v Trebovaniia k finansovym aktivam, v kotorye mogut razmeshchat'sia sredstva Rezervnogo fonda' (2008b), Government decree No. 805, 6 November.

'O vnesenii izmenenii v prikaz Ministerstva finansov Rossiiskoi Federatsii ot 16 ianvaria 2008 g. No 3' (2009a), Ministry of Finance decree No. 116, 24 February.

'O vnesenii izmeneniia v Trebovaniia k finansovym aktivam, v kotorye mogut razmeshchat'sia sredstva Fonda natsional'nogo blagosostoianiia' (2009b), Government decree No. 597, 22 July.

'Ob utverzhdenii Pravil perechisleniia v Stabilizatsionnyi fond Rossiiskoi Federatsii dopolnitel'nykh dokhodov federal'nogo biudzheta, ostatkov sredstv federal'nogo biudzheta na nachalo finansovogo goda i dokhodov ot razmeshcheniia sredtsv Stabilizatsionnogo fonda Rossiiskoi Federatsii' (2004), Governent decree No. 31, 23 January.

'Ob utverzhdenii perechnia inostrannykh gosudarstvennykh agenstv, v dolgovye obiazatel'stva kotorykh mogut razmeshchat'sia sredstva Rezervnogo fonda' (2008a), Ministry of Finance decree No. 5, 16 January.

'Ob utverzhdenii perechnia inostrannykh gosudarstvennykh agenstv, v dologovye obiazatel'stva kotorykh mogut razmeshchat'sia sredstva Fonda natsional'nogo blagosostoianiia' (2008b), Ministry of Finance decree No. 22, 24 January.

'Ob utverzhdenii normativnykh dolei razreshennykh finansovykh aktivov v obshchem ob"eme razmeshchennykh sredstv Fonda natsional'nogo blagosostoianiia i Poriadke rascheta fakticheskikh dolei razreshennykh finansovykh aktivov v obshchem ob"eme razmeshchennykh sredstv Fonda natsional'nogo blagosostoianiia i ikh privedeniia v sootvetstvie s normativnymi doliami' (2008c), Ministry of Finance decree No. 26, 24 January.

'Osnovnye polozheniia otcheta Pravitel'stva Rossiiskoi Federatsii o realizatsii mer po podderzhke finansovogo rynka, bankovskoi sistemy, rynka truda, otraslei ekonomiki Rossiiskoi Federatsii, sotisal'nomu obespecheniiu naseleniia i drugikh mer sotsial'noi politiki za pervoe polugodie 2009 goda i chetvertyi kvartal 2008 goda' (2009), 5 August, available at http://www.government.gov.ru/content/rfgovernment/rfgovernmentchairman/chronicle/archive/2009/08/05/5768549.htm.

'Ot redaktsii: za dvumia zaitsami' (2003), *Vedomosti*, 16 December.

'Ot redaktsii: oplata po faktu' (2005), *Vedomosti*, 11 March.

'Ot redaktsii: na smert' stabfonda' (2007), *Vedomosti*, 21 December.

Oxenstierna, Susanne (2009), 'Russia in Perspective. Scenarios of Russia's Economic Future 10 to 20 Years Ahead', FOI, Swedish Defence Research Agency, Stockholm, June.

Panov, Andrei, Boris Grozovskii and Mikhail Overchenko (2007), 'Fond "golubykh fishek"', *Vedomosti*, 22 May.

Petrachkova, Aleksandra (2006a), 'Uchites' u Kudrina', *Vedomosti*, 18 May.

Petrachkova, Aleksandra (2006b), 'Kak delit' biudzhet', *Vedomosti*, 26 October.

Petrachkova, Aleksandra and Aleksandr Bekker (2005), 'Pensionnyi stabfond', *Vedomosti*, 17 October.

Pis'mennaia, Evgeniia (2009), 'Zabud'te o pomoshchi', *Vedomosti*, 2 March.

Pis'mennaia, Evgeniia, Giuzel' Gubeidullina and Daniil Zhelobanov (2009), 'VEB rasprodast svoi portfel', *Vedomosti*, 22 October.

Pravitel'stvo Rossiiskoi Federatsii (2009), Rasporiazhenie No. 271-r, 10 March, available at http://gov.consultant.ru/doc.asp?ID=51251.

Programma antikrizisnykh mer Pravitel'stva Rossiiskoi Federatsii na 2009 god (2009), 19 March, available at http://www.kreml.org/other/207973731.

Putin, V.V. (2003), 'Biudzhetnoe poslanie Federal'nomu Sobraniiu "O biudzhet-noi politike v 2004 godu"', 30 May, available at http://archive.kremlin.ru/text/appears/2003/05/46347.shtml.

Putin, V.V. (2004), 'Biudzhetnoe poslanie Federal'nomu Sobraniiu "O biudzhet-noi politike v 2005 godu"', 12 July, available at http://archive.kremlin.ru/text/docs/2004/07/74379.shtml.

Putin, V.V. (2006), 'Biudzhetnoe poslanie Federal'nomu Sobraniiu "O biudzhet-noi politike v 2007 godu"', 30 May, available at http://archive.kremlin.ru/text/appears/2006/05/106175.shtml.

Putin, V.V. (2007a), 'Biudzhetnoe poslanie prezidenta Rossiiskoi Federatsii', 9 March, available at http://www.kreml.org/other/143944314.

Putin, V.V. (2007b), 'Poslanie Prezidenta RF Federal'nomu Sobraniiu ot 26 aprelia 2007g.', 26 April, available at http://www.kreml.org/topics/148082718.

Putin, V.V. (2009), 'Predsedatel' Pravitel'stva Rossiiskoi Federatsii V.V. Putin provel soveshchanie po voprosam osnovnykh napravlenii biudzhetnoi politiki i osnvnykh kharakteristik federal'nogo biudzheta na 2010 god i na planovoi period 2011 i 2012 godov', 21 July, available at http://government.gov.ru/content/rfgovernment/rfgovernmentchairman/chronicle/archive/2009/07/21/3928492.htm.

'Rossiia vlozhila v obligatsii Fannie Mae i Freddie Mac menee 30 mlrd. dollarov' (2008), *g2p*, 16 September, available at http://www.g2p.ru/publications/index.php?opn=55018&part=1.

'Russia Wealth Fund, Private Investors can Stabilise World Markets – Kremlin' (2008), *Thomson Financial News*, 20 February, available at http://www.forbes.com/feeds/afx/2008/02/20/afx4675511.html.

'Russian State Investments in Fannie Mae, Freddie Mac under $30 Bln' (2008), *RIA Novosti*, 16 September, available at http://en.rian.ru/russia/20080916/116844999.html.

'Sovokupnyi ob"em sredstv fonda', Ministry of Finance.

'Stabfondu ostalos' tri goda' (2006), *Kommersant*, 4 December.

Stanovaia, Tat'iana (2006), 'Promyshlennaia politika liberala', *Politcom.ru*, 5 May, available at http://www.politcom.ru/article.php?id=2667.

'Svedeniia o dvizhenii sredstv po schetu Federal'nogo kaznacheistva v Banke Rossii po uchetu sredstv Stabilizatsionnogo fonda Rossiiskoi Federatsii v rubli-akh za 2005 goda' (2005), available at http://www.minfin.ru/ru/stabfund/statistics/remains.

'U.S. Mortgage Giants' Share Drop Will Not Hit Russian State Funds' (2008), *RIA Novosti*, 12 July, available at http://en.rian.ru/russia/20080712/113839868.html.

Visloguzov, Vadim (2009), 'V Biudzhetnyi kodeks vveli chrezvychainye polozheniia', *Kommersant*, 28 March.

Voitenko, Marina (2009), 'Gospodderzhka bankov – novoe nachalo', *Politcom.ru*, 9 February, available at http://www.politcom.ru/7599.html.

'Vyskazyvaniia rukovodstva (2009)', Ministry of Finance, 24 March, available at http://www.minfin.ru/ru/press/speech/index.php?date_type4=p&afrom4=24.03.2009&ato4=24.03.2009&type4=1&src4=&id4=7201.

7
Some Macroeconomic Implications of the Future Fund

John Freebairn

Introduction

Up to 2005, most Australian public servants and the military received as a part of their remuneration a defined benefit superannuation payment in retirement[1]. At the time of employment, no funds were set aside for these future outlays. Rather, the payments were to be met when required on a pay-as-you-go form from recurrent government expenditure. In effect, the government was building up unfunded liabilities, or borrowing from its current employees. In May 2007 these unfunded liabilities were estimated at around A$103 billion, or 10 per cent of a year's GDP, and the liability is expected to grow to around A$148 billion by 2020 (Australian Government 2007). While some superannuation retirement benefits will be paid in the next few years, given the age distribution of expected retirements, a large proportion of these unfunded liabilities are not expected to mature until after 2020 (Au-Yeung et al. 2006). Financing these superannuation liabilities from recurrent funds as and when they are claimed is referred to as the business as usual (BAU) strategy.

The Australian government has established a Future Fund to bring forward the time of collection of public sector funds to pay for the unfunded superannuation liabilities of public servants and the military. The Future Fund strategy proposes to use government budgetary allocations over the next decade or so, revenue from the sale of the government's Telstra shares, and the investment returns on these funds, to meet the unfunded superannuation liabilities of public servants and the military. The Future Fund scheme was announced in 2004 and it has been in operation since April 2006. From the perspective of fiscal policy, the Future Fund idea means that over the next decade or two the budget surplus will be lower, or government expenditure will be lower, or tax rates will be higher, or a combination, and then the reverse will happen from about 2020 onwards, compared with the BAU policy strategy of funding the superannuation claims out of current revenue on a pay-as-you-go basis.

This chapter explores the fiscal policy implications of the Future Fund versus the BAU policy strategies, and then it assesses the likely comparative implications of the two opposing strategies and associated fiscal outcomes for the broad macroeconomic aggregates.

Background and policy scenarios

From a fiscal policy perspective, the key difference between the Future Fund (FF) strategy for meeting the promised retirement incomes of public servants and the military, relative to the BAU strategy, is that the call on government funds is brought forward to between now and 2020. At the same time, the FF strategy means a smaller draw on government funds after 2020 when compared with the BAU strategy.

Table 7.1 provides a simple comparison of the FF and BAU strategies. For both strategies, in the previous period up to 2005, denoted P_p, unfunded superannuation liabilities were accumulated. In the next period, denoted P_n, say up to around 2020, there are few government pay-as-you-go outlays for superannuation under BAU, but there is a big shift of government funds into the Future Fund under FF. The future period, denoted as P_f, say after 2020, is when most of the unfunded superannuation liabilities become payable. Under BAU, these payments come from recurrent government expenditure, and under FF they come from the Future Fund with no draw on recurrent government expenditure. For our analysis of differences in fiscal policy and its macroeconomic implications, the key difference between the two strategies is that relative to BAU, the FF strategy brings forward from P_f to P_n the government funding of the A$148 billion of unfunded superannuation liabilities. In effect, this is an intergenerational switch in the

Table 7.1 A simple comparison of the policy scenarios

	Business as usual (BAU)	Future Fund (FF)
Previous period, P_p	Super debt built up	Super debt built up
Next period, P_n		Extra government saving
Future period, P_f	Extra government expenditure Repay super debt	Repay super debt

funding of superannuation liabilities, or of government debt, between the P_n and P_f generations.

The budget options for funding the Futue Fund can be assessed from the textbook government budget identity for a particular year:

$$G - T = D \tag{7.1}$$

where G is government expenditure, T is taxation (and other) revenue, and D is the budget deficit. If we make SL the explicit payment of superannuation liabilities, or the deferred income paid to public servants and the military, and FFC explicit government payments into the Future Fund, and G' becomes other government expenditures, the expanded budget identity (7.1) becomes:

$$G' + SL + FFC - T = D \tag{7.2}$$

Government can fund the FF, that is, by making payments FFC in (7.2) over the next decade or so, either by:

- running a larger budget deficit, D, or a smaller budget surplus, while holding T and G' constant
- reducing government expenditure in other areas, G', while holding D and T constant
- raising more taxes, T, while holding G' and D constant, or
- a combination of the above.

In the future period after 2020, the reverse happens under the FF scenario relative to the BAU scenario.

In the future period under BAU, the SL payments in (7.2) have to be met from government funds, as a larger D, smaller G', larger T, or a combination.

For simplicity of analysis, the chapter will consider the case of a consistent approach to the funding of the superannuation liabilities, or fiscal stance, across both periods P_n and P_f. For example, for the case where government uses higher taxes, T, up to about 2020, or in P_n, to fund the FFC with no change in G' and D, then relative to the BAU scenario, it would have lower taxes, T, after 2020, or in P_f, with no change in G' and D.

Before analysing these policy strategy options, it will be helpful to have some background on the macroeconomic context in which the options will be evaluated. Currently, government (at the Australian, state, territory and local levels) expenditure and taxation is about the equivalent of 31 per cent of GDP. Assuming a continuation of current government expenditure programmes and entitlements, government expenditure, G' of (7.2), is projected to increase in the areas of health care (because of ageing of the population and technological change), and in aged care and aged pensions (because of demographic changes resulting in a doubling of the population aged 65 and over by 2046–47), with only small changes in other government outlays such as education. The Treasury in its *Intergenerational Report* (Commonwealth of Australia 2007)[2] projects an increase in Australian government expenditure as a share of GDP by the equivalent of 4.75 per cent of GDP to nearly 36 per cent of GDP by 2046–47. One of the several motivations for the Future Fund was the desire to bring forward the collection of funds for the unfunded superannuation liabilities before these other extra expenditure calls on future generations materialise.

Fiscal policy in Australia, especially at the federal level, has a strong bipartisan agreement for a medium term target of fiscal balance on average across the economic cycle. In practice, there has been a strong preference for a surplus in most years. Apart from the automatic stabilis-ers,[3] active fiscal policy plays a small role in short-term macroeconomic management. Rather, monetary policy is assigned the principal short-term macroeconomic instrument,[4] and fiscal policy is assigned to meeting medium- and longer-term objectives for expenditure, taxation and national saving.

A continuation of this medium-term fiscal policy strategy means that adjusting the expenditure, G', and tax, T, instruments in (7.2) are likely to be more important than adjusting the deficit, D, instrument in the funding of government employees' superannuation liabilities. Under this assumption that the BAU and FF strategies have little net effect on the net fiscal outcome and on aggregate demand, both before and after 2020, there will be only small differences in the effects of the two strategies on short-term macroeconomic outcomes. Rather, the focus of the comparative assessment is the effects of changes in levels of taxa-tion and government expenditure across the P_n and P_f generations on longer-term factor supply and productivity, and then GDP.

Effects of different Future Fund funding options

This section compares the effects of the FF and BAU strategies on GDP over the next decade or so, and then in future decades, via their comparative effects on incentives to work and to invest. The budget accounting identity (7.2) forms the framework for comparing the FF and the BAU scenarios. In particular, the comparative assessment distinguishes between the cases in which funds for the Future Fund under FF collected in the next period, or for the superannuation liabilities under BAU collected in the future period, are financed by additional debt, a higher tax burden or lower government expenditure.

Higher deficit

If funds for the FF over the next decade or so are to come from a larger budget deficit (or a smaller surplus) than under the BAU strategy, with G' and T unchanged, there is a simple swap on the liabilities side of the government balance sheet. Up to about 2020 when the Future Fund is being built up, the $X increase in FFC in (7.2) and reduction in unfunded superannuation liabilities is matched by an $X increase in D. Effectively, the unfunded superannuation liability is transferred to a larger budget deficit. After about 2020, the $Y billion fall of SL (now paid from the FF) is matched by a $Y decrease in D. Only in the unlikely situation of money illusion so that 'debt ain't debt' would we expect this FF funding option to have any macroeconomic effects relative to the BAU strategy.

Higher tax burden

Under this option, with G' and D held the same under the BAU and FF strategies, the tax burden under FF is higher during the next period and lower in the future period. For example, the next period tax burden as a share of GDP of around 31 per cent would be 0.5 to 1.0 percentage points higher, and the future period rate of around 36 per cent would be 0.5 to 1.0 percentage points lower. In principle, the tax changes could be to income taxation that falls on both labour and capital income, they could apply to the GST that falls on consumption and exempts saving, or other indirect taxes such as the excise duties, and the choice would have different effects on labour supply and investment decisions. The more likely tax to be changed would be income taxation given its importance in the Commonwealth government's revenue and its relative ease of being changed. Then, for changes in income taxation, relative to the BAU strategy, the FF strategy would increase the tax wedge for labour and capital inputs in the next decade or so during the FF accumulation phase and then lower the wedge in the future decades when superannuation liabilities are paid out. Then, using taxes to fund the FF may have factor supply and economic efficiency effects in addition to the straight intergenerational redistribution effects.

In an extreme world of Ricardian equivalence,[5] these changes in the timing of tax collections would have no effects on the real economy. Under the Ricardian equivalence assumptions of a lifetime optimisation model and with perfect foresight, rational decision-makers 'see through' differences in the timing of tax collections so that their timing has a minimal effect on the lifetime budget constraint and consumption and factor supply decisions taken. However, such extreme assumptions are not supported by the data.

Consider next the other extreme set of assumptions of naïve expectations and where decisions for each period are based only on that period's tax rates. During the next decade or so of build-up of the Future Fund, the higher (income) tax rates under the FF strategy relative to the BAU strategy would reduce the supply of labour and capital inputs, with a resulting smaller GDP. While the labour supply effect may be relatively small because of the low labour supply elasticity (generally regarded as not being greater than 0.2), the investment and capital stock effects are likely to be much larger. Largely, Australia as a small trader in a large global capital market, and with a relatively open economy, faces a highly elastic supply of world savings at the world-required after-tax rate of return.[6] An increase in Australian taxation on investment in Australia increases the required pre-tax return on investment in Australia. The result is a fall in investment and a lower capital stock under the FF strategy relative to the BAU strategy over the next decade or so.

In the future period the reverse happens, with the lower tax burden under the FF strategy encouraging larger supplies of labour and capital, and a larger GDP. Effectively, the FF relative to BAU lowers economic growth in the next period when higher tax revenues are collected to build up the Future Fund, and it increases economic growth in the future when the Future Fund, rather than higher taxes under the BAU strategy, meets the unfunded superannuation liabilities.

When the next and future periods are considered jointly, the FF strategy results in tax smoothing relative to the BAU strategy. For example, under the BAU strategy and with the *Intergenerational Report* projections (Commonwealth of Australia 2007), the average tax rates would be around 31 per cent and 36 per cent of GDP in P_n and P_f, respectively; but under the FF strategy the average tax rates would be around 32 per cent and 35 per cent, respectively. Since the factor supply response effects and distortion costs of taxation rise more than proportionately with the tax rate[7] (see, for example, Stiglitz 2000), tax smoothing under the FF strategy, relative to the BAU strategy, would result in a smaller fall in factor supplies and GDP, and in deadweight costs of tax distortions, over the next decade or so relative to the gains in the future period.

Lower expenditure

Under the FF strategy, government expenditure, G', is lower during the next decade or so and higher in the future, with T and D the same in both periods as under the BAU strategy. The macroeconomic effects of the FF strategy will vary with the type of expenditure affected. For example, if most of the expenditure to be reduced is considered of little economic social value, and hence a waste, for example, infrastructure projects designed primarily to win votes in marginal electorates and which have a low social benefit to cost ratio, the FF offers a net gain during the future period for little cost in the next period. Unfortunately, given the political processes and reasons that drive such expenditure programmes, there has to be only a low probability that economic wasteful expenditures, but political valuable expenditures, would be targeted to be reduced as a way of generating funds for the Future Fund.

Another category of government expenditures to be changed could largely have private good properties,[8] such as much government expenditure on tertiary education, health and housing. Here, private supply and public supply are considered very close substitutes. In this case, any reduction (or increase) in government supply is matched by an increase (decrease) in private supply. This expenditure switching may crowd-out other private consumption or reduce private saving during the FF build-up phase, and in the process reduce aggregate demand; and vice versa in the future period.

The more likely government expenditure options for changing under the FF strategy are the supply of goods and services to correct for market failures and those for social security payments to meet equity objectives. A lower supply of goods and services complementary to private investment, such as basic R&D and some infrastructure with a high social benefit to cost ratio, lowers the productivity of private investment, and in turn its level. Less expenditure on public goods, such as defence and law and order, and lower social security payments, reduce national welfare. For both of these types of expenditures, the FF strategy, relative to BAU, has adverse effects during the next decade or so, and favourable effects in the future.

Composition of investment and saving

The supporting legislation and charter for the Future Fund is very pre-scriptive (Future Fund 2006). Among other things, while it is owned by the Commonwealth government it has an arm's-length independent Board of Guardians, it is limited to investing in financial assets, it cannot make direct investments in infrastructure or property, it cannot assume control of listed or unlisted companies, it has employed a private funds manager to invest its funds and it is charged with maximising returns over the long run (with a targeted real rate of return of 4.5 to 5.5 per cent per annum). Its objectives and modes of operation are similar to those of private company and industry superannuation funds used by private sector employees.

In this context, the Future Fund is not expected to have significant effects on the composition of national investment and saving. As already noted, it has similar objectives and modes of operation as existing private sector superannuation funds. Even though the Future Fund will be a large player with control of up to 10 per cent of all Australian superannuation funds, the superannuation industry itself has to operate in a much larger and highly competitive finance industry in Australia, and the Australian finance industry is integrated into a much larger global finance industry. In this larger competitive market context, any idiosyncratic investment choices, including the possibility of directed investments by future governments, such as the proposed investment by the government in broadband, by the Future Fund will be offset by the investment choices of other players seeking to maximise long-run returns.

Some other considerations

A possible advantage of the FF strategy is that by bringing forward the time of collection of funds to cover superannuation liabilities, the strategy reduces risks and budget vulnerability to unforseen adverse cir-cumstances. Given the zero debt position of the Australian government, arguably this precaution is of limited value and it is unlikely to affect the credit ranking or cost of borrowing funds in the future if contingencies occur.

On the other side, it might be argued that a tighter budget situation during the build-up of the Future Fund, whether financed by higher T, lower G' or a larger D, makes it more difficult to achieve necessary structural reforms to the taxation and expenditure systems. Here the argument runs that it is easier to make structural changes that raise over-all productivity and effectiveness if there are enough available funds to leave almost everyone as a winner. To illustrate, the GST tax reform of 2000, which included a rationalisation of inefficient indirect taxes and a more controversial and a debatable partial change in the tax mix from an income base to a consumption base, involved a net additional cost to government outlays of about A$6 billion to minimise the number of 'losers' from the reforms.

Intergenerational comparisons

A key result from the previous discussion of using higher taxation, lower government expenditure or a combination over the next decade or two to provide funds under the FF strategy to meet already incurred unfunded superannuation liabilities, relative to the BAU strategy of waiting well into the future to fund these liabilities when they occur on a pay-as-you-go basis, is the intergenerational transfer. The FF strategy disadvantages the current generation relative to the future generation, although tax smoothing suggests a small positive sum game outcome when summing across the generations.

From a society social welfare assessment perspective, whether the losses to the current generation exceed the gains for the future generation under the FF scenario relative to the BAU scenario depends on the social discount rate.[9] One way to compare the different time profiles of outcomes of the two scenarios is to compute the present values. For a zero sum game, if the social discount rate is about the same as the rate of return on the funds invested in the Future Fund, there would be little to choose between the FF and the BAU scenarios; if the discount rate is higher, the BAU scenario is preferred, and vice versa. To the extent that the FF scenario offers a positive sum game, say because of tax smoothing, a higher discount rate could be sustained for a net social welfare gain for the FF over the BAU scenario. Alternatively, given that future generations almost certainly will have higher per capita real incomes (with the Treasury projecting an average gain of 1.6 per cent per year (Commonwealth of Australia 2007)), and that the marginal utility of money declines with the income level, it could be argued to use a higher discount rate to favour the current generation, and hence the BAU scenario is more likely to become the favoured scenario. Unfortunately, there is no general agreement on the social discount rate when it comes to drawing comparisons across generations.

Conclusion

The FF is a strategy for bringing forward the allocation of government funds to meet the unfunded superannuation liabilities of public servants and the military. Under special circumstances the strategy will have few or even benign macroeconomic effects. These include if the funds come from a bigger budget deficit (or smaller surplus) than otherwise, from wasteful expenditure, or if strict Ricardian equivalence applies to changes in tax burdens.

More likely, most of the funds for the Future Fund will come from a combination of higher taxes and less than full Ricardian equivalence, or from reduced government expenditure on goods and services subject to market failure or for equity reasons. In addition to the intergeneration direct income transfers, there will be indirect adverse effects on the aggregate level of economic activity during the next decade or so, but with benefits in the future.

Acknowledgements

With the usual caveats, I gratefully acknowledge the comments on an earlier draft of Jeff Borland and a referee.

Notes

1. In recent years and into the future, government employees have been shifted to an accumulation scheme, with funds drawn from budget outlays as the liabilities are accrued.
2. Similar projections were made by the Productivity Commission (2005). Studies by state governments project an increase in their expenditure, but by smaller amounts than for the Commonwealth.
3. Here automatic stabilisers mean that in times of recession, tax revenue collections fall and social security payments increase, and vice versa in times of a recovery.
4. For simplicity, the chapter ignores any different responses of monetary policy to the different budget options for providing funds to the FF.
5. The central proposition of the so-called Ricardian equivalence is that, under a specific set of circumstances, it actually makes no difference to the level of aggregate demand throughout the economy if the government finances its outlays by debt or by taxation. The underpinning assumption is that the issue of public debt in the current period is always accompanied by a planned increase in future collections, which would be needed to service this higher level of public indebtedness. Because debt financing is perceived by rational agents only as a change in the timing of taxation, expansionary fiscal policy has no important effects on the economy (see Barro, 1974).
6. For some supporting evidence, see Industry Commission (1991).
7. Strictly speaking, the factor supply effects depend on both the marginal and average tax rates, and the tax distortion costs depend only on the marginal tax rates. In most cases, and specifically in the case of a progressive income tax rate schedule, the marginal rate exceeds the average rate.
8. In particular, we refer to the properties of rival consumption and ease and low costs of exclusion.

9. Recall that we want to compare the present value of an \$X today allocation to the FF with a future \$Y payout on the superannuation liability under BAU. The \$X accumulates at $\$X\,(1 + r)$, where r is the rate of return on funds invested. The present value of the \$Y is given by $\$Y\,/\,(1 + d)$, where d is the social rate of time preference.

References

Au-Yeung, W., J. McDonald and A. Sayegh (2006), 'Future Fund and Fiscal Policy', *Economic Roundup*, Winter, pp. 27–37.

Australian Government (2007), 'Future Fund', March, available at http://www.futurefund.gov.au.

Barro, R. (1974), 'Are Government Bonds Net Wealth?', *Journal of Political Economy*, 82(6), pp. 1095–117.

Commonwealth of Australia (2007a), *Intergenerational Report 2007*, April, Canberra, available at http://www.treasury.gov.au/igr.

Future Fund (2006), *Annual Report 2005–06*, Australian government, Canberra, available at http:// www.futurefund.gov.au.

Industry Commission (1991), *Availability of Capital, Report,* No. 18, AGPS, Canberra.

Productivity Commission (2005), 'Economic Implications of an Ageing Australia', Draft Report, Melbourne.

Stiglitz, J. (2000), *Economics of the Public Sector*. New York: Norton.

8
The Political Economy of Australia's Future Fund – The Political Dimension

Richard Eccleston

In September 2004, the then Treasurer Peter Costello announced the creation of a new state-owned investment fund designed to 'to meet the long-term costs associated with Australia's ageing population'.[1] The Future Fund (FF) was formally created in May 2006 and as of late 2009 managed assets of A$85 billion and thus represents a significant development in Australian budget politics and management (Future Fund 2009). This chapter builds on the economic analysis presented by John Freebairn in Chapter 7 by exploring the political circumstances that led to the FF's creation as well as the economic and political consequences of its short history. The chapter argues that despite the FF's distinctive rationale and structure, many of the debates concerning the governance of 'conventional' sovereign wealth funds (SWFs) are also relevant to the political economy of Australia's FF. The central issues here are whether the creation of a state-run investment fund will enhance long-term national economic growth and the extent to which the fund can be used for political purposes.

At a more general level, the chapter argues that the creation and evolution of the FF provides significant insights into the Australian budget politics and political economy. Yet despite the success of the FF and the broad-based political support it enjoys, given the profound impact of the global financial crisis (GFC) on the public finances it is unlikely that the FF 'experiment' will be emulated in Australia or other advanced economies. The FF should be regarded as the product of unique political and economic circumstances of the early 2000s rather than a wider trend in public finance.

The political origins of the Future Fund

In many important ways the FF is both exceptional and confounding. It is exceptional because it is almost unprecedented for the government of a mature and diversified economy to establish a state investment fund to finance medium- to long-term financial liabilities and policy agendas. At the level of fiscal theory it is confounding for a liberal democratic government to tax today's citizens to fund future liabilities. Indeed the creation of the FF challenges the dominant public-choice literature on budget politics and its central claim that democratic governments face strong political incentives to fund current expenditure through deficit financing (Brennan and Buchanan 1980). Taxation is the most significant and consequential contract between citizens and government and given the FF challenges our understanding of this relationship, it is important to closely examine the politics surrounding its creation.

The Australian government's desire to establish the FF can be explained in terms of three sets of factors. Overtly the FF was developed as a policy response to the medium- to longer-term costs associated with Australia's ageing population. Across the industrialised world there has been a good deal of debate about the impact of an ageing population on public finance, the labour market, service provision and society more generally. In the Australian context the extent of the demographic challenge was outlined in the Treasury's *Intergenerational Report 2002–03*, which argued that the ageing population will result in lower workforce participation rates reducing the long-run growth potential of the economy (Gruen and Sayegh 2005, p. 629). On the expenditure side, the ageing population will result in increased demand for pensions, nursing and health services, which according to the Productivity Commission (2005) will cost an additional 6 per cent of GDP by 2045. While these issues have been on the policy agenda since the 1980s, and were important drivers of the superannuation reforms of the period, since the publication of the Treasury's *Intergenerational Report 2002–*03 they have had a major impact on the management of Australian fiscal policy (Treasury 2002).

It was in this context that the Howard government (1996–2007) developed a long-term strategy to put fiscal policy on a more sustainable footing and the FF was framed as being central to this goal. Treasurer Costello emphasised this point when he announced his intention to create the FF in September 2004:

> We know from the intergenerational report that a huge gap is going to open up in ten, twenty, thirty and forty years' time, between

revenues and expenses. If we start building a Future Fund now, we can start narrowing this gap.

This is the most dramatic response to the intergenerational report which we can now put in place as a consequence of Australia's strong economic position. We will be setting future generations up by funding the liabilities that are being incurred today, with money from today, rather than leaving the future generations to find it.

(Costello 2004)

In addition to making a down payment on the federal government's unfunded superannuation liability, the creation of the FF was also designed to ensure the viability of Australia's sovereign debt market. Australia's net government debt had been reduced from A\$96 billion in 1996 to A\$20 billion by 2004. While eliminating government debt was seen as being politically desirable, financial markets and policy-makers were concerned this would seriously undermine the market for Australian bonds. This in turn would impact on a key segment of the financial services industry, discourage foreign portfolio investment and potentially impact on the dynamics and liquidity of foreign exchange markets. Once these risks had been documented in a 2003 Treasury report (Treasury 2003), a decision was made to maintain a net public debt of approximately A\$50 billion, which in turn raised the issue of how to utilise anticipated future budgets.

At this time Australia was in an extremely enviable position as far as public finances were concerned, although as some analysts have noted, there are unique challenges associated with managing budget surpluses. On the expenditure side the availability of large surpluses will increase demands for new spending initiatives, while from a revenue perspective, surpluses tend to amplify demands for tax cuts and reform. Finally, in competitive two-party systems such as Australia's, governments are reluctant to accumulate large surpluses that can be used by opposition parties to credibly fund alternative policy programmes (Wanna et al. 2000, p. 294).

The problem of excessive surpluses can be addressed by either increasing expenditure or cutting taxes, but because it is politically difficult to cut established programmes or increase taxes such a course of action is only prudent if a surplus is *structural* – that is, likely to be maintained across the economic cycle. If a surplus is *cyclical* – the product of unsustainable economic growth – then permanently increasing expenditure or cutting taxes can lead to a rapid deterioration in public finances as economic activity slows, a dynamic that has been borne out in both the USA and the UK in the aftermath of the GFC. In Australia's case, the somewhat prophetic view held by policymakers was that while strong economic growth had been sustained since the late 1990s, this growth was the product of an unprecedented housing boom early in the decade before being supplemented by a commodities boom from 2002. In short, there was a view that the strong economic and revenue growth experienced from 2001 was exceptional and unlikely to be sustained.

In practice, the goal of Australian fiscal policy in 2001–02 and the onset of the GFC were to achieve an underlying cash surplus (UCS) of approximately 1 per cent of GDP with excess revenues being redistributed to citizens via income tax cuts (Eccleston 2007). While Treasurer Peter Costello argued that this was an appropriate goal of fiscal policy, representing a balance between the needs of today's taxpayers and future generations, by 2004 the government needed a clear strategy for maintaining a surplus of the order of 1–1.5 per cent of GDP.

Ultimately, the creation of the FF was a politically savvy response to the circumstances confronting the Australian government in 2004. The FF could be used to quarantine surpluses and temper demands for increased spending and/or tax cuts. An added advantage of the FF (unlike assets managed by the Reserve Bank) is that earnings on assets under management are not included in the budget's widely reported underlying cash balance (UCB), further reducing this influential measure of Commonwealth revenues.[2] Second, by establishing a clear objective for the fund – to meet the unfunded superannuation liability of federal public servants by 2020 – it could be argued that the government was taking concrete policy measures to address the medium-term fiscal challenges associated with Australia's ageing population.

Finally, the creation of the FF consolidated the Coalition government's all important reputation as a sound economic manager. Having established the FF it could claim not only that had it reduced Commonwealth debt, but it was now willing to forego current spending or tax cuts in pursuit of long-term national goals. This fiscal discipline clearly contradicts traditional theories of economic voting and their assumption that popular support for government is determined by the short-term financial benefits they can offer voters (Eccleston 1999). However, it is consistent with the new economic orthodoxy which had become established in Australia by the late 1990s whereby voters rewarded governments who could deliver 'The circle of virtue; low inflation, low interest rates, solid growth, strong investment, a budget surplus and falling public debt' (Kelly 1999, p. 11). Given this context there was little surprise when in March 2006 the Future Fund Act 2006 was passed by the federal parliament with bipartisan support (Hansard 2006).

Is the Future Fund an SWF?

A central aim of this book is to highlight the wide variety of SWFs currently in existence. However, the diversity of SWFs raises fundamental conceptual issues. For example, how do we distinguish between SWFs and state-owned pension funds, especially given that more traditional pension funds continue to dwarf SWFs in terms of the value of assets under management?[3] It is especially important to clarify such definitional issues when analysing Australia's FF given that its origins, structure and objective are unique.

In broad terms, the FF is an independently managed but state-owned investment fund. It has been capitalised from a combination of the cash surplus from Australia's federal budget as well as the sale of the final state-owned tranche of Telstra, the dominant telecommunications company in the Australian market. The investment mandate of the FF is commercial rather than strategic in that it must invest across a range of asset classes and is prohibited from assuming a controlling interest in any one firm. The FFs intended purpose is quite specific in that the assets under management are intended to meet the hitherto unfunded superannuation of Commonwealth public servants, a liability expected to reach A$162 billion by 2020 (Treasury 2009a).

The most influential definition of an SWF has arguably been provided by the recently established International Working Group (IWG) on SWFs. The IWG defines an SWF as a special purpose state-owned fund used for a range of strategic economic purposes including fiscal stabilisation, economic development, managing balance of payments imbalances and creating pension reserve funds without explicit pension liabilities (IWG 2008). In addition to these broad characteristics, the IWG argues that SWFs can be defined by their distinctive purpose in that they are 'commonly established out of balance of payments surpluses, official foreign currency operations, the proceeds of privatisations, fiscal surpluses, and/or receipts resulting from commodity exports' (IWG 2008). Finally, most of the literature argues that a clear distinction needs to be established between SWFs and currency reserve assets held by monetary authorities as well as pension funds managed for the specific benefit of individuals.

We have noted that Australia's FF may be unique in terms of its creation, structure and objectives, yet it clearly has the key attributes of an SWF. At the most elementary level the FF is a state-owned but independently managed investment fund used for the purpose of creating a general pension reserve for the purpose of meeting hitherto unfunded superannuation liabilities. Significantly, the FF can be distinguished from traditional pension funds because while the FF was created for the purpose of meeting superannuation liabilities, the superannuants who are the intended beneficiaries of the fund have no direct legal claim on its assets (Clark 2009). The FF was not created to develop long-term income streams from finite resources, it was created to manage excess revenue from Australia's recent housing and commodity boom.

Unlike many other SWFs discussed in this volume the FF was not created to manage large current account surpluses. Indeed, Australia is one of the few debtor nations that has created an SWF. However, and as will be discussed in greater detail below, by 2007 the FF was being used as a macroeconomic policy instrument with budget surpluses being invested in the fund to reduce inflationary pressures in the Australian economy (Eccleston 2007). So, while the FF is unique in a number of important regards, it does fall within the IWG's widely accepted definition of an SWF. Indeed, Australia has been a major player in the IWG's creation and the development of the 'Santiago Principles'. David Murray, the chair of the FF's Board of Guardians, served as the inaugural chair of the IWG (Monk 2009).

Governance and evolution

Australian governments of all political persuasions have been strong proponents of financial liberalisation since the 1980s. Given this strong support for private investment and reducing the state's direct ownership of financial assets, the proposal to create a state-owned investment fund created a good deal of attention and debate. Critics argued that a large state-owned investment fund had the potential to distort local financial markets while politically there were concerns about conflicts of interest between the government's role as a regulator and an investor. Perhaps the most prominent concern raised by critics of the proposed FF was the risk that investment decisions may be influenced by political rather than commercial imperatives.

Given such concerns there are a number of provisions in the Future Fund Act 2006 to ensure the fund's statutory independence. Key features include establishing an independent and expert Board of Guardians to manage all investment decisions, a clear investment mandate and policies complemented by rigorous reporting requirements (described in the previous chapter). Indeed the governance of the FF is widely regarded as representing best practice, having been ranked equal first in the Petersen Institute's assessment of SWF transparency and governance (Truman 2007). The researchers from Oxford University's SWF project rate the FF as 'amongst the very best institutions we have known and have evaluated' (Clark 2009, p. 15). Yet, despite this robust governance framework there remains some scope for the Australian government to modify the fund's mission and objectives. Indeed, in the FF's three years of operation there have been subtle changes in the fund's management and structure. The following section assesses both how the FF has evolved since its inception and some of the minor controversies that have surrounded its operation.

The most obvious mechanism through which government could influence the fund's investment decisions and management objectives is through amending the 2006 Act. At the time of the fund's creation there was an active debate as to whether contractual or constitutional provisions should be implemented to ensure that the structure and aims of the FF could not be altered by subsequent parliaments. In keeping with the Westminster tradition of parliamentary sovereignty, it was rightly decided not to attempt to prevent future governments from amending the original Future Fund Act 2006 (Clark 2009, p. 20). While future Australian governments may be at liberty to amend the Act, the reality is that they are politically constrained by the clear commitment to dedicate the funds under management to meeting the superannuation liabilities of Commonwealth public servants from 2020 onwards.

As Clark (2009, p. 6) argues, clearly earmarking a long-term investment fund for a principled, legitimate purpose 'may effectively constrain the temptation of giving in to claims for current consumption'. In practical terms, the Rudd Labor government (elected in 2007) has upheld the Howard government's commitment to devote funds managed in the FF to meeting future superannuation liabilities (Tanner 2009). This is despite the fact many economists (see Freebairn in the previous chapter) question the economic benefits of using SWFs to improve the welfare of future generations at the expense of current consumption and investment. Indeed this point was raised by the Labor Opposition (now government) in parliamentary debate in early 2006 when it argued that 'unfunded obligations could be paid for out of future economic growth encouraged by a Future Fund focused upon investment in infrastructure' (Hansard 2006).

Although the Rudd government had a clear commitment to increasing public investment in economic infrastructure it resisted any temptation to use the FF for such purposes. This policy was affirmed in a speech on the governance and performance of the FF by the Labor Finance Minister, Lindsay Tanner, in which he argued that the 'Future Fund will ensure that our children will not have to worry about paying the bill for public sector superannuants.... Through our savings and investment today, we are relieving them of a future fiscal burden' (Tanner 2009).

On the critical question of whether there should be more public investment in infrastructure to allow higher economic growth or whether there should be more mandated savings to offset mounting budget liabilities (as per the FF), the Finance Minister argued that Australia must do both: 'The Howard Government failed to actively invest in infrastructure, and the Rudd Government is now working hard to restore that balance.' (Tanner 2009). It seems that the existing funds invested in the FF will be quarantined to fund the government's unfunded superannuation liability as intended, but that this initiative will be supplemented with greater funding in social and economic infrastructure. The clearest example of this subtle shift in policy has been through the restructuring and expansion of the Howard government's Higher Education Endowment Fund (HEEF).

The HEEF, established in the final year of the Howard government, represents a clear example of how the objectives of SWFs often evolve with the changing political and economic landscape. To be clear, while the capital invested in the HEEF was managed by the FF, it was actually a separate investment fund established to 'enhance infrastructure and research facilities in the Australian university sector' (Bishop 2007). While the intention of the Howard government was that the HEEF would be a perpetual fund with only investment income being available to fund university infrastructure, within six months of assuming office the Rudd Labor government abolished the HEEF and replaced it with three separate national building funds: The Education Investment Fund; The Building Australia Fund; and the Health and Hospitals Fund.

The intention of these three new funds was to accumulate budget surpluses for specific investment projects over the short to medium term. At the level of macroeconomic policy these funds had a strong countercyclical role in that they were designed to accumulate budget surpluses during times of high growth with a view to investing in infrastructure as the economy slowed (Swan and Tanner 2008). Politically these decisions are significant because they clearly demonstrate that government is willing to adapt old (the HEEF) and develop new SWFs to meet emerging policy challenges. While these developments have not compromised the integrity of the original FF per se, it is important to note that approximately A$15 billion surplus funds from the 2007–08 financial year were allocated to the new Building Australia Funds that may otherwise have been allocated to the original FF or used to fund other spending and/or tax initiatives. This budget decision suggests that the Rudd government shared its predecessor's strategy of investing surplus funds in SWFs designed to meet long-term economic objectives, albeit with an emphasis on infrastructure investment rather than meeting unfunded budget liabilities.

The Telstra divestment

The most significant controversy during the FF's short history has been its management of a 17 per cent stake in Telstra corporation transferred to the FF in February 2007. This transfer came about as a result of the Howard government's 2005 commitment to sell its remaining 51 per cent holding in the former state-owned Telco. After the government sold 34 per cent of shares on issue during a public offering conducted during 2006, it was decided that the remaining 17 per cent of Telstra still owned by the government would be transferred to the FF.[4] While this decision was applauded to the extent that it effectively ended any direct public holding in Telstra it did create dilemmas for FF management. More specifically, the large Telstra holding distorted asset allocations within the FF, yet if the Board of Guardians decided to diversify their holdings they ran the risk of severely distorting the politically sensitive market for Telstra shares. To mitigate these risks FF management separately listed their Telstra holdings in their financial reports and, by Ministerial declaration, were prevented from selling Telstra shares for a period of two years (expiring in November 2008). Beyond these provisions, David Murray, chairman of the Board of Guardians, made it clear that after the embargo period the FF would reduce its Telstra holdings in the interests of building a more diverse investment portfolio:

> In November 2008 the Board's holding of Telstra shares, representing some 16% of the company's issued capital, will be released from escrow. Thereafter the Board will manage this holding in line with its investment mandate and with a view to its obligations to maximise

long-term value with acceptable risk and to avoid causing abnormal
volatility in the market.

(Future Fund 2008, p. 16)

Despite this well-documented intention to reduce its Telstra holding
an announcement that the FF had sold A$2.4 billion worth of Tel-
stra shares at A$3.47 each on 20 August 2009 attracted unprecedented
attention. The controversy escalated on 15 September when the government announced that it intended to force the structural separation of
Telco in the hope of reducing its monopoly power and creating a more
competitive telecommunications market. While this is a laudable policy
objective it undermined the Telstra share price, which fell to A$3.10 after
the announcement (Whitley 2009). The concern here was that the FF
may have benefited from prior knowledge of the government's intention
to separate Telstra by reducing its holding in the stock ahead of the public announcement. Family First Senator Steve Fielding was particularly
critical of the sale accusing the FF and the government of insider trading on a grand scale. While a subsequent senate inquiry cleared the FF of
any wrongdoing, the episode highlights the potential conflict of interests facing government when regulatory and policy decisions impact on
the financial performance of SWFs. As Monk observed:

> Given the high standards of governance at the Future Fund, and its
> clear separation from political influence, I'm of the mind that it is
> innocent. However, the investigation raises an interesting issue. If a
> quick phone call from a politician to a SWF manager can mean the
> difference between hundreds of millions of profit or losses, there will
> undoubtedly be the temptation to call. In countries with less robust
> governance and legal rules than Australia, will the temptation be too
> great?
>
> (Monk 2009)

The Costello appointment

The independence and performance of an SWF is critically dependent
on the quality of its management team and the structure and composition of its board. In this regard, the FF is widely regarded as being
both innovative and effective (Clark and Monk 2009, p. 18). The fund
is managed by a small, expert Board of Governors whose tenure is
between three and five years. In terms of specific personnel, there is
wide acceptance that the credibility and independence of the FF was

greatly enhanced by the appointment of David Murray as the inaugural chairman of the Board of Governors. Murray is widely regarded as one of Australia's most experienced and respected bankers, having been CEO of the Commonwealth Bank of Australia for more than 13 years. If anything, Murray's reputation has been enhanced by the FF's exemplary performance during the GFC.

Despite this enviable record and reputation, the November 2009 announcement that former Treasurer Peter Costello would be appointed to the Board of Governors attracted a good deal of attention. Most of the commentary focused on whether a Labor government should appoint former adversaries to high government office with former Labor Prime Minister Peal Keating making a typically colourful contribution:

> The prime minister's goodie two-shoes approach of appointing former opponents of the Labor Party to important public jobs is no substitute for thoughtful and mature reflection as to the public requirement of those positions.... Costello was a policy bum of the first order who squandered 11 years of economic opportunity.
>
> (Keating 2009, p. 1)

However, beyond the partisan politics of the appointment, the real significance of the Costello appointment is that it provides the former Treasurer and architect of the FF with an opportunity to protect his legacy from political interference and to this extent promises to consolidate the political interference of the fund.

Conclusion: the future of the FF

In many ways, Australia's FF is an anomaly in the world of SWFs. Unlike the majority of cases in this volume, Australia has a mature and diversified economy, sophisticated financial markets and has experienced consistent current account deficits. However, despite these circumstances, the FF does have many of the key characteristics of an SWF in that it was established to save the dividends of a cyclical housing and commodities boom to meet long-term budget liabilities. In addition to this overt financial goal, this chapter has also argued that the FF and the subsequent Nation Building funds created by the Rudd government had a clear political rationale.

More specifically, the FF was created in 2006 to consolidate the Howard government's economic management credentials and to temper demands for unsustainable new spending or tax cuts. When the

Labour Party assumed office in October 2007, they chose to supplement the existing FF with additional Nation Building funds that would be used to invest in economic and social infrastructure when the inflationary pressures then present in the Australian economy abated. How then should we interpret these innovative aspects of the FF and its derivatives? Could it be that the SWFs structured along the lines of the FF will be created in other advanced economies to manage budget politics, to help meet unfunded budget liabilities and to improve macroeconomic coordination?

One conclusion which can be drawn from the comparative study of SWFs presented in this volume is that the considerable variation in SWFs can only be explained with reference to the distinctive political and economic circumstances prevailing when a particular fund was created. In the Australian case, the creation of the FF was the product of an unusually sustained economic boom, the projected elimination of net Commonwealth debt and a government (and Treasurer Costello in particular) determined to contribute to hitherto unfunded budget liabilities rather than invest in economic and social infrastructure.

In the five years since the FF was created, political and economic circumstances have changed dramatically both in Australia and abroad. Undoubtedly, the most significant development has been the profound impact of the GFC on public finances with the budget position of all developed economies deteriorating significantly as a consequence of a combination of unprecedented expenditure on stimulus programmes and recapitalising the financial institutions combined with dramatic falls in tax receipts. In Australia, Commonwealth debt is now forecast to peak at 9.6 per cent of GDP in 2013–14 (this is modest compared with US$ 9.1 trillion or 65 per cent of GDP in the USA) before gradually declining to 3.7 per cent of GDP in 2019–20 (Treasury 2009b). Given this fiscal outlook, it is extremely unlikely that surplus funds would be available for allocation to the FF on any other SWF for at least a decade.

Clearly it will be some time before the governments of advanced economies have to confront the politics of budget surpluses. Even if funds were available, in the Australian context at least, it seems unlikely that the current Labour government would be interested in creating an investment fund for the purpose of meeting future budget obligations. As evidenced by the creation of Australia's Nation Building Funds there is a strong preference for current investment in infrastructure just so long as it is economically prudent to do so.

The creation of Australia's FF was a political masterstroke and its reputation has only grown on the back of its exceptionally solid financial performance during the GFC. Yet, despite this success the fund should be regarded as being an experiment in budget politics and management best suited to the final years of Australia's long economic boom that ended with the GFC. Given this context, it is unlikely that the SWFs along the lines of the FF will become commonplace in industrial economies in the high-debt post-GFC landscape.

Notes

1. I would like to acknowledge Tim Wolley's research assistance and input from various Australian Government officials familiar with the Future Fund's origins and operations. Any errors remain my responsibility.
2. This is the case until assets managed by the FF are transferred back to the federal budget. It should be noted that FF earnings are included in the Headline Cash Balance (HCB).
3. In Chapter 1 it was noted that as of 2007 pension funds had an estimated US$21 trillion under management whereas SWFs managed an estimated US$3.1.
4. The majority of the cash proceeds of the Telstra privatisation were also deposited into the FF.

References

Bishop, J. (2007), 'Media Release – The Higher Education Endowment Fund', 8 May, available at http://www.dest.gov.au/ministers/Bishop/budget07/bud03_07.htm (accessed 21 December 2009).

Brennan, G. and J. Buchanan (1980), *The Power to Tax: Analytical Foundations of a Fiscal Constitution*. Cambridge: Cambridge University Press.

Clark, G.L. (2009), 'Temptation and the Virtues of Long-term Commitment: The Governance of Sovereign Wealth Fund Investment', Oxford SWF Project Working Paper Series, February, available at http://papers.ssrn.com/sol3/papers.cfm?abstract_id=1349123 (accessed 22 December 2009).

Costello, P. (2004), 'Transcript the Hon Peter Costello Treasurer', Press Conference Treasury Place, Melbourne, 10 September, available at http://www.treasurer.gov.au/DisplayDocs.aspx?pageID=&doc=transcripts/2004/119.htm&min=phc (accessed 22 December 2009).

Eccleston, R. (1999), 'Democratic Paradox? The Impact of Ideational Change on Economic Voting', *Journal of Australian Political Economy*, 44, pp. 30–45.

Gruen, D. and A. Sayegh (2005), 'The Evolution of Fiscal Policy in Australia', *Oxford Review of Economic Policy*, 21(4), pp. 618–35.

Future Fund (2008), *Future Fund Annual Report 2007–08*. Canberra: Future Fund Board of Guardians.

Future Fund (2009), http://www.futurefund.gov.au (accessed 22 December 2009).

Hansard (2006), *House of Representatives Official Hansard*, 1, 7 February, pp. 42–97, available at http://www.aph.gov.au/Hansard/reps/dailys/dr070206.pdf (accessed 22 December 2009).

IWG (2008), *Sovereign Wealth Funds generally accepted principles and practices 'Santiago Principles'*, http://www.iwg-swf.org/pubs/eng/santiagoprinciples.pdf (accessed 3 June 2010).

Keating, P. (2009), 'Costello a "policy bum" who grew debt: Keating', *The Age*, 1 November, p. 1.

Kelly, P. (1999), *Future Tense: Australia beyond Election 1998*. Sydney: Allen and Unwin.

Monk, A. (2009), 'Insider Trading', Oxford SWF Project, 26 October, available at http://oxfordswfproject.com/tag/future-fund/ (accessed 22 December 2009).

Productivity Commission (2005), *Economic Implications of an Ageing Australia*, Melbourne: Productivity Commission.

Swan, W. and L. Tanner (2008), *Budget: Budget Strategy and Outlook Paper No 1. 2008–09*. Canberra: Commonwealth of Australia.

Tanner L. (2009), 'The Future Fund: Delivering for Australia', Speech to the National Press Club, 25 November, available at http://www.financeminister. gov.au/speeches/2009/sp_20091125.html (accessed June 3 2010).

Treasury (2002), *Intergenerational Report 2002–03: Budget Paper No 5*, Canberra: Commonwealth of Australia.

Treasury (2003), *Commonwealth Budget 2003–04: Budget Paper No 1*, available at http://www.budget.gov.au/2003-04/bp1/html/bst7.htm. (accessed 3 June 2010).

Treasury (2009a), *Commonwealth Budget 2009–10: Statement of Assets and Liabilities*, available at http://www.ato.gov.au/budget/2009-10/content/bp1/downloads/bp1_bst7.pdf (accessed 20 December 2009).

Treasury (2009b), *Mid-Year Economic and Fiscal Outlook 2009–10*, available at http://www.budget.gov.au/2009-10/content/myefo/html/part_3.htm (accessed 20 December 2009).

Truman, E.M. (2007), 'A Scoreboard for Sovereign Wealth Funds', Peterson Institute for International Economics, available at http://www.petersoninstitute. org/publications/papers/truman1007swf.pdf (accessed 22 December 2009).

Whitley, A. (2009), 'Australia's Future Fund to be Probed, Senator Says', *Bloomberg Online*, available at http://www.bloomberg.com/apps/news?pid=20601081&sid=aBbqKARUGy2o (accessed 22 December 2009).

9
Aboriginal Investment Funds in Australia

Ciaran O'Faircheallaigh

Introduction

The sovereign funds discussed elsewhere in this volume are operated by governments on behalf of 'peoples', defined as populations contingent with the states concerned. This chapter discusses a somewhat different situation, in which long-term investment funds are operated directly by distinct 'peoples' *within* a nation-state, in this case Aboriginal peoples in Australia. The rights of indigenous peoples within states have won increasing recognition in domestic law and in international forums, an important recent example of the latter being the United Nations Declaration on the Rights of Indigenous Peoples, adopted by the United Nations General Assembly in September 2007. Growing recognition of the rights of indigenous peoples is reflected in turn in their increased capacity, after centuries of economic marginalisation, to win a share of the wealth extracted from their ancestral lands. The investment funds discussed here are a product of this development.

Aboriginal investment funds are currently modest in scale, with the larger funds holding assets valued in the tens of millions rather than the billions. As a result, and because they are not operated by national governments, some of the issues raised by state sovereign funds do not arise in relation to Aboriginal funds. For instance, the macroeconomic impact of the latter's investment decisions is not a major issue, nor is the possibility that they may be used in pursuit of national strategic interests. However, they deserve attention because of their importance for the indigenous groups concerned (see below), and because they do raise issues that are also relevant to sovereign funds, in part because they share with sovereign funds a focus on managing wealth for the benefit of peoples rather than of individuals. These issues include investment strategies; the question of inter-generational equity; allocation of income to current consumption versus long-term investment; utilisation of income generated by capital funds; and, in relation to certain sovereign funds, the finite nature of natural resource endowments that generate fund income.

Other issues, unique to Aboriginal investment funds, also require attention. These include the challenge of designing institutional structures than can operate in a cross-cultural context, and the lack of geographical and political 'fit' between populations entitled to share in the income from investment funds and those affected by resource development activity.

This chapter provides a preliminary examination[1] of Aboriginal investment funds. The next section briefly outlines how the opportunity to create these funds has arisen, and their rationale. The following section provides key contextual information for a discussion of the funds. I then examine three general issues raised by their establishment and management: the definition of fund beneficiaries; decision-making structures used in managing them; and alternative uses for fund income. The discussion is then illustrated by reference to two specific Aboriginal investment funds.[2]

Aboriginal investment funds: opportunity and rationale

Aboriginal investment funds arise from negotiation of legally binding agreements between Aboriginal landowners (referred to as 'Traditional Owners') and private corporations and governments, agreements that increasingly govern the terms on which commercial development, and especially mining, occurs on Aboriginal land in Australia. The negotiation of such agreements reflects the growing legal recognition of indigenous rights in land, marked in particular by the High Court's 1992 *Mabo* decision that indigenous people had inherent rights in land and sea ('native title') resulting from their occupation of Australia prior to white settlement. *Mabo* was given legislative expression in the Commonwealth Native Title Act 1994. This confers on indigenous groups that have lodged native title claims or had their native title claims determined a 'Right to Negotiate', which provides them with an opportunity to negotiate agreements with companies that wish to exploit resources on native title land. These agreements usually include financial payments or 'quasi-royalties', some of which may be channelled into investment funds.

Agreements between Aboriginal groups and mining companies are usually confidential, as are the details of investment funds arising from them, which constitutes a major obstacle in seeking to quantify their scale and economic significance. However, the available information indicates that while Aboriginal funds are small in comparison to sovereign wealth funds, they are substantial relative to the scale of the populations they may affect, especially given their economic status. One fund established in 2001, for instance, is currently valued at more than A$50 million, while the Aboriginal communities involved have a combined population of between 3000 and 4000 people. As most Aboriginal people and communities in Australia have limited incomes and employment opportunities and experience under-provision of services such as housing, health and education (Productivity Commission 2007), investment funds on this scale have the potential to contribute positively to economic and social welfare. On the other hand, if that potential is not realised, the opportunity cost is significant.

Given that Aboriginal people and communities have urgent and immediate need for incomes and basic services, why do they allocate a share of payments from mining projects to investments funds where they may be 'frozen' for extended periods of time? One obvious reason is to ensure that a source of income remains after mining ends. All mineral deposits, even very large ones, have a finite life, and Aboriginal people are often concerned to ensure that when a deposit is exhausted there is an alternative source of income to replace a royalty stream. In addition, income from mining projects can be highly variable due to instability in markets and prices, creating a risk that even where mines still operate, they will generate little income over extended periods. A secure and ongoing source of income can be created by allocating a proportion of royalty payments to an investment fund during periods when payments are substantial.

This consideration is especially important given that any specific group of Traditional Owners may have only one major resource project on their land. Unlike state/provincial or federal governments, which typically have a stream of projects developed within their jurisdictions over time, Traditional Owners may not be able to rely on income from new projects to replace income from depleted mines.

Closely related to the finite nature of mineral resources is the issue of inter-generational equity. Modern mining projects tend to have lasting and sometimes massive impacts on the environment and landscapes, impacts that will continue to be felt by future generations. If all income from projects is consumed by current generations, their children and grandchildren will pay part of the costs arising from mining projects but will not share in the financial benefits. Future incomes from investment funds will allow them to do so. More generally, Traditional Owners often express a strong desire to ensure that the lives of future generations are more economically secure, and offer greater economic and social opportunities, than their own. The need to give effect to this desire is often articulated as a key rationale for establishing investment funds.[3]

In relation to some Aboriginal groups, the desire to ensure prudential and effective use of resources can also be a motivating factor. Many Aboriginal people have had little opportunity to gain expertise in managing and applying substantial flows of money. Many Aboriginal people are well aware of cases where income from mining projects has been dissipated and created no lasting benefits as a result of financial mismanagement or a lack of commercial acumen (see, for example, O'Faircheallaigh 2002, ch. 7). Thus, some groups are inclined to allocate a portion of their income to investment funds, where it will be 'safe', while they develop financial and commercial expertise, in part by managing the portion of income that is allocated for current spending.

Economic, social and political context

The social, cultural and political landscape in which Aboriginal investment funds are established is complex and may be unfamiliar to many readers. This section seeks to outline key aspects of this context. In doing so, the dangers of oversimplification must be recognised. Aboriginal Australia is highly diverse, reflecting Australia's large size, its widely varying climatic and environmental conditions, and the quite different contact histories of different regions. This qualification should be kept in mind in what follows. It should also be noted that the analysis focuses on areas of Australia where large-scale mining occurs (that is, outside major urban concentrations).

In demographic, social and cultural terms, an important consideration is that there is rarely a neat spatial coincidence between the residential communities where Aboriginal people usually live, and their traditional land and sea 'country'.[4] Nearly all Aboriginal groups suffered significant dislocation as a result of colonisation and later social and economic pressures and opportunities, and as a result many Aboriginal people no longer reside on their traditional lands. Thus, a resource project which is located on the land of a particular native title group, let us say Group X, may be adjacent to Community Y whose population includes members of Group X but also of many other native title groups whose traditional lands may be located well away from the project. Group X may rely on Community Y's elected council and other community organisations for delivery of basic public services such as housing, sewerage, roads and power. Conversely, many members of Group X, while maintaining cultural and spiritual ties with their traditional country, may live elsewhere, possibly in major regional centres, and derive no benefit from the services provided by Community Y.

This situation creates significant complexities and competing political pressures, given that agreements are generally negotiated with land-owning groups. All Community Y members will be affected by a major industrial project located nearby and community councils and other organisations will face additional pressure on their resources. Therefore, there will be pressure for Community Y to share in project benefits, including in income from investment funds. All members of Group X will feel entitled to share in the benefits generated from mining on their traditional lands, regardless of where they reside, and may resist allocation of benefits to a community in which they do not live and which does not provide them with services.

More generally, given the limited economic opportunities and services available in many Aboriginal communities, the allocation and utilisation of benefits from agreements and investment funds is intensely political. Central to Aboriginal politics is the ongoing negotiation and renegotiation of *relationships*, including the relationship of individuals to kin, to wider social formations such as family or clan, and to 'country'; relationships between families, clans and in some cases language groups; and relationships between such groups and particular areas of land or 'estates' (Myers 1980; Anderson 1998; Merlan 1998; Rose 2001). The economic benefits generated by mining projects and associated investment funds both become absorbed into, but also have the potential to change, existing social, cultural, economic and political relationships.

Another and key contextual factor involves the nature of Aboriginal land tenure systems, that is, the way in which people relate to land and define interests in it. This raises major issues about the nature of land tenure systems and rights and responsibilities in land, which will not be pursued here. However, it is important to briefly note a number of complexities that have a major bearing on management of financial flows and investment funds.

A critical point is that interests in land are often complex and multi-dimensional. One individual may claim primary affiliation to a specific area of land through one parent but have other affiliations through the second parent, through traditional adoption or through grandparents. It is common for Aboriginal people to make statements of the following sort. 'I go with my father's side, and so my country is "A". But I also have ties to country "B" because of my mother, and to country "C" through my mother's mother.' If pressed in a meeting about benefit payments, for example, to identify which land they are 'owners' of they may say 'A'. Yet such statements usually represent the making of a *definitive* claim to have the *major* say in relation to area 'A', not an abrogation of interest in relation to areas 'B' and 'C'. In addition, an area of land or sea may hold cultural or spiritual sites which have significance for, and whose management requires the involvement of, groups beyond the 'primary' Traditional Owner group.

Thus, any one area of land will encompass overlapping multi-layered rights and interests held by an array of individuals and groups, while any individual or group will have interests in a number of different areas of land. This reality does not sit comfortably with a legislative system for recognising and determining native title that seeks to neatly divide Aboriginal people into mutually exclusive groups of native title claimants and holders. Nevertheless, it is a reality that cannot be ignored and should be recognised in the structure of investment funds (see below).

Another critical part of the context for Aboriginal investment funds involves the need to adjust to the requirements of the non-indigenous legal and policy regime and employ non-indigenous structures that may be ill-suited to Aboriginal priorities and values. A good example is provided by the issue of taxation of income streams into, and later out of, investments funds. Currently, such income streams are taxable, unless they accrue to a trust established for 'charitable purposes' as defined by Commonwealth tax legislation and the Australian Taxation Office. As a result, many recent agreements establish charitable trusts to act as the vehicle for investment funds. But the need to restrict the use of fund income to specific purposes, such as the relief of poverty, can seriously reduce the ability of Aboriginal groups to use their income in the variety of ways they might wish, for instance, to establish business enterprises. Even more seriously, charitable trusts are required to distribute income within set time frames, whereas Aboriginal groups may wish to accumulate income over extended periods of time to help build the investment fund more quickly (FHCSIA 2008, p. 15).

Issues in establishing and operating funds

Definition of beneficiaries

A key issue involves the definition of the individuals and groups which will benefit from fund income. Responses to this issue can be considered along a spectrum. At one end is a narrow definition focusing on Traditional Owners with primary responsibility for the land on which a mining project is physically located; at the other a much wider definition that also includes other Aboriginal landowners with rights and interests in land and water affected by the mine's environmental and cultural 'footprint', and members of Aboriginal communities that experience the social impacts of mining.

A narrower definition appears on the face of it to recognise the special position of Traditional Owners with a close connection to the land most affected by mining and to favour their interests. But matters may not be so simple. These Traditional Owners do not often live in isolation, but rather have complex networks of relationships with kin and others with whom they share interests in country. They may face considerable pressure from members of culturally related land-owning groups or/and other community members to share resources. Refusal to share is likely to threaten social relationships and disrupt social harmony because of the resentment this creates within the wider Aboriginal community, including among people who have clearly recognised, but less direct, interests in areas affected by mining.

From this perspective, landowners might gain from a more inclusive approach that allows a wider group to share in the benefits of investment funds, as this may relieve pressure on them from kin and other community members. On the other hand, agreeing to share with a substantial number of people can quickly dissipate resources, and a broadly based definition of beneficiaries can cause serious tensions if Traditional Owners feel that benefits are being spread too widely and that they were missing out as a result. It may be possible to manage this tension through having a 'layered' or 'stratified' approach that explicitly recognises different categories of beneficiaries and levels of benefits, a possibility illustrated below in considering specific examples of investment funds.

Decision-making

The first issue in this area involves the question of who participates in decisions on management of investment funds and application of the income they generate. The range of possible options ranges from the entire membership of the beneficiary group to an individual or small number of individuals nominated to manage the fund. Where the fund is established through a trust, decision-making is in the hands of trustees who usually (though not always) represent Aboriginal groups that are signatories to the relevant agreement. The trust deed may require that trustees consult with the groups they represent to establish their views and preferences, but in practice there may be considerable variation in the extent to which this occurs. Trusts create a form of corporate governance derived from mainstream society, and there is no guarantee that they will be consistent with the cultural, social and political norms of Aboriginal groups.

The second dimension of decision-making involves the basis on which decisions are made. At one end of the spectrum, decisions may reflect the consistent application of explicit rules and formulae for the allocation of funds. At the other end of the spectrum, decisions may be made in an ad hoc manner and reflecting the political and other circumstances that apply at a specific point in time. Trusts tend to be marked by application of clear and explicit rules regarding the purpose to which funds can be put and the identity of beneficiaries. However, it is important to recognise that, as in any institutional environment, there may be significant divergence between formal rules for decision-making and the basis on which decisions are actually taken.

The third dimension of decision-making involves the degree of transparency involved, or the extent to which people affected by decisions can easily comprehend how they are made and clearly see the link between decisions and subsequent outcomes. This second point should be stressed. Transparency is not just about how a decision is initially made. It is also about the existence of a visible link between that decision and outcomes 'on the ground' over the subsequent time period. In general, transparency is greater when decision-making is participative and rule based. However, allowing participation and following rules does not of itself guarantee transparency. Highly complex decision-making systems may provide multiple points for participation but lack transparency, and adopting rule-based decision-making only contributes to transparency if all participants understand the rules and if constituents can see the link between the operation of rules and outcomes that affect them. Intricate rules, or rules that are very general and so leave room for considerable interpretation as they are implemented, are unlikely to contribute to transparency.

Utilisation of income from investment funds

Given the recent origin of Aboriginal investment funds, the question of how income from them should be utilised has not received a great deal of attention. However, a number of funds will soon reach the point when they can start distributing income and will have a capital base capable of generating substantial income flows. Therefore, this issue requires careful attention.

There are four basic ways in which income from investment trusts can be utilised:

- To make cash payments to individuals.
- To provide services such as education or health, support cultural or land management activities or develop community infrastructure such as sporting facilities.
- To purchase or develop businesses in the locality or region in which recipients of benefit payments reside.
- To continue to build a capital base by being reinvested in the investment fund.

Individual payments result in positive outcomes to recipients in that their incomes are higher than would otherwise be the case. Nevertheless, individual payments are subject to income tax and can adversely affect entitlements to pensions and social welfare payments, with the result that recipients may receive little if any net financial gain. In addition, any positive effects on income tend to be one-off and temporary, as individual payments may be quickly dissipated because of low existing income levels, demands from kin and the lack of alternative uses for funds. Finally, where individual payments are not generally available they can cause resentment in the wider community and lead to social disharmony, imposing significant costs on recipients.

Considerable controversy surrounds the use of mining payments to fund service provision or community infrastructure (see O'Faircheallaigh 2004 for a detailed discussion). Key issues are that mining payments may be utilised to provide services that government has a responsibility to provide to all citizens; and the possibility of a 'substitution' effect, where government reallocates existing expenditures to other regions or communities that are not in receipt of mining payments. If this occurs, the mining payments allocated to service provision create no net benefits for the Aboriginal recipients.

It is not inevitable that government expenditure will be cut, and indeed allocation of mining payments to service provision may lead to higher public spending where they can be used to 'leverage' additional financial commitments from government. Where a net addition to services does occur, the benefits tend to be spread widely among local Aboriginal populations, compared with any other use of investment fund income, because many services, particularly in areas such as education, health and sport and recreation, tend to be available to all Aboriginal people residing in an area. In addition, investment fund income may be used to pay for services that government would not support, and allow access to services more quickly than would otherwise occur, the latter a critical issue in relation, for instance, to certain health services such as kidney dialysis.

Against this background O'Faircheallaigh (2004) recommends a careful calculation of whether allocation of mining payments to services and infrastructure provision is likely to generate net benefits in particular cases. He suggests that positive outcomes are likely to be achieved if one or more of questions 1–5 below can also be answered in the affirmative.

1. Is investment fund income being spent on services that are highly valued by potential beneficiaries and that government will not provide?
2. Is income being applied in a way that attracts additional government expenditure into the activity concerned?
3. Is income being spent to ensure a *form* of service provision that will create substantially greater benefits than the equivalent service provided by government?
4. Is income being spent to provide a level of service provision higher than the standard level provided by government in comparable situations?
5. Is income being applied to ensure access to a service substantially *sooner* than would occur if government provides the service?

Investment of fund income in local and regional business enterprises also raises complex issues. If businesses are successful, use of income in this way can serve both to expand the total pool of available resources and to spread them widely. A thriving business can generate substantial employment, and creates the potential for development of spin-off economic activity in other enterprises that provide goods and services to the new business. A successful business builds an economic asset that creates incomes for future generations and, where the business has a diversified revenue base, can outlive the mining project that originally provided the capital to establish it.

On the other hand, Aboriginal ownership of businesses does not of itself guarantee these benefits. Most jobs may be held by non-indigenous people, either because Aboriginal people do not have the required skills or are not attracted to the type of work available. Critically, history makes it abundantly clear that it is difficult to establish profitable businesses in regions remote from major population centres (O'Faircheallaigh 2002). The available investment opportunities are often limited, with the result that the only opportunities available to Aboriginal groups may be risky. The economies of remote regions are usually reliant on industries which are volatile such as mining and tourism, so that even if an investment appears sound on the basis of all available information, its profitability may later be undermined by factors which are outside the control of Aboriginal organisations. Finally, extensive managerial and financial skills are required to establish and maintain a new business, particularly in a remote area and with a volatile business climate, and Aboriginal groups may at least initially lack the expertise required.

The final option is to use fund income to continue to build a capital base. This creates an opportunity cost in the contemporary period, as Aboriginal people who would otherwise experience benefits forego them. Opportunity costs have already arisen as a result of the initial decision to channel payments under mining agreements into an investment fund, and it can be argued that once a fund is in a position to generate significant income, this should be utilised to create immediate benefits, especially given the economic and social disadvantage faced by most Aboriginal peoples. However, the force of this argument will depend on the needs of individual groups and communities, and the extent to which they have alternative sources of income both in the contemporary period and into the future.

Investment funds: specific examples

Two examples illustrate the way in which the issues discussed above have arisen in particular cases, and the ways in which Aboriginal Traditional Owners and communities involved have tried to deal with some of them.

The Western Cape Communities Coexistence Agreement

The first example involves the Weipa bauxite mine in Western Cape York, far north Queensland. The Weipa mine was established in the early 1960s by Comalco Ltd, a subsidiary of Rio Tinto. Aboriginal peoples and communities affected by the project experienced significant environmental and social impacts over the following decades, but gained little of the wealth it generated.

In the late 1990s, Rio Tinto initiated a corporate policy of trying to establish positive relationships with all indigenous communities affected by its operations, regardless of whether a legal requirement existed to do so. In 2001, the Western Cape Communities Coexistence Agreement (WCCCA) was concluded between Comalco Ltd, the Traditional Owners of its mining and ancillary leases, four Aboriginal communities affected by its operations and the State of Queensland. Under the WCCCA, Comalco makes payments related to bauxite output and market conditions, while Queensland contributes a proportion of the statutory royalties it receives from Comalco.

Comalco's leases covered a large area, and as a result 11 Traditional Owner groups are signatories to the WCCCA. Their members mainly reside in four Aboriginal communities, Aurukun, Napranum, Mapoon and New Mapoon, and the elected local government councils of these communities are also signatories. As usually occurs, these communities include a substantial number of indigenous people who are not Traditional Owners for Comalco's leases.

The Traditional Owners decided, after extensive consultations and with the assistance of expert advice made available through the regional land organisation, the Cape York Land Council, to invest 60 per cent of their annual income under the project in a long-term investment fund. The capital of the fund is preserved, and all income from it reinvested in the fund, for 20 years. At the end of the 20 years, the same proportion of annual payments made under the WCCCA continues to be invested in the fund, but income from the fund becomes available for allocation to current expenditures. Sixty per cent of the income will be allocated for the economic, social and cultural benefit of Traditional Owner groups; and 40 per cent for community development purposes in the four affected Aboriginal communities.

This represents a specific compromise between meeting the needs of Traditional Owners on whose land mining occurs and those of communities affected by mining. The Traditional Owners adopted this approach in recognition of the fact that many of them derive significant benefits from their membership of these communities, and that the communities as a whole, and not just Traditional Owners, experienced substantial impacts from mining. For example, the Queensland government closed the Mapoon community in 1963 and forcibly removed its members to the tip of Cape York, hundreds of kilometres away, when it appeared that the bay on which Mapoon was located would be required for a second port to service the bauxite mine. Mapoon had been established as a Christian mission in the late 1890s, and many people from elsewhere in Cape York were relocated there in the decades that followed. Two or three generations later their descendents regarded Mapoon as home, and Traditional Owners recognised that their forced removal had cost them dear and that they deserved to now share in the benefits of the WCCCA.

Payments under the WCCCA must be made to a trust for public charitable purposes as defined under the Income Tax Act, with income allocated for the alleviation of poverty or distress and for community development purposes. The trust is a proprietary company, with the shares allocated so that the majority are held by the Traditional Owner groups. The Board of the trustee also has a majority of Traditional Owner members, with the remainder appointed by the Aboriginal community councils. Decisions are made by majority vote. Subsequent to the signing of the agreement, the signatories agreed that three sub-trusts would be established based on the southern, central and northern portions of Comalco's leases. Traditional Owner and community trustees sit on the sub-trust for the region in which their traditional estates and communities, respectively, are located (WCCCA Trust 2003). There is no provision in the WCCCA allowing for wider participation of Traditional Owners or community members in decision-making by trustees. The WCCCA is silent on how trustees are to be selected. This is left to the individual Traditional Owner groups and communities.

The WCCCA trust has already accumulated substantial funds and at the end of the 20-year 'income reinvestment' period will have a significant capital base. If sufficient income continues to be reinvested to maintain the real value of this fund, Traditional Owners will derive an income from the trust well into the future and possibly long after mining has ceased.

One issue that has arisen in relation to the trust involves its investment strategy. The trust is limited to investing in limited classes of financial institution deposits and securities and in land, and it can be argued that this has unduly limited its capacity to generate substantial returns on the funds invested. On the other hand, this approach does limit the vulnerability of the fund and income on it to fluctuations in global stock exchanges, including the recent 'global financial crisis'.

Four other issues have arisen in relation to the share of income from the WCCCA that is allocated for current spending, and these are also likely to be major issues in relation to income from the investment fund, when it becomes available for spending in 2021. The first involves allocation of income between affected groups. There is some resistance to the all-inclusive and equitable approach adopted in the WCCCA, under which all groups that have traditional interests in Comalco's lease areas are included on essentially the same basis. Some groups experience major impacts on their land and sites because bauxite mining currently occurs on a substantial proportion of their clan estates; others will not experience impacts until many years into the future because their land is not currently needed for mining; others experience only minor impacts because only a small part of their estates overlap with mining leases or because their land is used only for ancillary activities such as transport corridors. Some of the groups most directly affected have objected to this arrangement, arguing that income should be allocated proportionately to the scale, timing and severity of impacts experienced by individual groups.

A second issue involves the fact that to ensure the charitable status of the trusts, there are limits on the way in which income from the WCCCA can be applied. Some Traditional Owners have reportedly been unable to obtain funding support for activities they see as a high priority, for example, establishment of commercial enterprises. The third issue involves the basis for decision-making about proposals for expenditure. It has been suggested to the author that some trustees and administrative staff regard compliance with the trust rules as more important than the inherent quality of the proposed expenditures in terms of the social and economic benefit it can generate. Some applications have reportedly been successful because they clearly comply with trust rules even though the substantive benefits they offer are limited, with others being rejected because of a failure to comply with the letter of the trust rules, despite offering substantive benefits. This has reportedly led to a belief among some Traditional Owners and community leaders that decision-making lacks transparency and that form is more important than substance, leading to disillusionment with the trusts.[5] This in turn creates a risk that people will try to find ways of circumventing trust rules, leading to the danger of misallocation or misappropriation of funds.

Finally, it is not clear whether the WCCCA's decision-making structures, established to comply with non-indigenous legal forms and requirements of taxation and other legislation, can be reconciled with the political and social imperatives that drive Aboriginal people and groups, as discussed earlier in the chapter. There is an important issue for future research on Aboriginal investment funds.

The Argyle Diamonds Agreement

The second example involves the Argyle diamond mine in the Kimberley region of north-west Western Australia. Established in the early 1980s, the project had made regular, though ad hoc, payments to three Aboriginal communities located close to its operations, but had not allocated payments specifically to the Traditional Owners of its mining lease.[6] Community payments have all been utilised to help fund current expenditures. In 2001, Argyle was considering whether to extend the life of its operations by switching from open-pit to underground mining, which would involve substantial capital investment. It was anxious to secure a legally binding agreement with all relevant Traditional Owner groups prior to committing itself to the investment, and funded the regional land council, the Kimberley Land Council (KLC), to facilitate that agreement.

Supported by the KLC, Traditional Owners undertook an extensive process of consultation and internal discussions to establish negotiating positions on key issues and to define the groups with interests in land covered by, or affected by, Argyle's leases and operations. A consensus was reached that seven Traditional Owner groups were involved; two 'inner' or 'core' groups on whose country the bulk of Argyle's interests were located and were most affected by its operations; and five 'outer' groups who either had varying degrees of interest in the lease areas or whose traditional lands and cultural sites were affected by Argyle's operations. It was also recognised that the wider language peoples to which these Traditional Owners belonged, in particular the Mirriuwung and Gidja, were also affected, in part because of the regional significance of some of the cultural sites affected by Argyle's operations. This consensus formed the basis for negotiating arrangements for distribution of benefits arising from an agreement with Argyle.[7]

The establishment of the trust structures under the Argyle Diamonds Agreement reflects this consensus, and also a desire to achieve some flexibility in the purposes for which trust income could be applied, and an explicit strategy for using part of trust income to leverage additional expenditure by government. About one-third of payments are allocated to the Kilkaya Trust, a 'special purposes trust' which is not restricted by the requirements of a charitable trust, and operates specifically for the benefit of Traditional Owners. One-half of funds is allocated in equal parts to the two 'inner' groups; and the other half in equal parts to the five 'outer' groups. The remaining payments are allocated to the Gelganyem Trust, controlled by Traditional Owners but with a wider focus in terms of allocation and activities. The bulk of funds, particularly after the fifth year of the agreement, is allocated to a sustainability fund, all the income of which is reinvested until the end of mining. The capital of the fund must then continue to be preserved, but the entire income it generates may be distributed. The sustainability fund operates as a charitable trust.

During the first five years of the agreement a portion of payments accruing to the Gelganyem Trust is allocated to a Mirriuwung and Gija Partnership Fund. This supports initiatives designed to create wider regional benefits and where a contribution of at least an equal amount is available from government or the private sector. The fund has been used to considerable effect. For instance, it secured a co-commitment of A$300 000 from the Commonwealth government for an education initiative in 2005, while in 2008 more than A$5 was contributed by government and private groups for each A$1 committed by the fund for a development programme for teenage girls (Argyle Diamonds Ltd et al. 2004; Harvey and Nish 2005; Gelganyem and Kilkayi Trusts 2008).

The investment strategy followed by the sustainability fund is somewhat more flexible than that set out in the WCCCA, with allowance for low-, medium- and high-risk investments, the latter only after the first five years of the fund's operations and only to a limit of 25 per cent of investments. Despite the absence of high-risk investments, the trust funds incurred losses in 2007–08, reflecting the start of the global financial crisis, though their limited extent (equivalent to about one-eighth of the original value of the trust) (Gelganyem and Kilkayi Trusts 2008, p. 7) does reflect a relatively conservative approach to investment.

The trusts established under the Argyle Agreement are governed by a Board of Directors. Unlike the board for the WCCCA trust, the Aboriginal members of the Board of Directors are all Traditional Owners, reflecting the fact that community councils are not signatories to the agreement and that the funds they receive are paid to them directly and not via the trusts. The Board of Directors has two members nominated by each of the two 'inner' Traditional Owner groups, and one each nominated by the five 'outer' groups. It also has two independent members, chosen for their experience in business and community development. To date, both positions have been occupied by non-indigenous people. Decisions require the support of a majority of members, and this majority must include at least the two independent directors, three of the four 'inner group' directors and two of the five 'outer group' directors. There is a provision allowing attendance of up to 20 Traditional Owners who are not directors at board meetings, or of a larger number at the discretion of the chairman of the board (Argyle Diamonds Ltd et al. 2004, Schedule 10). As with the WCCCA, the Argyle Diamonds Agreement is silent on the manner in which Traditional Owner groups select their directors.

The Argyle Diamonds Agreement sets out the 'charitable purposes' for which sustainability fund income can be employed. These involve creating benefits for 'indigenous persons' by providing support for their education and training, for community development, for the promotion of art, (customary) law and culture, for the relief of poverty and sickness, and for the protection and enhancement of the natural environment (Argyle Diamonds Ltd et al. 2004, Schedule 1 to Schedule 10). The special purposes trust has a considerably wider range of purposes because the nominated purposes do not limit the discretion of the Board of Directors in determining how funds can be used to benefit the Traditional Owners (Argyle et al. 2004, Schedule 11).

Again, the issue arises as to whether trusts established to conform with non-indigenous legal forms and requirements can be consistent with and allow expression of Aboriginal social and political imperatives. However, in this case the initial structure of the trusts and allocation of benefits from them do reflect a consultative process that gave expression to Aboriginal cultural, social and political values. This is evident in the 'layered' approach in which the special position of Traditional Owners with primary responsibility for the site of Argyle's operations is recognised; the interests of five other groups of Traditional Owners is also recognised; and the wider cultural links of Traditional Owners and the regional significance of some of Argyle's cultural impacts is acknowledged through the Mirriuwung and Gidja Partnership Fund. In addition, the use of the special purposes trust in addition to the charitable trust provides greater flexibility in the allocation of resources, and so creates ongoing opportunities for recognition and renegotiation of social and cultural obligations.

Conclusion

Aboriginal investment funds are a relatively new phenomenon in Australia, but their number and the financial resources they receive are increasing rapidly. This reflects the growing recognition of indigenous rights in land, and the desire of Aboriginal people to ensure that mining projects continue to generate an income after resources are depleted and that resource exploration, with its attendant environmental and cultural impacts, benefit future as well as current generations.

Most funds established to date are still in a 'capital building' phase and have yet to generate substantial income flows. They will do so in coming years, at a level which has the potential to generate substantial benefits for affected Aboriginal landowners and communities. Significant issues arise in ensuring that these benefits are realised. One of the most important is to ensure that investment funds, and the income that flows from them, are managed in ways that recognise the specific cultural, social and political imperatives that characterise Aboriginal society. A particular challenge is to ensure that the use of non-indigenous legal forms and structures, designed in part to minimise tax liabilities, operate in a way that is consistent with Aboriginal priorities and values. Information sharing between Aboriginal groups is vital in this regard. The WCCCA trustees shared information and experiences with Argyle Traditional Owners while negotiation of the Argyle Agreement was under way, and this helps explain certain specific differences between the WCCCA and Argyle trust structures. In addition, sustained research is required to identify and develop legal forms and institutional structures that give expression to Aboriginal priorities and values, yet recognise that Aboriginal investment funds can benefit from features of mainstream legal and financial systems, such as charitable status (see, for example, FHCSIA 2008; Native Title Payments Working Group 2008; Strelein 2008).

The investment strategies that are appropriate for Aboriginal funds require careful consideration, to achieve an appropriate balance between preserving their capital value while at the same time providing some exposure to investments that carry greater risk but higher returns. Attention also needs to be paid to options for using future income from investment funds. Individual payments can generate significant benefits for Aboriginal people on low incomes, but tend to be quickly dissipated. Use of income to support service provision and infrastructure development requires a strategic approach, designed to ensure that resources are directed to areas that government will not fund, and/or that they do not displace existing government funding and, if possible, leverage additional government spending. Use of income to help develop Aboriginal enterprises can generate significant benefits, but given the remote location of many Aboriginal communities affected by mining and the limited economic opportunities available to them, great care must be taken in considering potential business investments.

In the longer term, establishment of Aboriginal investment funds may have wider political implications. While the funds are established by and for Aboriginal 'peoples', they result from a recognition of indigenous rights by the Australian state that is fundamentally economic in nature and devoid of any concept of political sovereignty. Thus, native title rights are essentially rights to negotiate commercial benefits, not to exercise political autonomy, an approach in marked contrast to that adopted in Canada, for instance, where land claim settlements typically involve creation of indigenous governments as well as recognition of rights in land (Gibson and O'Faircheallaigh 2010). An important issue for future research is whether Aboriginal peoples in Australia, possibly by combining their resources on a regional basis, can utilise their growing economic leverage to negotiate a degree of political independence, or whether investment funds will simply reinforce a characterisation of indigenous rights as narrowly economic.

Notes

1. The author has recently been awarded, with colleagues at Melbourne University and the Australian National University, an ARC Linkage Grant within which the author's research will focus on the management of financial payments, including payments to investment funds, that are made under agreements between indigenous groups and resource developers in Australia and Canada (LP0990125: 'Poverty in the Midst of Plenty: Economic Empowerment, Wealth Creation and Institutional Reform for Sustainable Indigenous and Local Communities').
2. As mentioned below, the establishment and operation of Aboriginal investment funds are generally surrounded by confidentiality requirements. This inevitably means that in writing this chapter I have had to rely to some extent on information gained in advising Aboriginal groups on negotiating agreements with resource developers and on establishing and managing investment funds. Where specific funds are discussed, the relevant information is in the public domain. Where the discussion is based on confidential information, the identity of the funds involved is not revealed.
3. For example, Traditional Owners for the Weipa bauxite mine and the Argyle diamond mine in Western Australia constantly reiterated to me their determination to ensure that mining on their traditional country improve not only their own lives but those of their grandchildren and great-grandchildren.
4. 'Country' is a term used by Aboriginal people to encompass more than the physical dimension of land and sea. It denotes the unity of land, sea, sites, knowledge, law, culture and people.
5. Traditional Owners and trustees, personal communication, September 2009, November 2009.
6. With one exception – from 1995, the company made individual cash payments to a small number of individual Traditional Owners who had signed an agreement with the company, under controversial circumstances, in 1980.
7. The funds that had previously flowed from Argyle Diamonds to Aboriginal community councils continue to be paid to them, and they continue to be used solely for current expenditures.

References

Anderson, C. (1998), 'All Bosses are Not Created Equal', in W.H. Edwards (ed), *Traditional Aboriginal Society*. Melbourne: Macmillan, pp. 197–212.

Argyle Diamonds Ltd, Traditional Owners and Kimberley Land Council Aboriginal Corporation (2004), 'Argyle Diamond Mine Participation Agreement – Indigenous Land Use Agreement', available at http://www.atns.net.au/agreement.asp?EntityID=2591 (accessed 19 January 2009).

FACHSIA (Department of Families, Housing, Community Services and Indigenous Affairs) (2008), 'Optimising Benefits from Native Title Agreements', Australian Government Discussion Paper, available at http://www.ag.gov.au/www/agd/agd.nsf/Page/Indigenouslawandnativetitle_Nativetitle_Discussion Paper-OptimisingbenefitsfromNativeTitleAgreements (accessed 26 October 2009).

Gelganyem and Kilkayi Trusts (2008), *Annual Report July 2007 to June 2008*, Gelganyem and Kilkayi Trusts, Kununurra, Western Australia.

Gibson, G. and C. O'Faircheallaigh (2010), *Negotiating Impact and Benefit Agreements: A Toolkit for Communities*. Ottawa: Gordon Foundation.

Harvey, B. and S. Nish (2005), 'Rio Tinto and Indigenous Community Agreement Making in Australia', *Journal of Energy and Natural Resources Law*, 23(4), pp. 499–510.

Merlan, F. (1998), *Caging the Rainbow: Places, Politics and Aborigines in a North Australian Town*. Honolulu: University of Hawaii Press.

Myers, F. (1980), 'The Cultural Basis of Politics in Pintupi Life', *Mankind*, 12(3), pp. 197–214.

Native Title Payments Working Group (2008), *Native Title Payments Working Group Report*, available at http://www.ag.gov.au/www/agd/agd.nsf/Page/Indigenouslawandnativetitle_Nativetitle_DiscussionPaper-OptimisingbenefitsfromNativeTitleAgreements (accessed 26 October 2009).

O'Faircheallaigh, C. (2002), *A New Approach to Policy Evaluation: Mining and Indigenous People*. London: Ashgate Press.

O'Faircheallaigh, C. (2004), 'Denying Citizens their Rights? Indigenous People, Mining Payments and Service Provision', *Australian Journal of Public Administration*, 63(2), pp. 42–50.

Productivity Commission (2007), *Overcoming Indigenous Disadvantage: Key Indicators 2007 Report*. Canberra: Commonwealth of Australia.

Rose, D.B. (2001), 'The Silence and Power of Women', in P. Brock (ed.), *Words and Silences: Aboriginal Women, Politics and Land*. Sydney: Allen and Unwin, pp. 92–116.

Strelein, L. (2008), *Taxation of Native Title Agreements*, Australian Institute of Aboriginal and Torres Strait Islander Studies, Canberra.

WCCCA Trustees (2003), 'The Western Cape Communities Coexistence Agreement: Presentation to Argyle Traditional Owners', unpublished.

10
Norway – The Accidental Role Model

Bent Sofus Tranøy

Introduction

In the last 35 years, Norway has changed from a rather frugal, mid-income northern European social democracy into one of the world's most prosperous countries. This is reflected in its purchasing power parity (PPP)-adjusted GDP per capita, where Norway usually ranks first among the 'real' states and only lags tax heavens and even more oil rich Qatar, 'and in the size of its sovereign wealth funds (SWF), which as of December 2009 was valued at just below 2600 billion Norwegian krone (NOK), an equivalent of roughly US$450 billion.[1] Financial strength has not, however, placed Norwegian technocrats in a carefree position. Since the early 1970s when it became clear that Norway's oil and gas resources would bring hitherto untold riches, transforming resource assets into income has been recognised as a potential force for destruction; that it can also be a blessing has been more of an afterthought.

Norway has a bumper SWF that goes under the name of the Government Pension Fund – Global (GPF-G), formerly called The Petroleum Fund of Norway. Because SWFs are routinely interpreted as expressions of state power in the global political economy, they can be portrayed as a threat to the existing liberal financial order, as discussed in Chapter 1. However, this chapter argues that treating the Norwegian SWF in this light is misleading in terms of both intention and function. Norway's GPF-G is a strictly portfolio-oriented, relatively transparent institution. It is therefore more accurately appraised as supportive of a market-based financialised world economy as I explain in this chapter.

Instead of analysing this SWF as an instrument of foreign policy, we are better placed by considering the historical trajectory that eventually led to the establishment of what used to be called 'The petroleum fund'. This trajectory reveals Norway's GPF-G as the product of struggle to avoid the 'natural resource curse' in the form of 'Dutch Disease', that is, a bloated public sector that crowds out the export sector through wage inflation, transfers and appreciation of the real exchange rate. In this sense, the fund is just the latest – and seemingly most successful – means for achieving an end: a means for pursuing a motive that is 20 years older than the fund itself.

Norway's struggle to contain the pressure wrought by petro-wealth is fundamentally a story of domestic politics: a continuous effort to integrate rent-based revenues into an established domestic order with an older governance, production and distributional structure. The main pillars of this structure were parliamentary (social) democracy, a state-dominated but mostly privately owned export sector based largely on hydro-electric power, corporatist labour market institutions and a generous, universalistic welfare state. In this chapter I argue that the essence of foreign economic policy in small corporatist states, which Peter Katzenstein (1983, 1985) captured with his notion of flexible adjustment, still holds, as my analysis of the Norwegian SWF demonstrates. In an age of financial globalisation, protecting the domestic political economy by establishing a fund is a corollary well suited to pursuing a combination of international competiveness and domestic compensation of those who lose out as a result of structural adjustment.

This privileging of domestic policy and politics generally also holds when considering the motives behind the often highlighted, and sometimes celebrated, ethical standards of the fund. Since the beginning of the twenty-first century, the Norwegian fund has adopted a strategy of implementing ethical standards based on three pillars: active management of ownership rights, negative screening and divestment. This may be a standout feature of the fund as an SWF. Certainly it has some impact on the fund management industry as other private sector funds piggyback the decisions of the GPF-G. Still, the strategy is riddled with inconsistencies and implementation problems, and, predictably, has had little impact at the ultimate level of outcomes: the workings of global corporations. The strategy of establishing ethical standards should thus be seen as primarily a defensive measure – a strategy intended to pacify a domestic constituency while helping to uphold Norwegians' understanding of their country as fair-minded and peace-brokering.

Discussion in the rest of this chapter proceeds as follows. In the next section I present a 'Katzensteinian' conceptual framework, linking the fund to a strategy of flexible adjustment. The Norwegian fund has been around for awhile and at each step of its development, it was animated by a struggle to preserve the essence of Norway's long-standing corporatist welfare model in the face of increasing affluence, as I explain in the following section. The fourth section introduces the fund's investment strategy. A strict portfolio approach puts the maximum holding in any given company at 10 per cent, but the average is less than 1 per cent. Direct control or anything resembling foreign direct investment is not part of the practice of GPF-G. Before the financial crisis in 2008, however, willingness to assume risk in search of greater yields had gradually increased.

In the fifth section I introduce the two most important domestic debates inspired by the management of petro-riches. One is the debate on ethical investment and corporate social responsibility. The second is the debate driven by groups that are less worried about catching 'Dutch Disease' than they are about the country's ruling technocratic and democratic elites, which I refer to as the 'invest (and spend) more at home now' position. As I explain, both tensions have been alleviated through highly elaborate institutional constructions. Adoption of an ethical strategy has catered to the moral concerns of the political left and introduction of a spending rule allowing for a gradual phasing in of petroleum revenues has appeased the groups clamouring for more spending. In the sixth section I briefly discuss the fund's international standing and how the Norwegian state has sought to manage this standing, before concluding the chapter in the final section.

Theory: small, open, vulnerable and rich

Most, if not all, countries stricken by the kind of resource curse that leads to gross corruption – kleptocracy and even civil war – had weak institutions and no real democracy when the resource in question was discovered (Karl 1997). In contrast, when oil was discovered in Norway, the country was a mature democracy with not only established routines and institutions for policymaking in general, but, more importantly, pursued liberal open economic policy. The best description of foreign economic policy in small, open economies is Peter Katzenstein's concept of 'flexible adjustment', most thoroughly developed in his book *Small States in World Markets: Industrial Policy in Europe*, published 25 years ago and, indeed, its 25th anniversary had just been celebrated at the time of writing this chapter.

Katzenstein originally developed this concept to understand the origins and rationale of the foreign economic policies of seven small, northern European states in the post-war era (Katzenstein 1985). His conceptualisation has four main analytic components: adjustment, flexibility, domestic compensation and corporatism.

The 'flexible' part of the formula captured an institutionally determined capacity to prioritise competiveness through tying real wage increases in the economy as a whole to productivity gains in the export sector. Sector-based pattern bargaining is used to achieve a compressed wage structure within a corporatist framework of incomes policy. Defending competitiveness this way can be termed a flexible strategy because it does not equate with avoiding structural change. To the contrary, levelling wage levels across economic sectors entailed privileging highly productive sectors and entities (that paid below their capacity) while punishing the less productive ones. This stimulated the transfer of labour to highly productive sectors (Moene and Wallerstein 1997). The struggle to shield the domestic economy from the potentially inflationary effects of spending oil riches at home can thus be seen as directly continuing a policy tradition of giving highest priority to the export sector to maintain the sector's competiveness.

The 'adjustment' component derives from recognition that because the national economy is so small that economic change is a fact of life. These small economies did not choose it; it is thrust upon them. 'These states, because of their small size, are very dependent on world markets, and protectionism is therefore not a viable option for them' (Katzsenstein 1985, p. 24). They cannot shape the external environment, which must therefore be taken more or less as a given. From the vantage point of the late 1970s and early 1980s, the natural focus for adjustment was trade policy. Here Katzenstein argued that 'smallness' creates a functional need for an open economic policy on both the import and export sides of the equation.[2] More importantly, their open economies and industrial adjustment fostered an interest in and loyalty towards international regimes, because small, not very powerful, actors are less vulnerable in a world where stable rules place at least some limits on how large states can treat smaller ones. If we transpose onto today's financialised world economy this logic of taking the economic environment as a given while promoting rule-following in the political environment, the functionally equivalent strategy is arguably to be a transparent portfolio investor. The choice to prioritise transparency reflects an orientation towards observing rules. The choice to limit oneself in portfolio investment is to avoid antagonizing larger states, like the US, that do not like foreign takeovers of important firms.

Economic openness often involves asymmetrical distribution of costs and benefits: small groups suffer when industries decline and lose out to international competition, even though the majority of society reaps the benefits of an open economy and free trade. Thus, the domestic compensation element of the strategy refers to the socialisation of risk through a generous welfare state designed along universal lines. The macroeconomic regime, of which the GPF-G is an important part, seeks to achieve a gradual phasing in of petroleum revenues for welfare purposes. As I return to discuss in the next section, the fiscal rule that regulates use of these revenues limits the non-oil deficit to 4 per cent of the fund on average over the economic cycle. Here the aim is to continually support and develop the welfare state in line with a general increase in living standards and expectations without causing undue harm on the private sector.

In Katzenstein's schema, the institutional mechanism that transferred all these functionally determined needs into wilfully pursued deeds was corporatism. Corporatism, as developed in response to the inter-war crisis that engulfed parts of Europe between World Wars I and II, differs from the democratic corporatism in small European countries in both the institutional arrangement and the intention. In small European countries, democratic corporatism has three distinct characteristics:

> an ideology of social partnership, a centralized and concentrated system of economic interest groups, and an uninterrupted process of bargaining among all of the major political actors across different sectors of policy.
>
> (Katzenstein 1985, p. 80)

At a more abstract level, we can speak of a system that gives priority to establishing and maintaining consensus on important issues in general and on foreign policy in particular. Norwegian elites have throughout post-war era sought to establish broad domestic alliances and agreements on matters deemed important for national security and social stability. They have seen consensus as both a value in itself and a means to achieve long-term stability and predictability.

One group of actors whose role is underplayed in Katzenstein's conceptualisation is the technocrats. In Norway, the economics professionals gained considerable influence on economic policymaking in the immediate post-war period (Bergh and Hanisch 1984; Lie 1995).

Observers commonly speak of an 'iron triangle' running between the Ministry of Finance (MoF), Statistics Norway and the Central Bank, ranked in that order. A strong technocracy generally sits well with a consensus-oriented corporatist polity. It provides factual premises – or constructs reality – for processes such as wage negations (for example, measures of productivity growth) and a common analytical framework and language within which economic events can be interpreted and decisions structured. The notion of 'oil rents' and the idea that these can easily result in catching 'Dutch Disease' are both ideas brought into the debate by economists, to present two clear examples.[3]

This picture of corporatist bliss, collective rationality and consensus should not, however, be painted in strokes that are too broad to capture important tensions. We need to appreciate that three tensions in managing Norway's oil wealth lurk beneath this abstract model of Norway's political economy.

At the parliamentary level, the game between government and opposition changes with the availability of oil rent. In the first couple of decades after World War II, the Norwegian government established a tradition of fiscal frugality. That is, in normal years the government budgeted with a small surplus. There was also a tradition of responsible opposition in fiscal matters, based on the shared premise that both the state's coffers and the population's willingness to pay tax were limited. Introducing (the promise of) petro-wealth blurred this line and opposition parties on both sides of the left–right divide began to behave more aggressively in fiscal matters. From the mid-1970s, this effect could be observed in several rounds of what, compared to earlier practice, seems like fiscal irresponsibility (Lie 2001, pp. 196–7).

The second tension stems from the fault line between public sector workers (typically female service providers) and those employed in the export sector (typically male blue-collar workers). Although public sector unions make-up the vast majority of the Norwegian Confederation of Trade Unions (*Landsorganisasjonen i Norge* or LO), export industry workers have held on to their predominant control within the labour movement, and most LO leaders are recruited from their ranks. Also, even though the phrase 'sector-based pattern bargaining' sounds benign, in practice, export workers bargain first, setting the limit for what everyone else could get. Over time, this has translated into greater wage growth for the economic sectors that are competitive. Wage bargaining is not the only issue at stake, since public sector employees tend to argue for greater welfare spending than their private sector counterparts do.

The third tension is created by the problems of consensus-oriented politics in negotiating institutional change. Consensus systems can create many de facto veto players. These systems work best when policy continuity and stability are desirable (Tranøy 2000). Nevertheless, like so many other social democratic political economies, Norway also went through a period of both credit and product market liberalisation in the 1980s. Problems with veto players made it difficult to sequence reforms. Housing and credit markets were liberalised, while interest rates were regulated downward and tax breaks were not reduced.

History: retaining values while becoming rich

Norwegian oil and gas production began in 1971. This section provides a brief history of the management of Norwegian oil wealth across the three decades until the fund was fully integrated into the Norwegian macroeconomic regime in 2001. This discussion demonstrates how the motives and tensions identified in the previous sections have been played out across time.

When production of oil and gas began, the now defunct planning section of the MoF began working on a White Paper, exploring how the petroleum sector should be integrated into Norwegian society over time (St. meld nr. 25 1973–74). The White Paper conveyed two main messages, one that history would prove to be unique to this report, and another that has become a mainstay in the documents churned out by the technocracy.

The original line of argument, in which the MoF has since lost interest, was that not only should the people of Norway spend oil wealth on material goods, but also governments should seek to help build 'a qualitatively better society'. Here the ministry foreshadowed themes that would later gain currency in other circles, such as green concerns, encouraging more time for people to take care of each other, and other topics that are traditionally considered too 'soft' for a finance ministry to make its business. The second line of argument was that Norway should seek to extract its petro-resources slowly. This seemed particularly important in a context where Norway enjoyed full employment and labour was on the verge of becoming a scarce resource.

In an interview given 30 years after initiating the report, Per Schreiner, the bureaucrat who led the project, stated that at the time, the report had made a few wrong calls about the immediate future.[4] The most serious of these was underestimating the severity of the economic downturn in the mid-1970s that followed the initial production of oil and gas at the start of that decade. The report also failed to foresee the steep rise in the oil price after what has come to be known as OPEC I in 1972–73, and it overestimated the speed at which oil fields would be ready for exploitation.

These developments that moved beyond the report conspired with other factors to knock fiscal policy off balance in the following years. The mid-1970s downturn created demand for a fiscal stimulus, the size of which was influenced by the impression of impending wealth for Norway created by the oil price rise. The slower than anticipated development of the North Sea oil fields also meant that by 1983, when the next big effort to systematise government plans for the management of oil wealth was made, it could still be argued that the best way to avoid 'Dutch Disease' was to keep extraction rates low. The Norwegian public report whose title translates into *The Future of the Petroleum Sector Activity* outlined two strategies for controlling the pace of transforming wealth into income: one was to create a fund, and the other was to carefully pace petroleum exploitation itself (NOU 1983, p. 27).

The report presented plans that foreshadowed many specifics of the current fund-based regime, but it concluded then that this was not a realistic option. Influenced by the fiscal generosity of the mid-1970s, it believed that the political system or the electorate would not remain passive if governments put aside billions in an investment fund while problems remained unsolved in Norwegian society. Instead, the committee recommended a slow extraction rate in the North Sea.

As the 1980s progressed, the evolution of the oil industry proved the report's analysis of the dynamics of the Norwegian political system to be somewhat misguided. In fact, how events transpired turned the analysis on its head. Investments in and their corollary from oil and gas extraction grew at such a phenomenal rate that the idea of saving by keeping oil in the ground was no longer a viable option. Meanwhile, the idea of establishing a fund gained currency, at least metaphorically.

It is a noteworthy anecdote that Jens Stoltenberg, the current Prime Minister and also the chief architect of the current macroeconomic regime when it was established in 2001, wrote his Masters thesis in economics in the mid-1980s. His thesis sought to calculate two optimal rates, one for extraction of the resources and the other for spending the revenues they generated. His key assumptions were that although future oil prices were highly uncertain, revenues could be placed in foreign securities at a certain rate of return. He concluded that the more a government is risk averse, the faster it should transform oil resources into financial wealth (Reinertsen 2009).

During the mid-1980s the Norwegian economy boomed liked never before. After OPEC II, oil investments accelerated to a degree that surprised the MoF. This and the corresponding increase in revenues contributed to the boom. The bigger picture is that economic policy took a bumpy ride through the 1980s as it suffered from the badly sequenced reforms noted above. This included chaotic credit market conditions, pro-cyclical monetary and fiscal policies and an asset price bubble. When the price of oil (and the value of the pricing currency, US dollars) collapsed in the winter of 1986, the ensuing train of events ended in an uncomfortable landing for the Norwegian economy around the turn of the decennium, encompassing not only a banking and a debt crisis, but also a housing price crash, rapid growth in unemployment and quickly deteriorating state finances.

This in turn paved the way for a comprehensive reform programme through which a new macroeconomic policy regime gradually found its shape. One main lesson was that, as a mistress, oil not only corrupts, but is also unfaithful. There was thus more to fear than 'just' 'Dutch Disease' and a resulting cost explosion. There was also a fear of vulnerability in case of another oil price fall. Shielding or delinking the economy and the state's fiscal position from the vagaries of the oil market became an urgent concern.

In 1988, a major review of Norwegian stabilisation policy led by a professor of economics from Norway's main business school, Erling Steigum, produced a conceptual exercise that provided further arguments for establishing a fund (NOU 1988, p. 21). The key notion was that when extracting oil and gas, one was not earning an income, rather one was transforming a given wealth from one type of asset to another. According to the report, this kind of wealth transformation does not in itself create room for increased spending.

Even though low oil prices and the precarious state of the Norwegian economy at the end of the 1980s meant there was no surplus to be saved at this point, a fund was still enacted in January 1990. Creating the fund was primarily about establishing an institutional mechanism, and substance was of less concern then. The main principle was that all petro-income was to be transferred to the fund. The fund would then cover the fiscal deficit that arose before counting in oil revenues. According to the White Paper that introduced the Bill to parliament (Ot.prp. nr. 29 1989–90), this approach would improve long-term management of fiscal policy beyond the routine then in place, particularly through two mechanisms. First, it would lead to better medium-term planning vis-à-vis the spending of oil revenues, and a stronger commitment to these plans. Second, the spending of oil revenues would need explicit budgetary decisions and these decisions would have to be made in light of prior planning decisions.

The world oil market in the 1990s was nothing like that of the previous 11 years from 1974 to 1985, or the decade that followed in the 2000s. Oil price collapsed, plummeting from the average of US$24 per barrel in current price (in 1974-85to US$18 per barrel in current price (in 1986-99. In the first decade of 2000s the oil price climbed again, from US$28.5 per barrel in 2000 to US$97 in 2008 (BP 2009). No event in the 1990s matched the producer bonanza created by the supply-side shocks of the 1970s, or the demand-side shock of the early 'noughties'. Nevertheless, the Norwegian economy gradually picked up after reaching a nadir in 1992–93. Interest rates fell; the failed banks were restructured and returned to health; unemployment went down; and the fiscal position gradually improved. In 1996, the first transfer was made into the fund to the tune of 2 billion NOK, all of it, like currency reserves, invested in 'secure' government bonds.

Almost immediately, the Central Bank began to argue that it should be allowed to place a fraction of the fund in stocks. In 1998, it was granted permission for 40 per cent of the portfolio to consist of stocks. From then on, Norges Bank Investment Management (NBIM) started to grow as a major separate unit inside the Central Bank. Today NBIM employs more than 200 people. While the main office is in Oslo, it also has offices in New York, Shanghai and London, as it engages a global network of external investment managers who are given specific mandates tied to predetermined benchmarks. It also outsources many aspects of its back office functions.

The 1990s were marked not only by relatively low oil prices but also by a distinctive set of problems created by managing a fixed exchange rate in a world of increasingly volatile capital flows. Norway had tied the NOK to the ECU (later the euro), but was increasingly 'out of sync' with the large continental economies. This made for a recurring problem of importing pro-cyclical monetary policy impulses, which in turn affected incomes policy (Tranøy 2000). In January 1999, the incoming Central Bank governor, former MoF top mandarin, Svein Gjedrem, took things into his own hands. He (re)interpreted the exchange rate regulation that had hamstrung his predecessors and declared that in order to keep a stable exchange rate over time, Norway needed to pursue inflation targeting. This dramatic move created a need for post hoc formalisation and helped motivate another review of Norway's macroeconomic regime.

In the spring of 2001, a large parliamentary majority agreed to a fiscal guideline that implies the annual non-oil deficit should, on average over the economic cycle, be limited to 4 per cent of the fund. Four per cent was assumed to be the long-term real return on the fund, and the target is used with some discretion, but in a symmetrical fashion so that spending can be above 4 per cent in a downturn while it should be below 4 per cent when demand is strong and the economy is booming. Between 2001 and 2009, four successive governments were faithful to this guideline. While the 2009 budget deviated from the guideline in response to the global financial crisis, it enjoyed a substantial majority backing in the Norwegian parliament. In early 2010, efforts were being made to return to 'the 4 per cent trajectory'. Only one party refused to accept the spending rule – the right-wing populist Progress Party, which I discuss below.

The 2001 spending rule was part of a larger package encompassing not only fiscal but also monetary policy. In short, while committing to its voluntary constraint, the parliament at this point – after 51 years of pursuing a fixed exchange rate (with variable commitment) – equipped the Central Bank with the interest rate weapon. The Central Bank could use this to cajole and threaten the two other major macroeconomic policymakers – parliament and the executive themselves, on the one hand, and the peak-level wage negotiators, on the other – to maintain a 'responsible' stance.

This new regime represented a concession (within boundaries) to the pressure to 'spend more now' that had gradually grown in strength after the fund started to expand in 1996. Between 1996 and 2001, the rule was to spend as little as possible, projecting the impression (although strictly speaking, it was not quite the case) that all petro-revenues were saved. Norway was now moving towards a policy of what we might call 'responsible spending'. The spending guideline was to serve as a focal point for parliamentary decision-makers, while the empowered Central Bank's role was to police the new regime.

Specifically, the Central Bank was given a symmetrical inflation target of 2.5 per cent. The official argument behind this was to maximise currency stability, or at least maintain as orderly a relationship as possible with the euro, Norway's most important trading partner currency. It was argued that Norway needed an inflation target slightly above that of the European Central Bank to 'create room' for the phasing-in of oil incomes.

Investment strategy: an elaborate portfolio approach

Since Norway is a small, relatively easily run country that scores highly on measures of interpersonal (and inter-elite) trust, its political system has been characterised by a fairly low level of formalisation, not least in many aspects of economic policy. Corporatism does not equate with formalism, and certainly not with transparency.[5] Over the last 20 years or so, this tradition has been modified under the influences of EU law (and 'juridification'), new public management and what some call 'new constitutionalism'. In the case of the GPF-G, however, other motivations for moving economic policymaking towards formalism were more important than external impulses and governance fads.

Two matters are central to understanding the set-up of GPF-G. One is that the fund manages (relative to GDP and to most other meaningful measures) an enormous and fast growing fortune. It is therefore crucial for the legitimacy and future sustainability of the operation that it maintains a high standard of transparency and accountability. Transparency does not, however, mean posturing and maximising public conflict. Rather we can speak of a highly technocratic form of authority shielded from public and democratic scrutiny by the sheer complexity of its tasks. As we shall see below, the NBIM employs techniques and works according to risk management principles that ordinary Norwegians (including most members of parliament) have little chance of understanding.

The second matter key to understanding the set-up is the need to secure continuity. In Norway there is a strong tradition of seeking broad compromises and support for policies that need to be maintained in order to be effective. This 'rule' is upheld on issues such as pension and tax reform, and has also been applied to the fund. Therefore, even though from a technical legal/constitutional standpoint the fund can be dissolved by a new majority in parliament after an election, this is not a realistic political scenario. The fund's institutionalisation (in a broad sense) has been too successful to befall such an outcome.

A precondition for (formal) accountability is to have in place a clear division of responsibility and labour. Thus, the Central Bank operates according to a mandate given by the fund's formal owner, the MoF. The MoF determines a benchmark and establishes risk limits and guidelines. As the Central Bank sees it, how these risk limits are set means that 'most of the variation in the return of the fund is determined by decisions made by the Ministry' (Vikøren 2008, p. 72). In financial market parlance, the fund engages in both index- ('beta') and active- ('alpha') management of securities and bonds. Separate units have been built up for this management work.

Parliament receives an annual review of the fund's performance and management practices in the form of a 'White Paper' from the MoF. The fund's management model is meant to maximise transparency through liberal practices concerning the disclosure of information. For example, the fund's annual reports disclose a list of every single investment held at the end of the year, and report on the corporate governance work carried out by the NBIM (Vikøren 2008, p. 72).

Norway has chosen a strict portfolio model for its fund in the sense that the maximum holding in any given company is 10 per cent, while the average is less than 1 per cent. The limit used to be 5 per cent, but as the fund grew and moved into a broader range of equities, the Central Bank argued that the ceiling was set too low.

The portfolio strategy was chosen primarily because it was deemed attractive from a risk management perspective. One could probably also add that taking strategic positions in companies would have implied increased political risk (at home and abroad), while also requiring competencies different from those required for financially oriented capital management.

This strategy is crystallised in a benchmark portfolio set by the MoF. The benchmark portfolio serves at least two purposes: as a risk management tool and as a rod to measure NBIM's performance. The risk management demands further elaboration: to control risk, limits are set for the acceptable deviation between actual investments and the benchmark portfolio.

Since the fund routinely outgrew expectations over the past 11 years, its composition and strategy have been constantly on the agenda. Size brings its own problems, particularly for spreading risk over areas and asset classes. On the question of whether the fund should move into property markets, the official answer is yes, now. On whether it should move into US mortgage-backed securities, the official answer was yes, just before the market crashed in 2007–08. Consequently, the portfolio has gone through several changes since 1996, most often at the advice of the Central Bank and, if the change is substantial, subject to approval by parliament.

The NBIM is proud to have built a 'professional and business oriented investment culture' inside the staid Central Bank. The MoF has set the parameters of the fund's strategy in sophisticated risk management, according to the modern finance theories that have recently been discredited in the global financial crisis. In practice, however, investment strategy decisions always have to take into consideration political and social reality. The fund has not been able to avoid the influence of herd mentality; it decided to increase its exposure to both equities and mortgage-backed securities just as the market was about to turn.

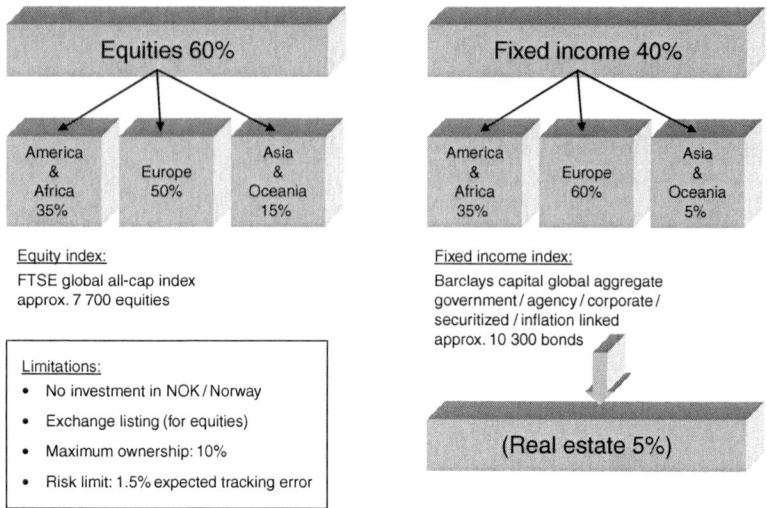

Equities 60%			Fixed income 40%		
America & Africa 35%	Europe 50%	Asia & Oceania 15%	America & Africa 35%	Europe 60%	Asia & Oceania 5%

Equity index:
FTSE global all-cap index
approx. 7 700 equities

Fixed income index:
Barclays capital global aggregate
government / agency / corporate /
securitized / inflation linked
approx. 10 300 bonds

Limitations:
• No investment in NOK / Norway
• Exchange listing (for equities)
• Maximum ownership: 10%
• Risk limit: 1.5% expected tracking error

(Real estate 5%)

Figure 10.1   Strategic asset allocation of Norges Bank Investment Management
Source: Norges Bank.

The composition of the (benchmark) portfolio is communicated most easily by way of a flow chart (Figure 10.1):

Over its first ten-year period, the fund averaged a real return of 4.5 per cent, of which the NBIM delivered half a percentage point, or some US$6 billion, from active management. This means that the fund continued to perform a little better than the rate of return stipulated by the spending rule. After the fund suffered serious losses in 2008, the picture changed for the worse. Even though results picked up in 2009 (the third quarter of that year was the best in the history of the fund) and the transaction costs are exceptionally low by private sector standards (0.09 per cent annually), with the losses incurred in 2008, the average annual net return of the fund between January 1998 and September 2009 was around 2.5 per cent.

The losses during the global financial crisis have motivated the fund's management to take a broad review of its active management strategy in particular and of its risk profile in general. This review was under way in 2010, and one interesting facet of the review is that it takes its point of departure in the efficient market hypothesis (EMH). This concept of market efficiency seems spectacularly heroic in the aftermath of the financial crisis of the late 'noughties'. But it is significant for other reasons as well: two key aspects of the analysis commissioned from established finance professors from the USA and the UK also hinge on this premise.[6]

First, the review asks, given that the EMH predicts it is impossible to beat the market in a systematic fashion, is there any point in pursuing alpha management at all? Second, and more indirectly, the review speaks of theoretically expected (and empirically detectable) premiums related to a long list of risk factors (volatility, credit, liquidity, value-growth and several others). It claims these should be sought through constructing an in-house factor-oriented benchmark instead of relying on standard, passive international (geographical) benchmarks such as the ones currently in use (FTSE for equities and Barclays Capital, Barcap–Lehman for fixed income papers).

Domestic debates: external ethics and domestic consumption and investment

An ethical investor

The debate about engaging in 'ethical' or socially responsible investing began almost as soon as the petroleum fund actually obtained monies to invest, in 1996. A long and heated debate followed. Initially the Central Bank was prone to ridicule the idea, and made it appear as the pipedream of 'irresponsible' left-leaning social democrats (of the Socialist Left Party. Gradually, however, the discourse changed. Two different processes help to explain this. One was set in motion by regular media coverage of how the fund was invested in companies engaged in politically unattractive or even illegal business, such as the production of landmines or exploiting child labour, which translated into unpleasant media exposure for whomever was minister of finance at the time of a given 'scandal'. The other was a gradual change in financial markets; the idea of ethical investment was gradually gaining a foothold within the peer community of the NBIM.

A committee led by law professor Hans Petter Graver was established in 2002.[7] Its proposals were largely taken onboard and enacted by parliament in 2003, and from 2004 a structure for ethical management of the fund was put in place. Three mechanisms, one positive and two negative, were established.

The positive mechanism was to begin exercising ownership rights to promote long-term financial returns based on internationally accepted standards, operationalised as the UN Global Compact and the OECD

Guidelines for Multinational Enterprises. For this purpose a new unit was set up within the NBIM, and its first head was a philosopher who specialised in Augustinian ethics, a man with no previous background in finance. The committee behind the plan had said that responsibility for promoting the ethical exercise of ownership rights should extend only so far as to remain consistent with achieving long-term financial return. The argument was that sound financial investment is an ethical obligation on par with principles of socially responsible investment (SRI), since the present generation has an obligation to future (Norwegian) generations in maintaining and increasing the wealth they will inherit. The committee also picked up on what was then a strengthening trend in international fund management, when it claimed that in many cases financial considerations are concurrent with ethical considerations.

Of the two negative mechanisms, one is negative screening to prevent inclusion in the investment universe of companies that produce themselves, or through entities under their control, weapons whose normal use violates fundamental humanitarian principles. The other is a facility for divestment/withdrawal from companies where owners systematically breach ethical norms: such as (a) gross or systematic violation of human rights, (b) gross violations of individual rights in war or conflict situations, (c) severe environmental degradation, and (d) gross corruption.

To help the MoF, as owner of the fund, to avoid the risk of moral complicity in particular problematic cases, the fund's Council on Ethics makes detailed assessments of individual cases. The council works in a very thorough manner, inviting to its hearings representatives from companies under review, and placing strict demands on evidence before allowing itself to recommend divestment.

In 2009 the ethical strategy of the fund was reviewed. The Minister of Finance behind this review was Kristin Halvorsen, leader of the left-wing social democratic party, Socialist Left Party (Party SV). Until this party helped to establish a red–green alliance in 2005, Party SV had never been in power. As a parliamentarian before her appointment as Finance Minister, Halvorsen was active in promoting the idea of ethical standards. The review of the fund in 2009 yielded a few additions to the strategy previously employed. A programme of positive selection directed towards green investment was implemented in 2010. It has encouraged efforts to review both the climate change strategy and use of financial havens by companies in which the GPF-G is invested. Another new approach, a 'naming and shaming technique', involves the publication of a list of companies considered borderline for divestment.

Despite these efforts, at the beginning of 2010, the well-established environmental and humanitarian NGO, Fremtiden i våre hender (The Future is in Our Hands), labelled the GPF-G 'ethics bad boy' of the year. Its main grievance was that four of the five largest absolute positions taken by the fund are in the international oil industry. The NGO also underlined that so far the fund had never divested from a company for having a poor climate change record.[8]

The latest addition to the ethical strategy is the parliament's decision to withdraw from 17 tobacco companies. This decision was made after being recommended by the fund's Council on Ethics, and it split the parliament along the left–right divide. The two right-wing parties (the Conservatives and the Progress Party) argued that as long as tobacco is a legal substance in Norway and the Norwegian state takes in significant revenues taxing its consumption, refusing to invest in the production of tobacco is a double standard. As we can see, their argument reverses the 'double standard' argument of the left. While the left is most often concerned with cases where the fund's investment policy lags behind traditional public or foreign policy, in this case the double standard emerges because the fund runs ahead of public policy.

Spend more now

As noted above, establishment of the regime in 2001 was motivated partly by the need to install a safety valve against the pressure to spend and invest more in the present time. It has been quite successful yet it has faced criticism from both the right and the left. Both sides' criticisms are grounded in opposition to prioritising the investment in financial saving abroad. While criticism from the right is directed towards the 'saving' side, critics on the left are more concerned with the 'financial' side. The left's concern centres on a demand to invest more in public infrastructure, but its demand has been largely contained because participation in current red–green, centre–left coalition limits what the left leaning politicians allow themselves to say. Criticism from the populist right centres on welfare spending, and what makes it a right-wing programme is its demand for the delivery of services through the market, with the state providing the financing. This criticism represents a different kind of challenge because it is articulated by the Progress Party, which although politically isolated by the other opposition parties, has grown into the biggest of all the opposition parties. Here I discuss the challenges arising from different political perspectives, moving from those of the right to those of the left.

The right-wing populist Progress Party has been clamouring for higher government expenditure in most sectors, always pointing to the big 'kitty' that the state has at its disposal but refuses to use. When speaking of the demand for increased spending on any given purpose, its politicians have made a habit of starting sentences with phrases such as: 'In one of the richest countries in the world, it is a scandal that we cannot even afford ...'. This strategy has paid off in opinion polls where the Progress Party regularly reaches support levels of 25 per cent or more and to a somewhat lesser degree in elections, where in 2009 it still scored almost 23 per cent of the vote.

The fund's fast growing rate of 4% provided the government with a degree of fiscal freedom that most other social democratic parties (or states for that matter) would envy. The Norwegian Social Democrats spearhead the centre–left coalition which has governed since 2005. Still, the Progress Party has continued to make inroads into the Labour Party's support base by maintaining its 'in one of the richest countries in the world' rhetoric.

The red–green coalition government since 2005 was re-elected in September 2009. It is dominated by the Social Democrats under Premier Jens Stoltenberg, but also includes the agrarian Centre Party and the leftist Social Democrats of Party SV. Inside this coalition, two main groupings cut across all three parties. The dominant group, which controls most of the ministerial posts, can be described as 'New Labour light', meaning that it has a solid belief in free markets and refuses to see the financial sector as anything other than just another sector. It is also committed to containing the growth of the public sector, in not only relative, but also absolute terms.

The Norwegian welfare state is, for reasons beyond the scope of this chapter, much heavier on transfers to individuals than investment in infrastructure. The left-leaning public sector union-dominated faction of the ruling coalition is concerned about this. The infrastructure agenda is reinforced by the environmental concerns that normally are close to the heart of those of a left of centre persuasion. Public transport is one concern. Norway is a train-laggard in a European context and the present plans – even though they represent real growth – secure this position, much to the chagrin of the majority of the supporters of SV. The debate over infrastructure has also reopened an almost closed fault line between old school Keynesians who insist it is important to distinguish between the 'real economy' and 'the financial economy', and 'new labour' types of a more neoclassical persuasion. The argument levelled by the opposition within the ruling parties is that saving by investing in the real economy is as productive as (and not morally inferior to) investing in securities abroad. In response to that argument, the author (and in the name of full disclosure: debate participant) has never been able to pick up a counter-argument based on economic reasoning. The true conviction behind the Stoltenberg-camp's opposition to investing in domestic infrastructure is probably based more on public choice. This camp does not trust the political system's ability to constrain itself in the absence of the 4 per cent focal point.

The fund's supporters inside and in close proximity to the technocracy at MoF have not sat by idly while opposition has mounted. From the mid-1990s onwards, they have built a second line of defence, effectively brick-by-brick. To the paramount issue of protecting the export sector, they have added an argument concerned with intergenerational equity and pensions. As early as in the mid-1990s, the MoF published its first intergenerational account. In 2001, a broad-based pension commission was established, producing a welter of standard neoclassical and demographic arguments for encouraging savings and for providing stronger incentives for workers to remain in the labour market. These have been backed up by a graph popularly labelled 'Jaws', depicting the ever-widening gap between oil revenues and future pension obligations.

In a loose sense, intergenerational equity means simply that some petro-wealth should be saved for later. In a stricter sense, it can mean intergenerational revenue neutrality, a way of thinking which can introduce serious constraints on pension policy. If one follows through on the logic, the implication is to move from 'pay as you go' to government funding. In this spirit the fund was renamed the (Government) Pension Fund – Global (GPF-G) in 2006 from its previous name Government Petroleum Fund of Norway. In the course of this move, a new superstructure was created above both the GPF-G and the older, smaller *'Folketrygdfondet'*, a government asset manager invested in domestic securities. This was done without actually changing the GPF-G's statues to tie the fund more closely to pension expenses. This change means that initially it was designed only as a symbolic move to show the fund's supporters that the government took seriously the wellbeing of future generations.

External impacts

In discussing potential external impacts of the Norwegian fund, it is useful to distinguish between two dimensions captured in current debates. One is on ethical investment practices, and the other is on SWFs as representatives of state power in a liberal market context. My discussion covers both issues.

A key argument presented in this chapter is that the main reason to emphasise ethical standards in GPF-G's operation is to quell domestic unease with operation of some companies in the world and to avoid some of the most embarrassing cases of double standards (for example, situations in which Norway is a major player in leading the global fight against landmines, while Norway as an investor is placing its funds in landmine production).

As the second largest SWF in the world, with corresponding human capital of staff and competence, GPF-G can have some impact as a role model in terms of its ethical work. It can be a standard setter in initiating ethically responsible investments. In this regard, the fund's Council on Ethics keeps an email list of 30 organisations that want to be informed whenever a divestment decision is made. The list features a diverse set of actors, ranging from other investment funds to NGOs.

For example, in November 2007, the MoF dropped the British mining and metals group Vedanta Resources from the fund's portfolio on the recommendation of the Council, which linked this mining group to environmental damage and human rights violations. The mining group had sought to use 723.343 hectares of land (including 58.943 hectares of reserve forest land) in India's Lanjigarh Tehsil of Kalahandi District to set up an alumina refinery. On rejecting Vedanta's application for the project on 23 November 2007, the Supreme Court of India referred to the recommendation of the GPF-G's Council on Ethics and stated:

> We do not wish to express any opinion on the correctness of the said Report. However, we cannot take the risk of handing over an important asset into the hands of the company unless we are satisfied about its credibility.
>
> (Quoted from Føllesdal 2009)

When analysing the more discrete and positive part of the ethical effort, we can start from the premise that corporate governance work is difficult. The influence of minority shareholders is low all over the world, as witnessed in the many failed cases where even fairly large blocks of shareholder votes have failed to reduce bonus and option programmes of corporate leaders in the USA, the UK, and for that matter in Norway. Corporate governance work is also more indirect, longer term and less visible and spectacular than dramatic divestment decisions concerning single companies, especially if these are global players with famous brands such as Wal-Mart.

Corporate governance becomes even more indirect and less visible when it addresses rules of the game rather than substantial issues. Given the state of corporate governance and ownership rights around the world, the corporate governance section of NBIM has been forced to take on these priorities. From the outside it is difficult to gauge the status of corporate governance inside the NBIM. Yet we can note that whenever the NBIM speaks of its ethical engagement, it is at pains to stress that in the long term the ethical strategy is also profitable (Reinertsen 2010).

As revealed in Chapter 1 in this volume, the spectre of SWFs arrived in earnest on the agenda of international relations in the latter half of the 'noughties'. Concerns about SWFs seemed particularly prescient in the autumn of 2007 when some SWFs started to take large shares in Wall Street institutions in response to the financial strain these institutions faced in the early stages of the global financial crisis. Analytically we can distinguish between several different concerns about SWFs and the heart of the debate is the SWF's motives. This was predominantly because many SWF-holding countries are non-OECD, surplus-running, and without well-embedded democratic traditions, and are investing mainly in democratic OECD countries. What is their motive? Are they seeking something more than investment? Are they interested only in reasonable risk-adjusted financial returns? Are they also motivated to pursue other strategic objectives? These questions give rise directly to a call for transparency, for if SWFs disclose what they are doing, perceptions can be replaced by knowledge, which will facilitate a more rational debate.

GPF-G found itself in a privileged position when this debate over SWFs flared. Put simply, it 'ticks all the right boxes'. First, it has a carefully selected portfolio, with the average holding, as noted above, less than 1 per cent. This seems to rule out any serious strategic ambition at the outset. Second, for domestic reasons outlined above, it was already highly transparent when the debate about SWFs began. Third, it is based in a democratic OECD country.

Talking to bureaucrats involved in handling and running the Norwegian fund, this author has a clear impression that Norway's fund has never been subject to any serious external pressure to reform or change its behaviour. A delegation representing the GPF-G travelled to the USA in March 2008 to provide a statement for relevant subcommittees of the Committee on Financial Services of the House of

Representatives. No serious concerns about its performance were raised; nor was its behaviour an issue during the discussion of the Generally Agreed Principles and Practices (GAPP) for SWFs. In the process of working out the GAPP and forming an international forum for SWFs, the GPF-G has been, if anything, held up as an example to others, and the GAPP enshrined in the Santiago Principles of 2008 demanded no substantial change on the part of the GPF-G.[9]

Conclusion

From this discussion of Norway's GPF-G, three related points are worthy of emphasis here. The first concerns the domestic politics versus international relations dimension. The second concerns democracy and the quality of institutions. The third is a reflection on power and governance in a (still) corporatist polity.

The most important point made in this chapter is that to understand the establishment and workings of the Norwegian SWF, one must grasp the domestic politics of handling petro-wealth in a corporatist state. In this light, the GPF-G is the latest and most successful attempt at creating a regime that phases petroleum revenues into the Norwegian economy at a pace that does not (quickly at least) destroy other sectors, and at the same time shields the Norwegian polity, economy and society from the volatility of international oil and gas markets.

Reflecting this fundamental motive, the fund has been set up in a way that disallows its use as a strategic tool of foreign economic policy. As a financial institution managing a large portfolio, Norway has seen itself as a price taker in the global financial market, and in effect a not very reflective contributor to the global 'savings glut', and to the associated development of a more 'financialised' capitalism. Consequently, in the debate on the motives of SWFs to pursue nationalism or capitalism, the Norwegian case delivers a slightly paradoxical answer. Although Norway's primary motives for creating a SWF were grounded in a desire to preserve its own corporatist brand of domestic capitalism, Norway's SWF paradoxically also helps to create solid support for a financialised capitalism at the global level. The GPF-G's commitment to transparency, counter-cyclical spending on equities (the 60–40 split dictates that the GPF-G buys more equities when prices are depressed) and provision of rich business for international fund managers and other services related to the global finance market solidifies this conclusion.

The strict portfolio approach also reduces the fund's potential to impact upon the ethics of corporations. Any impact is more likely to be indirect, through the GPF-G being a standard setter and part of an international movement towards more ethical investment practices.

Stretching the 'domestic politics' argument to its limits, one could even argue that the international environment in which the fund operates is in fact a domestically constructed perception of that environment. This should not be taken to mean that without domestic perceptions the external environment would cease to exist, but that how the external environment is perceived and interpreted domestically fundamentally shapes the relative attractiveness of political choices made in relation to the fund. Specifically, the Norwegian technocracy and its advisors' insistence on the EMH as an appropriate ontology and starting point for discussing investment strategy have a double impact. First, it makes the choice of actually having a fund seem more attractive, since it conveys the impression that global financial markets are fraught with *risk* (that is, something that can be calculated and used to make profit) rather than *uncertainty* (which frames the whole proposition as something of a gamble). Second, it reduces the legitimate role of active management.

The second point concerns how the trajectory of political and institutional development in managing petro-wealth in Norway was shaped fundamentally by Norway's circumstances when oil was discovered. Norway was then already a mature democracy with comparatively well-functioning and efficient societal and political institutions and a strong technocracy. This accounts for a story where the focus has remained on largely preserving an old order – changing it only very gradually rather than going flat out for a new growth model, or quite simply, as in some cases, letting the funds flow to a narrow kleptocratic elite.

The third and last point is that in this particular corporatist state, the historical evidence so far indicates it is easier to cap demands emanating from democratic channels (especially the pressure to spend more now) than pressures that stem from a coalition of industry, trade unions and regional politicians. A better understanding of the mechanism behind this outcome will be useful. One possible, but clearly insufficient reason is that the technocracy through the strength of the MoF wields a more direct influence on the spending habits of governments and parliaments than it does on the investment plans of an industry. However, this strategy of bearing the strain in the democratic channel comes at a cost. Transforming wealth from resources underneath the seabed into financial wealth increases both its visibility and its tangibility. This literal transforming of the nation's wealth has enabled the Progress Party to attack anti-spending rules by publicly emphasising just how much wealth Norway has. One day this party may gain enough power to break the hold of both the present regime and its 'slowly, slowly' approach to managing Norway's oil through the GPF-G.

Notes

1. At the exchange rate prevailing in mid-January 2010, 1 USD = 5.70 NOK. Historically the rate has varied between 10 and 5 NOK since the demise of the Bretton Woods exchange rate regime with the median and average being slightly below the 7 NOK mark (author's 'guesstimate').
2. The argument is that small economies can neither be self-sufficient across the broad spectrum of material wants that a modern society has, nor can they provide domestic producers (exporters) with a big enough market to sustain economies of scale.
3. From the 1980s, as economists began to take high profile jobs as commentators and 'talking heads', the profession changed and its members began to appear as a more diverse group. But as Lie (2001) has noted, this was primarily a matter of appearance and perception. Only a few voices really strayed from the broad consensus, and while news media looking for debates and conflict tended to amplify these voices, they were not particularly influential within the profession as such.
4. 'Var Ola Nordmann smart nok?' interview with Per Schreiner in *Fagbladet.* 2 (2002).
5. On the contrary, one of the strengths of corporatist structures has been considered to be the way it facilitates constructive consensus seeking through securing the privacy of elites who could 'talk shop' across the table instead of engaging in public posturing for the 'benefit' of their respective constituencies.
6. For a link to the main external review of the risk profile and strategy of the fund by Professors Ang, Goetzmann and Schaefer, see http://www.regjeringen. no/nb/dep/fin/tema/statens_pensjonsfond/publikasjoner-om-statens-pensjons fond—/reports-on-active-management-of-the-gove.html?id=588819 (accessed 22 January 2010).
7. NOU (2003), p. 22. Commonly known as '*Graver-utvalget'* after its leader.
8. ANB-NTB, 21 January 2010.
9. The Norwegian government itself notes this in its national budget for 2009 (Report no. 1 (2008–2009).

References

Bergh, Trond and Tore. J. Hanisch (1984), *Vitenskap og politikk, Linjer i norsk sosialøkonomi gjennom 150 år*. Oslo: Aschehoug.

BP (2009), 'Statistical Review of World Energy', June.

Føllesdal, Andreas (2009), 'Does Divestment Work? The Case of the Norwegian Government Pension Fund', in Driving Development: Business as a Force for Good?, Global Compact Network Nordic Countries, NHO, 18 May 18, available at http://www.gcnordic.net/ckfinder/userfiles/files/Oslo/FOLLESDAL. ppt (accessed 5 March 2010).

Karl, Terry Lynn (1997), *The Paradox of Plenty: Oil Booms and Petro-States*. Berkley, CA: University of California Press.

Katzenstein, Peter (1983), 'The Small European States in the International Economy', in John G. Ruggie (ed.), *The Antinomies of Interdependence*. New York: Columbia University Press.

Katzenstein, Peter (1985), *Small States in World Markets: Industrial Policy in Europe*. Ithaca, NY: Cornell University Press.

Lie, Einar (1995), *Ambisjon og tradisjon, Finansdepartementet 1945–65*. Oslo: Universitetsforlaget.

Lie, Einar (2001), 'Styringssvikt eller langsiktighet i den økonomiske politikken?', in Bent Sofus Tranøy and Øyvind Østerud (eds), *Den fragmenterte staten*. Oslo: Gyldendal Akademisk.

Moene, Karl Ove and Michael Wallerstein (1997), 'Social Democratic Labor Market Institutions: A Retrospective Analysis', in Herbert Kitschelt, Peter Lange, Gary Marks and John D. Stephens (eds), *Continuity and Change in Contemporary Capitalism*. Cambridge: Cambridge University Press, pp. 231–60.

Ot.prp. nr.29 (1989–90), Om lov om Statens petroleumsfond, Norges Bank (2008), NBIM Quarterly Report, Q3.

NOU (1983), *Petroleumsvirksomhetens framtid*.

NOU (1988), *Norsk økonomi i forandring. Perspektiver for nasjonalformue og økonomisk politikk i 1990-årene*.

NOU (2003), *Forvaltning for fremtiden. Forslag til etiske retningslinjer for Statens petroleumsfond*, p. 22.

Reinertsen, Maria (2009), 'Oljefondets utspring', *Morgenbladet*, 22 May.

Reinertsen, Maria (2010), 'Hvor kommer politikken fra?', manuscript prepared for *Samtiden*, Oslo.

St. meld nr. 25 for 1973–74, *Petroleumsvirksomhetens plass i det norske samfunn*.

Vikøren, Birger (2008), 'Norges Bank's Experiences With the Organisation of the Government Pension Fund – Global', in E. Gnan and M. Gudmundsson (eds), *Commodities, Energy and Finance*, SUERF Study 2008/2, Vienna, July.

Wolf, Martin (2007), 'We are Living in a Brave New world of State Capitalism', *Financial Times*, 17 October.

11
Nationalism or Capitalism? Sovereign Wealth Funds of Non-OECD Countries

Jørgen Ørstrøm Møller

Introduction

For many years sovereign wealth funds (SWFs)[1] lived a quiet life without attracting much attention. They were regarded as 'normal' investment funds shuffling the world's savings around like other financial institutions. The interest started to grow a few years ago for two main reasons: First, a total amount of SWFs – a potential of US$6–10 trillion by 2013, and US$12 trillion by 2015, – started to look big enough to influence international investment. Second, SWFs proliferated from a limited number and 20 new funds were set up between 2000 and 2008 (Jen 2007; Regling 2008). Finally, the Chinese government's decision to launch China Investment Corporation (CIC) triggered particular attention despite its limited size – US$200 billion. It did not take long for statements about the potential risks of sovereign wealth funds from leading politicians to reach the headlines, accompanied by various initiatives by international institutions 'to do something' about SWFs.

When the global financial and economic crisis erupted in 2008, these initiatives were put on the backburner. In the last year or two, activities to establish a regulatory framework for SWFs have waned, being replaced by frantic endeavours to get the financial markets back to normal, as SWFs stepped in and helped save the near collapsing Western financial system by injecting US$60 billion into US and European banks (Fotka and Meggison 2009).

Currently SWFs are not a hot issue among European Union/Organisation for Economic Cooperation and Development (EU/OECD) countries, but the situation might change any time because the fundamental issues concerning SWFs remain. They touched a raw nerve and caused serious concerns about the future role of EU/OECD countries in the global economy – the word 'angst' may be used in this context. The main problems embodied in the policy stance in EU/OECD countries towards SWFs are:

* questions about the management and investment policy of funds not subject to normal financial supervision (risk of politically motivated investment decisions)
* worries that countries operating SWFs wish to accumulate assets through deliberate low currency rates, thus distorting comparative competitive advantages
* unease that the shift from liabilities (bonds) to equities leads to opaque changes in corporate governance
* feelings that national security may be jeopardised
* presumed risk that the 'brain power' of enterprises would be moved out of home countries relegating them to 'producing' instead of 'inventing' countries.

The question this chapter tries to answer is whether the underlying skepticism and negative attitude towards SWFs is directed against the funds themselves or radiates a deeper anxiety among Europeans about the long-term position of Europe in the global economy.

The figures

At the beginning of 2009, the size of SWFs worldwide was between US$1900 and US$2900 billion (CRS 2009). This corresponds to a maximum of 44 per cent of global currency reserves standing at US$6531 billion (IMF 2008) and is equal to the combined assets of all hedge funds and private equity firms as of February 2008 (House of Commons 2008). Global equity market capitalisation is estimated to be approximately US$50 800 billion and bonds, equities and bank assets $US190 400 billion (IMF 2008); SWFs therefore represent only 5.8 per cent and 1.52 per cent, respectively, of these funds.

The EU (Eurostat 2007, 2008) was investing far more abroad in non-member states than it receives in inward investment. In 2006, outward foreign direct investment (FDI) was €206 billion and €157 billion inward FDI. At the end of 2006, EU outward FDI stocks were

€ 2649 billion and EU inward FDI stocks were €2057 billion – a net position of €592 billion. For the year 2005, outward FDI rose 16 per cent and in 2006 rose 11 per cent, while inward FDI flows rose 10 per cent in 2005 and 13 per cent in 2006. From 2002 to 2006, outward FDI rose 42 per cent and inward FDI rose 63 per cent.

Looking more closely at the composition of inward EU FDI stocks from 2001 to 2004, important changes emerge. North America's share falls from 62 per cent to 51 per cent, a significant change in a relatively short time span. Those having increased their share are non-EU countries from 16 to 20 per cent, South and Central America from 11 to 14 per cent and Asia up from 8 to 9 per cent. This trend continued in 2006, with North America's share falling to 50 per cent and non-EU countries rising to 22 per cent.

A further breakdown reveals that at the end of 2006 the top investors in the EU were:

Investor	Stocks in euro (€) billion	Share in per cent
USA	953.7	46.4
Central American countries	261.3	12.7
Switzerland	247.8	12.0
Japan	99.3	4.8
Canada	81.0	3.9
Norway	63.0	3.1
Singapore	40.0	1.9
Near and Middle East countries	35.2	1.7

Another classification reveals that offshore financial centres account for €393.8 billion, which explains the high figure of Central American countries and Singapore. Hong Kong, with €16.4 billion, also falls within that group.

The picture changes completely when one looks at growth rates for inward FDI. The following list shows absolute amount of FDI stocks at the end of 2006 (in parenthesis):

Turkey (€11.6 billion) with 300 per cent growth tops the list, followed by Brazil (€10.5 billion), Singapore (€40 billion), Norway (€63 billion), Russia (€12.7 billion), Iceland (€6.29 billion), Lichtenstein (€7.7 billion), Korea (€7.6 billion), Canada (€81 billion), USA (€953.7 billion), Japan (€99.39 billion), Switzerland (€247.89 billion), Mexico (€8.4 billion), Hong Kong (1€6.4 billion) with a growth rate of nil, and at the bottom of the top 15 comes Australia (€17.3 billion) – the first country whose FDI in the EU indeed declined.

There is little evidence that SWFs have controlled or are in the progressing of controlling a significant share of total economic activity in the EU, whether it is about the total stocks of FDI, or investment flows or specific economic sectors. Only Norway and Singapore among the well-known SWFs appear to be the large investors in Europe. Near and Middle East countries account for only 1.7 per cent of inward FDI stock. What attracted attention to the SWFs was probably the *growth* in their size and activities rather than their absolute size.

An analysis by The Monitor Group (2008) suggests an increasing difference in investment patterns by SWFs located in the Middle East and North Africa (MENA) versus those located in Asia. Those from MENA tend to direct their investment more towards North America and Europe than the Asian SWFs, which tend to invest in Asia. Since 2000, MENA-based funds have invested US$100 billion, out of which US$72 billon went to North America and Europe. There were 205 deals, with North America and Europe accounting for less than half of their total investment activities. SWFs domiciled in Asia invested US$150 billion, with US$74 billion going to North America and Europe; a total of 573 deals with 74 going to North America and Europe.[2]

Looking at the picture in the perspective of EU/OECD positions/reactions, the following observations are pertinent:

- the EU is and will continue for the foreseeable future to be a net creditor and a net investor abroad
- the size of SWFs may look large, but in the context of global equity markets they are not
- EU outward FDI stocks are at least equal to their total; they are not a significant share of EU inward FDI stock
- their limited size rules them out of having any consequence for EU/OECD economic policies
- the trend over recent years may disclose a somewhat stronger investment by SWFs, but this is not significant, and 2008 – dominated by the financial crisis – saw a sharp decline in SWFs' investment in OECD countries, which fell from US$37 billion in the first quarter of 2008 to US$9 billion in the second quarter and US$8 billion in the third quarter (Fotka and Meggison 2009)
- any concern about foreign direct investors and their possible impact on economic activity and business life in Europe should be directed towards offshore financial centres and hedge funds rather than SWFs.

The author is often struck by the apparent oddity that these funds are more acceptable than SWFs. The explanation may be that the Europeans feel that the money invested from offshore centres is European money – in reality recycled – making this a circuit to evade European tax, but still under European control and steered by commercial objectives.

The European reaction

The essential point is that the attitude of the EU and its member states towards SWFs inscribes itself in the normal political framework and manoeuvring of the Union. The logic of the integration imposes constraints on national policies while offering the benefits of common policies. Largely, the member states seek to pursue national interests inside the EU framework by influencing EU decisions. The European institutions (Commission, Council and Parliament) play a similar game to compete with each other and with the member states too.

The EU originally foresaw that movements of capital could cause, or threaten to cause, difficulties and a clause allowing precautionary measures to be introduced as a temporary measure was part of the Treaty of Rome of 1958. After the implementation of the Economic and Monetary Union, this clause was directed solely towards movements of capital to or from third countries. With the entry into force of the Lisbon Treaty, the scope of the Common Commercial Policy – where member states have pooled sovereignty to exercise it in common – is extended to cover 'foreign direct investment, the achievement of uniformity in measures of liberalisation'.[3] This is one of the explanations why EU institutions have taken an active line on the issue of SWFs.

The EU position towards SWFs was set out in the Presidency Conclusions, endorsed at the meeting of the European Council on 13–14 March 2008 (Council of the European Union 2008):[4]

The European Council welcomes the Commission Communication on Sovereign Wealth Funds (SWFs).[5] The European Union is committed to an open investment environment based on the free movement of capital and the effective functioning of global markets. SWFs have so far played a very useful role as capital and liquidity providers with long-term investment perspective. However, the emergence of new players with a limited transparency regarding their investment strategy and objectives has raised some concerns relating to potential non-commercial practices. The demarcation between SWFs and other entities is not always clear-cut. The European Council agrees on the need for a common European approach taking into account national prerogatives, in line with the five principles proposed by the Commission, namely: commitment to an open investment environment; support for ongoing work in the IMF and the OECD; use of national and EU instruments if necessary; respect for EC Treaty obligations and international commitments; proportionality and transparency. The European Council supports the objective of agreeing at international level on a voluntary Code of Conduct for SWFs and defining principles for recipient countries at international level. The EU should aim to give coordinated input to this ongoing debate, and invites the Commission and the Council to continue work along these lines.

The question of financial stability, the capital markets, international cooperation and a common EU position was on the agenda for the meeting of the European Council in March (Council of the European Union 2009a) and June 2009 (Council of the European Union 2009b). In both occasions, SWFs were not an important issue and they were actually conspicuously absent from the conclusions. This suggests that the global economic and financial crisis shifted parameters and attention, at least temporarily.

The same pattern is visible when looking at statements by leading European politicians who had discussed the possibility of setting restrictions on inward FDIs from SWFs. Since the spring of 2008, however, these voices have calmed down albeit they may still be espoused by left-wing political forces in particular.

French President Nicolas Sarkozy initially launched a vigorous attack on SWFs, but little more than six months later, he established such a fund to defend France's own interests. In January 2007, President Sarkozy stated: 'France must protect its companies and give them the means to develop and defend themselves' (Emmanuel and Hepher 2008), and 'I believe … in globalisation but I don't accept that certain sovereign wealth funds can buy anything here and our own capitalists can't buy anything in their countries. I demand reciprocity before we open Europe's barriers' (Reuters 2009a). These are strong statements; Sarkozy does not mince words. In November 2008, the French government announced a strategic industries fund estimated at €20 billion to invest in France's key industries to defend them against takeover bids by SWFs (*EUobserver* 2008). It became clear that the French government meant business when, in July 2009, 20 stakes in companies amounting to €14 billion were made public (Reuters 2009b).

German Chancellor Angela Merkel stated in July 2007: 'With those sovereign funds we now have new and completely unknown elements in circulation.... One cannot simply react as if these are completely normal funds of privately pooled capital' (Dougherty 2007). In Germany, but also in other European countries, the prospect of the Russian company Gazprom taking a share or buying national energy companies raised fear leading to proposals to block such plans (Twickel 2008; Walker 2008).

In Britain, Chancellor of the Exchequer Alistair Darling publicly distanced himself from the French position of defending selected key sectors and stated: 'Sovereign wealth funds or companies owned by governments need to play by the rules. We believe in a liberalised trade system. One of the reasons London is the number one financial centre in the world is because we have a very open economy.... [The worry is] if a company is behaving in a way which some might regard as not commercial but political' (Conway 2007). A few days later he was prompted to clarify this statement and did it in the following way: 'When a company is not acting in a commercial way or we have reason to believe it is going to make an investment where there is an issue of national security, then we have powers to take action'.[6] An article in the *Sunday Times* added: 'behind the scenes, his advisers were rather more explicit: if Russia's Gazprom has ambitions to take over Centrica, the parent of British Gas, then it can think again. No deal' (Laurence and Armstead 2009).

Analysing the French, German and British views, while they all pay lip service to the freedom of capital movements and maintaining the current international system, they all:

- focus upon national security as a concern that legitimises restrictions
- explicitly or implicitly mention the energy sector as an example of national security (it is interesting to note that the deregulation wave starting in the 1980s – that privatised what used to be public utilities – has brought, among other things, the energy sector in reach of private instead of public ownership)
- require the money spent by SWFs to be invested with them, beefing up their industries with more capital, provided that they have a hand in how the money is used – a somewhat conflicting policy as the investors obviously want a free hand themselves.

Behind these policies there seems to be a fine line of balancing fundamental economic interests with the activities of SWFs.

The British are influenced by London's role as a major financial centre. A large part of British industry has ceased to be competitive and/or has been sold to foreign investors (for example, the car industry), transferring the role as driver for the economy to oil and services. Britain is vulnerable to steps that might tempt international investors, including SWFs, to question their use of London as a destination point for their investments. Despite various attempts, neither Frankfurt nor Paris has succeeded in establishing themselves as a credible alternative.

Germany is a traditional supporter of a liberal global economy. A tough German line towards SWFs would not fit this image, and German industry may also welcome capital from abroad. Accordingly, Germany is soft-pedalling on restrictions while at the same time expressing anxiety about key industries. It is, however, careful to mention only the energy sector in this regard, not its manufacturing industries. The spring of 2009 saw a major investment (Reiter 2009) in what may be labelled Germany's most precious industrial asset – its industrial jewel – when Aabar Investments PJSC (an Abu Dhabi-based SWF) took a 9.1 per cent share in Daimler AG. Adding its shares to those already held by Kuwait (6.9 per cent) gives SWFs from the Middle East a 16 per cent ownership share. This was not regarded as a threat to national security, more an important boost for car production, research and development, and employment for the whole German economy. The reaction was unanimously self-congratulatory, with Daimler Chief Executive Officer Dieter Zetsche saying 'We are delighted to welcome Aabar as a new major shareholder that is supportive of our corporate strategy.... We look forward to working together to pursue joint strategic initiatives.' 'It's a win-win situation for both companies', stated Ferdinand Dudenhoeffer, director of the Center for Automotive Research at the University of Duisburg-Essen.

France's strategy is more difficult to gauge, possibly because it is more subtle. By asserting its position early on to establish its own fund and safeguard key industries in French hands, France conveys the message that any investment in France would have to sound out the French government prior to taking any initiatives. By applying such a policy, the French government wants to have its cake and eat it too. The SWFs have tempted to go along with this as there certainly must be French companies that are interested in their investment while at the same time they do not wish to antagonise the French government. Judged on the structure of political systems among the large European nation-states, France can get away with this; the British and the Germans probably cannot.

What these moves signal about France's economic and industrial policy is still open for interpretation, but it seems possible that the alleged threat of SWFs is used as a pretext to take state-owned shares in a number of key industries. Referring to SWFs may make these measures more palatable to the skeptical French public because the European Commission and other international organisations have been given the job of ensuring competition.[7]

The European Commissioner for Internal Market and Services, Charlie McCreevey, in January 2008, outlined a European approach:

> The freedom of capital movements is too precious to be jeopardised on the grounds of sudden unrest.... Some have argued that new legislation is needed to protect national security concerns of EU Member States. In reaction to this, I would like to stress that investments which have the potential to compromise national security can already be blocked. It is often forgotten that a Member State is entitled to restrict Treaty freedoms on the basis of legitimate national security concerns..... We must not allow the discussion on Sovereign Wealth Funds to be used as an excuse to raise unjustified barriers to investment and the free movement of capital.... I do believe there are issues relating to transparency and governance that we need to engage on with certain Sovereign Wealth Funds.... We need Sovereign Wealth Funds to be transparent in their operations, preferably on the basis of an international code of best practice.
>
> (McCreevey 2008)

The European Commission (European Commission 2008) sees benefits as well as concerns of specific relevance to the EU connected with SWFs, enumerates reasons and proposes five steps for a common approach.

- Benefits: SWFs have helped to keep the global financial system stable by recapitalising other financial institutions in difficulties and will probably help to strengthen the euro's role as an international reserve currency; even if this is not mentioned by the Commission, the bid of Frankfurt and Paris to be global financial centres may thus improve.

  Concerns: the opaque way of management of some funds. There is uneasiness that the funds want to give lower priorities to pure commercial purposes and accord higher priority to other purposes such as acquiring high technology or getting control over distribution channels. Political motivations could influence investment decisions spilling over into negative consequences for recipient countries. The Commission does not mention it, but abrupt selling of shares in a company trying to casts doubts over its viability falls into this category of potential uneasiness.

- The Commission is not oblivious to the strong interests of member countries, in particular the major member countries and enumerates the following three reasons for a common EU approach instead of letting member countries act on their own. First, multilateral solutions offer greater advantages than individual national responses. Second, maintaining a well-functioning internal market and non-discriminatory rules requires a common approach. Third, it will be difficult to open third country markets to EU investors if the EU or individual member countries were to be seen erecting barriers.
- A common approach should be built around five steps: First, commitment to an open investment environment. Second, support for multilateral work. Third, use of existing instruments. Fourth, respect for EU Treaty obligations. Fifth, proportionality and transparency.

In July 2008, the European Parliament, assuming more and more responsibility in shaping policies for the EU, adopted (with 661 votes for and 11 against) a resolution (European Parliament 2008) highlighting that:

> SWFs have not caused distortion of capital markets...is concerned about the lack of transparency...welcomes the Communication from the European Commission but regards it as a first step...requests the Commission to conduct an analysis of tools at the European Union's disposal in either Treaty provisions or existing legislation – such as transparency requirements, voting rights, shareholders' rights and golden shares – that would allow some reaction in the event of ownership problems due to SWF intervention.

The final phrase is the crucial one as it opens the door for 'reaction in the event of ownership problems' without specifying what kind of problems might give rise to the reaction.

At the OECD Ministerial Meeting in June 2008 (OECD 2008a) the chair summarised the discussion about SWFs in the following way:

> SWFs have become a key player in the new financial landscape. Ministers welcomed the benefits that SWFs bring to home and host countries and agreed that protectionist barriers to foreign investment

would hamper growth. They recognised the rapidity by which the OECD has responded to the mandate given by the G7 Finance Ministers and other OECD Members. Ministers praised the Report by the Investment Committee on SWFs and the guidance they give to recipient countries on preserving and expanding an open environment for investments by SWFs while protecting legitimate national security interests. They expressed their support for the work at the IMF on voluntary best practices for SWFs as an essential contribution and welcomed the continuing coordination between the OECD and the IMF. Ministers looked forward to future work on freedom of investment by the OECD, including surveillance of national policy developments. They adopted the OECD Declaration on SWFs and Recipient Country Policies and were joined by Ministers from Chile, Estonia and Slovenia, who adhered to the Declaration. This Declaration constitutes another example of the OECD's capacity to set international standards.

Since 2006, the OECD (OECD 2008b) has 'provided a forum for intergovernmental dialogue on how governments can reconcile the need to preserve and expand an open international investment environment with their duty to safeguard the essential security interests of their people' and finalised its work on guidance on sovereign wealth funds in October 2008. It consists of three parts.

- Declaration on recipient countries' policies with the core element that OECD countries should not erect protectionist barriers to international investment, should not discriminate among investors, and safeguards for national security reasons should be transparent and predictable, proportional to the concern and subject to accountability in application.
- A confirmation of investment policy principles reflecting the need to keep markets open and transparent.
- More detailed guidelines for recipient countries investment policies relating to national security aiming to strike a balance between legitimate concerns for the investor and the recipient countries by enumerating a number of steps to be complied with in case of restrictions motivated by national security.

The OECD guidelines are more complex and go indeed deeper into the matter than is the case for much of the work done in the EU. This can be explained by the non-binding character of OECD guidelines compared with the more intricate task of drawing up legal Acts for the EU fitting into the existing or planned regulation of the European capital market. The common denominator is the concern for national security where the EU concern goes deeper and further includes consequences for economic activity and ownership of investment under the auspices of SWFs.[8]

EU/OECD SWFs

The non-EU/OECD countries' funds are normally fed by strong export earnings that are expected to continue with an overall objective to invest over a long-term horizon without any specific purpose. The EU/OECD[9] countries' funds cannot count on export earnings, but are normally fed by public funds to act as a reserve when in a decade or two a higher absolute number and share of people above 65 years of age will shift the burden of financing to a smaller share of the population in the productive age.[10]

Australia. The Future Fund (see Chapters 7 and 8). Set up in 2006. Objective: to build up a buffer in view of the expected demographic evolution. Management through an independent board. As of 30 June 2008, the total portfolio was A$64 billion.

Belgium. Zilverfond. Set up in 2001. Objective: to fund claims for expenditure from 2010 to 2030 flowing from an ageing population. Management is linked to the Minister of Finance, who issues guidelines. Flexibility is limited as the fund invests exclusively in Belgian Treasury Bonds. As of 31 December 2009, the total portfolio was €15.5 billion.

France. The Strategic Industries Fund is mentioned above, but France also has Fonds de Réserve pour les Retraites (FFR) set up in 2001. Objective: to fund old age pensions. Management is under the supervision of a board composed by, inter alia, parliamentarians and representatives of ministries, but aiming for independence and transparency. As of 31 December 2008, the total portfolio was €27.7 billion.

Ireland. The National Pensions Reserve Fund (NPRF). Set up in 2001. Objective: to meet as much as possible of the cost to the state of social welfare and public service pensions to be paid from 2025 until at least 2055. Management is performed by seven members of the NPRF Commission appointed by the government. As of end-2007, the total value of NBRF was €21.150 billion.

Korea. Korea Investment Corporation (KIC). Set up in 2005. Objective: to manage public funds entrusted by the government and the Bank of Korea. Management is in the hands of a nine-member steering committee with public and private sector members. Initially KIC was entrusted with US$27 billion and as of end 2007 US$14 800 million was invested.

New Zealand. The New Zealand Superannuation Fund. Set up in 2001. Objective: to meet the cost of an ageing population. Management is handed over to a board (Guardians) who must manage the fund consistent with best practice portfolio management, maximising returns without undue risk and avoiding prejudice to New Zealand as a responsible member of the world community. The government plans to allocate about NZ$1.5 billion a year over the next 20 years. As of 31 May 2008, the value of the fund was NZ$14.7 billion.

Almost all the funds were established around 2001 to accumulate reserves deemed necessary to meet future pensions and possibly other social welfare expenditure, and they are institutionally linked to government supervision or guidance. As they belong to the public sector and are supposed to finance future public expenditures, they are basically an instrument for siphoning off some funds from the normal budget to special institutions that are allowed to invest in a different manner to the way in which they would invest if the money was kept inside the budget, where it would have improved the budget balance and public debt position.

The political consideration must have been that a deterioration of public finances *ceteris paribus* is worthwhile compared with another policy for disposal of public finances. This is of course why investment policies and transparency, in addition to accountability, become an interesting question. Whether or not it is a profitable or beneficial policy for society depends simply upon the portfolio performance compared with conventional management of the public debt/public assets. It looked a safe practice in 2001, but after the upheavals on global capital markets in 2007–09 (and the volatility will probably continue for at least another two years) many of the funds have suffered substantial losses that have to be recouped in the future.[11]

The philosophy of the funds may be to buy into tomorrow's production by shifting from bonds (mainly more conservative treasury bonds) to more aggressive equity shares as an investment objective. Without doubt, equity markets rise over the long term, but there have been long spells – several decades in fact – where the market did not move and of course not everyone selects equity shares that are going to grow in value.[12] It is not a foregone conclusion that a switch to new investment methods will increase the value of a country's savings allocated to meet future claims. Many governments were carried away by the euphoria of the equity market in the 1990s and decided to enter the market; they often did so when it had reached its peak.

What makes an SWF investment different from other inward FDI?

This section will analyse European skepticism, fear and outright negative attitudes towards SWFs compared with other kinds of inward FDI. SWFs appear to be easy to identify, but when we look at their effects from a recipient country's point of view, it is less simple. First, SWFs are different because of their country of origin. Second, what is the difference from the recipient country's point of view between an investment undertaken by an SWF or company that is fully or partly owned by a SWF? One of the least analysed but most important issues is the blurring of distinction between SWFs, state-owned enterprises and other enterprises in a country that has set up SWFs.

Defensive actions

1. Many EU/OECD countries have announced measures to protect themselves against FDI inflows, which might threaten national security or similar interests.[13] It is, however, an open question whether national security is threatened more or less by SWFs than by private investors. If a private foreign company obtains high technology that is vital for national security, it may not hesitate to sell it to other countries. Many countries need to defend themselves against industrial espionage gradually evolving into a policy instrument.

Suppose that private funds pursue a policy of maximising profits; then they would not hesitate to jeopardise a country's national security by, for example, selling 'high-tech' information. They might even postulate that such selling/buying is part of natural commercial operations and that inhibitions go against commitments undertaken under international treaties guaranteeing free trade in goods and services.

A sub question is the argument that SWFs would be more liable to steer investments towards companies having 'interesting' technology and offer a higher price than other bidders to acquire that technology. Such a policy would crowd out competitive bids for a 'high-tech' company pushing it towards SWFs as the only serious bidder on the price level set by its (allegedly) too high a bid. An 'unfriendly' SWF may prevent, for example, defence-related national companies from consolidating into one large company and in so doing, it may stand a better chance of surviving international competition. The remaining small- or medium-sized companies could subsequently be 'conquered' one by one.

There is little evidence to support the view that domestic, privately owned companies in possession of high technology or the knowledge and ability relevant for national security are open for outside bids.

Again, the question arises as to what the implications would be to national security of a takeover by a SWF instead of by a foreign privately owned company. The question can be posed differently in that a government might have more leverage in negotiation or in discussion with another government about national security than if it negotiated with a privately owned company.

National security may be threatened by outside FDI, but it is far from obvious that it is threatened more by SWFs than by foreign privately owned companies. If there is a need to protect national security it should be done by other measures, not by discriminating between SWFs and private investors.[14]

Until now, national security has been considered only in a conventional sense. We need to broaden the analysis and examine national security in terms of securing supplies, guaranteeing effectiveness of infrastructure, maintaining competitiveness and knowledge of ownership.

2. The question of securing supplies is much in the forefront of the debate on SWFs, but the focus is mainly on oil-exporting countries in the Middle East buying, among other things, agricultural land or in the case of China, buying minerals and oil. The large scale of Chinese investment in natural resources in Africa and Latin America and the latest controversy surrounding the Chinese investment in Rio Tinto (Cimilucca et al. 2009) highlight how important this issue will be. An increasing scarcity of commodities, such as food, means higher prices and more profitable investment in these sectors. EU/OECD countries, however, do not seem to be a target, as few of them possess energy resources and/or commodities. What they might fear is SWFs investing in third countries and eventually taking over traditional suppliers to EU/OECD countries.

3. The case of a Dubai consortium wishing to take over the operation of a number of US ports illustrates how sensitive EU/OECD countries

might be, fearing that vital infrastructure could come under the control of a foreign government. It is difficult to gauge what foreign ownership would mean for ports and other infrastructure if a recipient country wanted to 'mobilise' them to defend national security, but this is probably one of the few cases where SWF ownership might jeopardise national security.

At various points in the twentieth century, the British government subsidised the building of liners for the two main transatlantic ship owners – Cunard and White Star Line – conditional upon these ships being deployed as armed merchant cruisers in the event of national security. During World War I and World War II, the liners were used extensively as hospital ships and troop carriers. As late as 1982, *RMS Queen Elizabeth II* served as a troop ship in the Falklands War. Similarly *USS United States,* a passenger liner built in 1952, was a joint enterprise between the US military and United States Lines transatlantic shipping company and was designed as a troop ship with a capacity of 15 000 soldiers, although the ship served only as a liner until it ceased operating in 1969. There may or may not exist similar arrangements between governments and private companies in selected areas – not necessarily confined to shipping – and they might not be publicly known, but SWFs would not be allowed to invest in them.[15]

4. Maintaining competitiveness, or keeping what is regarded as a country's assets or 'crown jewels', can evoke, and has evoked a national security issue. An example is Groupe Danone, the French food company. It originates from a glass company (BSN), which, after failing in its attempt in 1968 to merge with another French giant glassmaker, Saint-Gobain, switched to food products and after a long string of mergers and takeovers became one of the world's biggest food companies. The French government's position was that, after efforts over many years to establish a food giant using France's position as an agricultural country, a takeover of Groupe Danone by a foreign company could not be tolerated. When rumours surfaced in the summer of 2005 that PepsiCo was weighing up a takeover bid, Prime Minister Dominique de Villepin pledged to defend Danone as one France's industrial 'jewels'(*DairyReporter* 2005).

The French position reflects its sentiment that some countries, for a variety of reasons, have a competitive advantage in selected areas and they cannot allow corporations to come under foreign control. It can be interpreted as a national security issue because those advancing this position regard it as necessary for the nation's pride and identity to develop their assets under national leadership. A more sophisticated interpretation points to the supply chain, as foreign ownership of some companies inevitably has negative consequences – in the case of Groupe Danone for French agriculture – and thus in the long term would undermine this sector's position as an integral part of the country's social fabric.

5. It is interesting to stop for a moment and ponder upon divergent views between governments and private companies in recipient countries. Governments may worry about inward FDI from SWFs and point to their national security concerns, but owners and management of many private companies may prefer capital injections from SWFs to capital from other companies or funds. They may see other companies or funds as predators in disguise looking for a bid to resell at a higher price or split the company into separate units to sell them one by one. The investing company may itself be a 'victim' of analysts on the stock market, who may conclude that breaking up the recipient company or selling some of its knowledge will be good for the share price and force management into such policies. Inviting capital from outside, and especially in the form of SWFs looking for long-term development of the recipient company, may help to fend off pressure from the stock market as outlined above. For example, Daimler AG did not hesitate to welcome a capital injection from SWFs, but it might have been wary about a private investor having links to companies interested in Daimler's expertise.

SWF – risk-taking profile

A great deal has been written about the risk-taking attitudes of SWFs, but there is little evidence that this is the case. The decisive question is, of course, whether the risk profile is such that they are ready to undertake investments, which could not find a 'normal' investor or whether they seek safe investments.

Danmarks Nationalbank (Schrøder and Humle Slotsbjerg 2008) has looked into risk management of SWFs compared with how central banks manage currency reserves, assuming that SWFs are an alternative to traditional management of currency reserves, and Danmarks Nationalbank draws the following conclusions:

> The primary difference between the investment strategies of central banks and SWFs is that central banks have to take monetary and foreign-exchange policy into account, whereas SWFs typically seek to achieve high returns and therefore have a greater risk appetite.

From a risk-management perspective, it might be appropriate for a SWF to diversify in the same way as, for example, pension funds.

SWFs with a long investment horizon have invested large sums in stocks and other, more risky assets in the expectation of achieving a higher return in the long run.

Turning to a comparison with other funds, the available evidence (Setser and Ziemba 2007; IMF 2008) reveals SWFs to be fairly prudent investors with a gradual rising share of equities in most portfolios.[16] The majority employ external fund managers and look to long-term and passive investment. In many cases, they diversify risks by investing according to a market index. If anything they seem to be more risk adverse and more prudent than many EU/OECD countries' private funds. An indication of the low willingness by SWFs to run risk is that their leverage seems to be low, separating them from hedge funds.

Most SWFs hold only minor stakes in companies and there are only a few cases of attempts to obtain control over companies. There is little evidence of SWFs seeking to take an active part in management of the company in which they invest (for example, by asking for a seat on a board or acquiring management responsibility). As minority stakeholders, they are less likely to influence management and the operation of the company they have invested in than many other funds without transparency and accountability.

Due to their ownership and origin, they are less transparent and less open to accountability than funds listed on Western stock exchanges. This is why critical observers point to the possibility that 'secrecy' may lead them into investments not open to, or likely to be pursued by, 'normal' funds. This argument, however, is flawed. Looking at the development of capital markets over the last decade it seems obvious that a number of funds domiciled in EU/OECD countries have been set up to avoid rules applicable for 'normal' funds. For example, pension fund A and pension fund B can set up pension fund C that is not under the same supervision and thus is able to undertake operations not open to the other pension funds.

It is wrong to conclude that SWFs are without accountability. The fact that many are not listed on the stock exchange (although some of them are), and because the home country does not operate a Western-style political system, does not mean that the political system neglects the sentiment of the population, who for obvious reasons are interested in how the wealth of their nation is managed.

It is clear that ownership of SWFs, although less transparent and with less accountability, does not necessarily represent pursuing investment policies that are different from most 'normal' funds. Unwanted repercussions in the recipient country are just as likely to occur from activities by 'normal' funds as from SWFs, although they may be of a different character.

SWFs – points of concern and answers

When a SWF obtains a controlling share in a company, there is a widely held concern that it could gradually transfer the 'brain' of the acquired organisation (strategic planning, 'high-tech', management knowhow and financial centre) into its own headquarters, and this could result in the recipient country being deprived of assets that are not only vital for the company being 'robbed', but also for the economic development of the recipient country.

Several points arise from these fears. First, SWFs have up until now primarily taken small stakes in companies. While this makes the risk of transferring vital assets away from the recipient country remote, it does not prevent this scenario from materialising at a later stage when SWFs have grown larger. In addition, it still leaves open the question of corporate governance.

What would motivate an SWF to pursue such a policy? It would only be profitable if the 'brain' produced a higher output in another country and although this cannot be ruled out (for example, if clusters of companies are created), it only seems feasible in a few cases.

The risk seems much more likely with inward FDI by a foreign company undertaking the investment on the basis of short-term calculations or for strategic reasons – for example, getting rid of competitors, or enlarging the research and development base.

It is not difficult to see why recipient countries react defensively to guard themselves against this kind of FDI, but it is difficult to see why SWFs should be more likely to entertain these methods than other companies or why they would be set up in a predatory way to buy and later deconstruct a corporation.

SWFs – perceived impacts

Finally, we come to the question of the impact of SWFs on economic policy, the national capital market and the currency rate.

Recipient countries, many of which are running a deficit on their balance of payment, would like the money controlled by SWFs to be invested with them. Without an orderly 'recycling' of money accumulated by SWFs the global capital market would be in difficulties.

Recipient countries might like to impose constraints on inwards FDI, but are prevented from doing so by international rules that were written by them in an age when they were global investors. They cannot violate, at least not openly, rules set by themselves; if they try to do so, they will disrupt the global capital market that is necessary for them to finance their deficits and/or channel capital into research and development for their enterprises.

As the almost catastrophic development on the US capital market, and to a certain extent the global capital market, illustrate that instability in financial markets comes from financial inventions initiated by institutions in the EU/OECD countries rather than by SWFs. The record of SWFs suggests that they are much more interested in keeping markets stable than in seeking short-term profits that would compromise the stability of the system.

The EU/OECD's negative reaction to SWFs in late 2007 and most of 2008 was replaced by a period of relief as a large number of Western financial institutions that had violated almost all the rules of good corporate governance were rescued by an injection of capital from SWFs.

An argument is sometimes promoted that an SWF may be used to destabilise another country's economic policy. There are many precedents where monetary policy in particular has been rocked by inward FDIs, but it is difficult to see how any destabilisation could have taken place because of an SWF in view of their limited investment. This brings us back to one of the major observations of fears: that growing SWFs may be able to destabilise another country's economic policy in the future. As outlined above, the size of SWFs is still limited and an attempt to influence economic policy (for example, by trying to push the exchange rate up or down or force interest rate adjustments) will require a massive effort.

It is also postulated that SWFs, by non-economic motivated operations, can create a negative sentiment around a country's industries and/or selected industries. When a company sells shares to an SWF, it might set in motion a wave of uncertainty about the future prospect of a company, thus destabilising it. This argument is unfounded as it rests upon the assumption that other investors and rating agencies are unaware that the selling was initiated by an SWF and that they are unable to decide whether they should sell shares or not.

Investment by an SWF might, in some cases, interfere with competition. For example, suppose that an SWF from a country that is among the world's biggest steel producers undertakes a large investment in iron ore suppliers. In these circumstances, it is not unthinkable that price and delivery may be slanted in favour of steel mills in the home country of the SWF.

For the EU there is a special concern as the European capital market is evolving and consequently a number of capital market provisions, including supervision, are being transferred from national to European level. Fundamentally, it is a problem of discrimination/non-discrimination. The European capital market is built to favour, or at least to accord preferential treatment to, European companies vis-à-vis non-member countries. On the one hand, the Europeans need to make sure that rules are drafted in such a way that foreigners do not reap benefits;[17] on the other hand, international commitments (for example, as undertaken in the OECD or World Trade Organisation) must be observed. At its core, the problem for the Europeans is to avoid a situation where SWFs unintentionally act as a spoiler in their endeavours to further European integration.

Conclusion

EU/OECD countries fear SWFs without explaining why they do so. These countries often put forward platitudes such as 'national security problems' with little evidence as to what the threat of SWFs actually is, apart from 'foreigners' owning domestic enterprises or having a stake in them. In practice, these countries find it difficult to come to terms with their declining role in the global economy as witnessed by a falling share of global GDP and the growing rate of outsourcing.

In addition, they fail to realise that a swing of global savings away from the EU/OECD countries to Asia and the Middle East necessarily and unavoidably means that ownership of a larger share of global economic activities will follow. Consequently, capital markets and the control over financial institutions move away from EU/OECD countries and are taken over by countries standing for the savings.[18]

In short, the problem is not about the power of SWFs, but the psychological barrier in acquiescing to the change of power in the global economy.

Acknowledgements

I am grateful to Ib Hansen and Frank Mols for a number of comments to the first draft. Klaus Regling and Ole Beier Sørensen helped me in my preparations.

Notes

1. The EU literature normally defines SWFs in this way: SWFs are generally defined as state-owned investment vehicles that manage a diversified portfolio of domestic and international financial assets.
2. Total figures are available for the first quarter of 2008 revealing US$58 billion, more than for 2000 to 2005 taken together. The figure for 2007 was US$92 billion.
3. I am grateful to Horst Krenzler for drawing my attention to this point.
4. The European Council is the highest political body of the EU. It comprises the Heads of State or Government of member states along with the President of the European Commission. It is assisted by the Foreign Ministers of the member states and one member of the European Commission. It meets at least twice a year, normally three times a year.
5. Communication from the Commission to the European Parliament, the Council, the European Economic and Social Committee and the Committee of the Regions, Com (2008) 115. *A Common European Approach to Sovereign Wealth Funds, Brussels*, available at http://ec.europa.eu/internal_market/finances/docs/sovereign_en.pdf .
6. The Enterprise Act 2002 (House of Commons Library 2008).
7. To put the size of these investments by the strategic industries fund in perspective, the total FDI liabilities for France at the end of 2005 were €144.5 billion, whereof €14.5 billion is held by the Near and Middle East countries and €4.4 billon by other Asian countries (Eurostat Pocketbooks, 2007, 2008).
8. As this paper deals with the EU/OECD attitude, the 'Santiago Principles' (Generally Accepted Principles and Practices) agreed October 2008 among 26 countries with SWFs including one member country (Ireland) of the EU and eight member countries of OECD is not incorporated. The paper, however, attempts to accommodate the concerns of recipient countries whereof 13 including the European Commission participated. The report also contains a useful list of SWFs. Available at http://www.iwg-swf.org/pubs/eng/santiagoprinciples.pdf.
9. In the following SWFs, those established by Canada (Alberta), Norway and Mexico are excluded as their operations are comparable to oil-exporting countries' SWFs and not EU/OECD countries' funds. It should not be overlooked, however, that the underlying idea behind the Norwegian, Canadian and may be also the Mexican funds are somewhat similar to funds in EU/OECD countries: namely to build up a reserve to finance social welfare in particular pensions.
10. Sources for the following short description are – unless otherwise specified – the 'Santiago Principles' and websites for the national funds.
11. France's FFR informs in its annual report for 2008 that the result for 2008 was minus 24.8 per cent and the annual performance since the fund's inception in 2001 is plus 0.3 per cent (see http://www.fondsdereserve.fr/IMG/pdf/FRR_RA_2008_version_fr.pdf).
12. The US Standard & Poors index hardly rose in 15 years from 1965 to 1980. From 2000 to 2007 it fluctuated around a stable trend and then fell to about the 1997 level.

13. Here I have chosen to focus on the political, economic and psychological aspects and do not enter into a discussion of limitations for discriminating between domestic investors and foreign investors, be they private companies or SWFs written in international treaties such as commitments undertaken under the World Trade Organisation (WTO) or Free Trade Agreements.

14. The EU when setting up rules for the internal, later single, market was aware of the need to build in a safeguard for security even if the words used are 'public security' and not 'national security'; see Articles 36 and 224 of the original Treaty of Rome.

15. This is mentioned as an illustration only. For the shipping sector, national legislation in a number of countries, including the UK and the USA, may give the government the right to requisition ships in case of armed conflict. For example, in the UK, the Crown has by right of its prerogative, a *jus angariae*, that is to say, a right to appropriate the property of a neutral where necessary in time of war. This right of angary can only be exercised subject to the right of the neutral owner to receive compensation, which may be enforced by legal process. See *Halsbury's Laws of England*, 49(1), 4th edn (LexisNexis 2005) at para. 410. I am grateful to Christopher Lau for helping with this point.

16. The studies available all examine behaviour prior to the economic/financial crisis starting summer 2007. This means that known investment practice for the SWFs were developed when equities were rising in value and appearing to be a good and safe long-term investment.

17. The cornerstone of the EU as economic integration is often misunderstood or misrepresented. The main idea is non-discrimination between member counties, but not necessarily according foreigners the same treatment – often labelled 'community preference'. Foreigners sometimes criticise this, but neither politically nor economically is there anything wrong with 'community preference', as long as it conforms with international commitments. There is no reason why the Europeans should accord preferential treatment to other countries without reciprocity. The basic idea of the WTO is to spread such quid pro quo arrangements, which explains why countries do not do it unilaterally. Several Free Trade Agreements enter into this area, but without exception they act in conformity with WTO commitments and normally the words 'WTO plus' are used to inform that preferential treatment is accorded on top of what WTO delivers and usually it is stipulated that in case of subsequent WTO agreements the Free Trade Ageements will be swallowed up by what WTO may agree upon.

18. China and Japan have for several years competed for the number two slot for global value of stock markets and in July 2009 China moved into that position again after Japan had been number two for 18 months. See *Bloomberg Online*, 'China's Market Value Overtakes Japan as World's No 2', 16 July 2009, available at http://bloomberg.com/apps/news?pid=20601087&sid=a_84o9PPPGqk. There are those who think that China's stock market is soon going to be number one. See *Bloomberg Online*, 'Mobius Says China Market Value to overtake U.S. in Three Years', 18 July 2009, available at http://www.bloomberg.com/apps/news?pid=20601080&sid=a4.VQEZdQ__M.

References

Cimilucca, Dana, Shai Oster and Amy Or (2009), 'Rio Tinto Scuttles its Deal with Chinalco', *Wall Street Journal*, 5 June.

Commission of the European Communities (2008a), 'Communication from the Commission to the European Parliament, the Council, the European Economic and Social Committee and the Committee of the Regions: A Common European Approach to Sovereign Wealth Funds, Brussels', available at http://ec.europa.eu/internal_market/finances/docs/sovereign_en.pdf.

Conway, Edmund (2007), 'Darling Warns Over Politically Motivated Bids', *Telegraph*, 20 October, available at http://www.telegraph.co.uk/finance/markets/2818013/Darling-warns-over-politically-motivated-bids.html.

Council of the European Union (2008b), 'Presidency Conclusions', Document 7652/1/08, Rev.1, Brussels European Council, 13–14 March, available at http://www.consilium.europa.eu/ueDocs/cms_Data/docs/pressData/en/ec/99410.pdf.

Council of the European Union (2009a), 'Presidency Conclusions', Document 7880/1/09, Rev. 1, Brussels European Council, 19–20 March, available at http://www.consilium.europa.eu/uedocs/cms_data/docs/pressdata/en/ec/106809.pdf.

Council of the European Union (2009b), 'Presidency Conclusions', Document 11225/09, Brussels European Council, 18–19 June, available at http://www.consilium.europa.eu/uedocs/cms_data/docs/pressdata/en/ec/108622.pdf.

CRS (Congressional Research Service) (2009), *Sovereign Wealth Funds: Background and Policy Issues for Congress*, Analyst Marin A. Weiss, Order Code RL34336, Updated 26 March 2009, available at http://assets.opencrs.com/rpts/RL34336_20080326.pdf.

DairyReporter.com (2005), 'Water Charge Batters Danone Profits', 21 July, available at http://www.dairyreporter.com/Financial/Water-charge-batters-Danone-profits.

Dougherty, Carter (2007), 'Europe Looks at Controls on State-owned Investors', *New York Times*, 13 July, available at http://www.nytimes.com/2007/07/13/business/worldbusiness/13iht-protect.4.6652337.html.

Emmanuel, William and Tim Hepher (2008), 'Sarkozy Vows to Defend France Against Wealth Funds', Reuters, 9 January, available at http://uk.reuters.com/article/idUKNOA93430220080109?pageNumber=1&virtualBrandChannel=0.

Euobserver.com (2008), 'Sarkozy Launches €20 Billion "Strategic" Industries Fund', 21 November, available at http://euobserver.com/9/27157.

European Commission (2009), *The So-called 'Sovereign Wealth Funds': Regulatory Issues, Financial Stability and Prudential Supervision*, Economic Papers 378, Brussels, April.

European Parliament (2008), 'Resolution on Sovereign Wealth Funds', RSP/2008/2589, available at http://www.europarl.europa.eu/sides/getDoc.do?pubRef=-//EP//TEXT+MOTION+B6-2008-0304+0+DOC+XML+ V0//EN and http://www.europarl.europa.eu/oeil/FindByProcnum.do?lang=en&procnum=RSP/2008/2589.

Eurostat Pocketbooks (2007), *European Union Foreign Direct Investment Yearbook 2007*. Luxembourg: Office for the Official Publications of the European Communities 2007, available at http://epp.eurostat.ec.europa.eu/cache/ITY_OFFPUB/KS-BK-07-001/EN/KS-BK-07-001-EN.PDF.

Eurostat Pocketbooks (2008), *European Union Foreign Direct Investment Yearbook 2008*. Luxembourg: Office for the Official Publications of the European Communities 2008, available at http://bookshop.europa.eu/eubookshop/download.action?fileName=KSBK08001ENC_002.pdf&eubphfUid=604157&catalogNbr=KS-BK-08-001-EN-C.

Fotka, Veljko and William Meggison (2009), 'Are SWFs Welcome Now?', *Columbia FDI Perspectives*, 9, 21 July, available at http://vcc.columbia.edu/documents/FotakandMegginson-Final.pdf.

Gugler, Philippe and Julien Chaisse (2009), 'Sovereign Wealth Funds in the European Union, General Trust Despite Concerns, NCCR Trade Regulation', Swiss National Centre of Competence in Research, Working Paper No. 2009/4, January.

House of Commons Library (2008), *Sovereign Wealth Funds*, Ian Townsend, Standard note SN/EP/4767, 1 July.

IMF (2008), *Sovereign Wealth Funds*. IMF, Washington, DC.

IMF, COFER tables, available at http://www.imf.org/external/np/sta/cofer/eng/cofer.pdf.

International Monetary Fund (IMF), *Sovereign Wealth Funds – A Work Agenda*, 28 February, available at http://www.imf.org/external/np/pp/eng/2008/022908.pdf.

Jen, Stephen (2007), 'Currencies: How Big Can Sovereign Wealth Funds Be By 2015', *Morgan Stanley Global Research*, 3 May, available at http://www.morganstanley.com/views/gef/archive/2007/20070504-Fri.html.

Laurance, Ben and Louise Armistead (2009), 'The Rising Powers of Sovereign Funds', *Sunday Times*, 28 October, available at http://business.timesonline.co.uk/tol/business/industry_sectors/banking_and_finance/article2752048.ece.

McCreevey, Charlie (2008), 'The Importance of Open Markets', Speech to Council of British Chambers of Commerce in Continental Europe (COBCOE), London, 10 January, available at http://europa.eu/rapid/pressReleasesAction.do?reference=SPEECH/08/4&format=HTML&aged=0&language=EN.

Monitor Group Assessing the Risks (2008), available at http://www.monitor.com/Portals/0/MonitorContent/documents/Monitor_SWF_report_final.pdf.

OECD (2008a), 'Chair's Summary of the OECD Council at Ministerial Level: Outreach, Reform and the Economics of Climate Change', Paris, 4–5 June, available at http://www.oecd.org/document/56/0,3343,en_2649_34487_40778872_1_1_1_1,00.html.

OECD (2008b), *Guidance on Sovereign Wealth Funds*, available at http://www.oecd.org/document/19/0,3343,en_2649_34887_41807059_1_1_1_1,00.html.

Regling, Klaus (2008), 'Sovereign Wealth Funds: Building Trust in a Changing Economic Environment', Speech given in Singapore to the 2nd meeting of the International Working Group of SWFs, 10 July 2008.

Reiter, Chris (2009), 'Daimler Sells Aabar a 9.1% Stake for $2.7 Billion', *Bloomberg Online*, 22 March, available at http://www.bloomberg.com/apps/news?pid=20601087&sid=a0eAzATgnNcU.

Reuters (2009a), 'Sarkozy Attacks Wealth Funds on Eve of Middle East Trip', Reuters, 12 January, available at http://www.reuters.com/article/oilRpt/idUSL1220023020080112.

Reuters (2009b), 'France in $19 Billion Strategic Fund Stake Transfer', Reuters, 6 July, available at http://www.reuters.com/article/innovationNews/idUSTRE5651ZT20090706.

Setser, Brad and Rachel Ziemba (2007), 'Understanding the New Financial Super-power – The Management of GCC Official Foreign Assets', *RGE Monitor*, December, available at http://www.cfr.org/content/publications/attachments/SetserZiembaGCCfinal.pdf.

Schrøder, Søren and Esben Humle Slotsbjerg (2008), 'Foreign-Exchange Reserves and Sovereign Wealth Funds', *Danmarks Nationalbank Monetary Review*, 2nd Quarter, available at http://www.nationalbanken.dk/C1256BE9004F6416/side/Monetary_Review_2008_2_Quarter/$file/kap05.html#_ftn3.

Twickel, Nikolaus von (2008), 'Barriers Going Up All Over Europe', *Moscow Times*, 13 March, available at https://www.usrbc.org/resources/russiannews/event/1366.

Walker, Marcus (2008), 'Germany Tinkers with Foreign-Takeovers Plan', *Wall Street Journal*, 14 January, available at http://online.wsj.com/article/SB120027192850787365.html.

12
The USA's Policy on Sovereign Wealth Funds' Investments

Gawdat Bahgat

As the world's largest economy, the USA plays a leading role in the global financial system. As the world's largest importer of goods and natural resources, Washington has run increasingly large current account deficits since the early 1990s. In contrast, Asian emerging markets and oil-exporting countries have accumulated substantial current account surpluses. A large proportion of these foreign currency accumulations have been allocated to sovereign wealth funds (SWFs). By investing in the US markets, and other foreign markets, these funds generally seek to maximise their profit.

Generally, the USA welcomes all kinds of foreign investments including those from SWFs. Washington has long been open and receptive towards foreign investments as has been demonstrated by several US administrations in various statutory frameworks, policy measures and in international agreements. In the last half century, the USA has entered into several treaties with other countries and international organisations that acknowledge its commitment to openness to foreign investment and free market principles and encourage other countries to reciprocate. Generally, these treaties grant foreign investors the same investment opportunities enjoyed by domestic investors. In addition, the USA is a member of two international organisations – the Organisation for Economic Cooperation and Development (OECD) and the World Trade Organisation (WTO) – that advocate open investment related policies, including policies that are transparent and non-discriminatory.

The challenge facing the USA and the international financial community is how to make the world safer for SWFs while maintaining an open market-based regime in which private sector actors are the major players (Truman 2008). More than most developed countries, the USA has been a strong advocate of a free market economy and critical of any governmental intervention in the economic system. The question, then, becomes how to reconcile the need for foreign investment without compromising the basic cores of the US political and economic regulations and philosophy.

In the following sections, I examine the US general policy on foreign investments particularly those by the SWFs. This will be followed by an analysis of the laws and regulations that govern these investments. I also discuss the main US government entity in charge of monitoring and regulating foreign investments, mainly the Committee on Foreign Investment in the United States (CFIUS). The following section will focus on how regulations vary from one economic sector to another. In the concluding section, I summarise the main findings and provide an assessment of the overall US policy on SWFs' investments.

Foreign investment – data limitations

Two US agencies, the Treasury and Commerce's Bureau of Economic Analysis (BEA), collect and report aggregate information on foreign investment in the USA that includes SWF investments. This process of collecting and reporting investment data is regulated by the International Investment Survey Act of 1976 (subsequently broadened and redesignated as the International Investment and Trade in Services Survey Act) (Office of the Law Revision Counsel 2009a). The Act requires that a benchmark survey of foreign direct investments and foreign portfolio investments in the USA be conducted at least once every five years. Foreign direct investment is defined as the ownership of 10 per cent or more of a business enterprise. The BEA collects data on direct investment in the USA by both public and private foreign entities, which by definition would generally include SWFs, by surveying US companies regarding foreign ownership.

The Treasury collects data on foreign portfolio investment in the USA through surveys of US financial institutions and others. These surveys collect data on ownership of US assets by foreign residents and foreign official institutions. Officials from these agencies use these data in computing the US balance of payments accounts and the US international investment position and in the formulation of international economic and financial policies. The data are also used by agencies to provide aggregate information to the public on foreign portfolio investments.

SWF investment holdings are included in the foreign investment data collected by the Treasury and BEA, but cannot be specifically identified because of data collection limitations and restraints on revealing the identity of reporting persons and investors. BEA's foreign direct investment data do not identify the owner of the asset. BEA also aggregates the holdings of private and government entities for disclosure purposes. As a result, the extent to which SWFs have made investments of 10 per cent or more in a US business, while included as part of the foreign direct investment total, cannot be identified from these data.

The Treasury's portfolio investment data collection and reporting separates foreign official portfolio investment holdings, which include most SWFs, from foreign private portfolio investment. The information that is reported to the Treasury, however, does not include the specific identify of the investing organisation; thus the extent of SWF investment within the overall foreign official holdings data cannot be identified. In addition, some SWF investments may be classified as private if the investments are made through private foreign intermediaries, such as investment banks, or if an SWF is operated on a sub-national level, such as by a state or a province of a country. These types of organisations are not included in the Treasury's definition of official government institutions.

In 2007, foreign investors, including individuals, private entities and government organisations, owned assets in the USA valued at approximately US$20.1 trillion. Foreign official portfolio investment holdings, which include SWF investments, totalled US$3.3 trillion in 2007, up from US$1 trillion in 2000. (Government Accountability Office 2009a) In short, the data shows that the USA has been receiving more investment over time from countries with SWFs and from foreign official institutions.

Sovereign wealth funds

The US Department of Treasury uses the term SWF to mean 'a government investment vehicle which is funded by foreign exchange assets, and which manages those assets separately from the official reserves of the monetary authorities (the Central Bank and reserve-related functions of the Finance Ministry).' SWF managers, the Treasury asserts, typically have a higher risk tolerance and higher expected return than traditional official reserve managers. Finally, the Treasury classifies SWFs into two categories based on the source of the foreign exchange assets: (a) commodity funds are those established through commodity exports. They serve different purposes, including stabilisation of fiscal revenues, inter-generational saving and balance of payments sterilisation; (b) non-commodity funds are typically established through transfers of assets from official foreign exchange reserves. Large current account surpluses have enabled non-commodity exporters to transfer 'excess' foreign exchange reserves to SWFs (Department of Treasury 2009c).

Since 2000, the USA has attracted the largest volume of cross-border SWF investment, totalling approximately US$48 billion. Roughly US$43 billion of this value reflects investment in 2007 and early 2008, largely consisting of deals involving financial sector entities (Government Accountability Office 2009b). SWFs from China, Kuwait, Singapore and the United Arab Emirates (UAE) were among the top investors. They bought assets in Citigroup Inc., Merrill Lynch & Co. Inc., Morgan Stanley & Company Inc. and Blackstone Group LP, among others.

Regulating foreign investment

There are no federal laws that specifically target SWFs investing in the USA. However, some laws specifically target foreign investment, which include SWFs. These laws regulate foreign investments regardless of the economic sector. They are mainly driven by national security considerations and the desire to protect the nation's industry. The list includes: Agricultural Foreign Investment Disclosure Act of 1978, Magnuson-Stevens Fishery Conservation and Management Act of 1976, Communications Act of 1934, Submarine Cable Landing License Act of 1921, Atomic Energy Act of 1954, Deepwater Ports Act of 1974, National Industrial Security Program, International Banking Act of 1978 and International Emergency Economic Powers Act of 1977, among others.

The Agricultural Foreign Investment Disclosure Act of 1978 requires foreign investors who acquire, transfer or hold an interest in US agricultural land to report such holdings and transactions to the Secretary of Agriculture. The data gained from these disclosures are used in the preparation of periodic reports to the President and Congress concerning the effect of such holdings upon family farms and rural communities (Office of the Law Revision Counsel 2009b).

The Magnuson-Stevens Fishery Conservation and Management Act stipulates that foreign vessels are not permitted to fish commercially within the boundaries of any state. However, they can fish within an area that is contiguous to the USA's territorial sea and extends 200 miles from the shore, called the Exclusive Economic Zone (EEZ), but only after issuance of a permit by the Secretary of Commerce. Foreign vessels fishing in the EEZ are also subject to annual quotas (National Oceanic and Atmospheric Administration 2009).

The Communications Act stipulates that certain communication licenses – including broadcast, wireless personal communication systems, cellular and aeronautical fixed – may not be granted to any alien individuals or their representatives, any corporation organised under the laws of foreign government, any corporation of which more than one-fifth of the capital stock is owned or voted by aliens or their representatives or by a foreign government, any corporation directly or indirectly controlled by any other corporation of which more than one-quarter of the capital stock is owned or voted by aliens, their representatives or by a foreign government (Federal Communications Commission 2009a).

The Submarine Cable Landing License Act of 1921 stipulates that no person shall land or operate in the USA any submarine cable directly or indirectly connecting the USA with any foreign country unless a written license to land or operate such cable has been issued by the President of the USA (Federal Communications Commission 2009b).

The Atomic Energy Act of 1954 requires that civilian uses of nuclear materials and facilities be licensed and it empowers the Nuclear Regulatory Commission to establish and enforce such standards to govern these uses in order to protect health and safety and minimise danger to life or property (Nuclear Regulatory Commission 2009).

The Deepwater Ports Act of 1974 authorises the Secretary of Transportation to issue licenses to US citizens for the construction and operation of deepwater oil or liquid natural gas ports beyond state seaward boundaries and beyond the territorial limits of the USA. The Act allows foreign investors to own interest in a license-holder through stock ownership so long as the licensee is incorporated under US law and its president or other executive officer is a US citizen (Maritime Administration 2009).

The National Industrial Security Program authorises the Secretary of Defense, Secretary of Energy, Nuclear Regulatory Commission and Director of Central Intelligence to issue and maintain a National Industrial Security Program Operating Manual. The manual prescribes specific requirements, restrictions and other safeguards that are necessary to preclude unauthorised disclosure and control authorised disclosure of classified information to contractors, licensees or grantees (National Archives 2009a).

The International Banking Act of 1978 stipulates that, with limited exception, no foreign bank may establish a branch or an agency, or acquire ownership or control of a commercial lending company without the prior approval of the Federal Reserve Board (FRB), which is prohibited from approving such an application unless it determines that the foreign bank is subject to comprehensive supervision of regulation on a consolidated basis by the appropriate authorities in its home country (Federal Deposit Insurance Corporation 2009).

The International Emergency Economic Powers Act (IEEPA) authorises the President to declare the existence of an unusual and extraordinary threat to the national security, foreign policy or economy of the USA that originates in whole or substantial part outside the USA. It further authorises the President, after such a declaration, to block transaction and freeze assets to deal with the threat. In the event of an actual attack on the USA, the President can also confiscate property connected with a country, group or person that aided in the attack (Department of Treasury 2009a).

The Committee on Foreign Investment in the United States (CFIUS)

In 1975, President Gerald Ford issued Executive Order (EO) 11858 establishing the CFIUS mainly to monitor and evaluate the impact of foreign investment in the USA. The EO emphasises that international investment in the USA promotes economic growth, productivity, competitiveness and job creation. The EO further underscores that it is the policy of the USA to support unequivocally such investment, consistent with the protection of the national security. The EO authorises the CFIUS to undertake an investigation of any transaction that might threaten or impair the national security of the USA and send a report to the President. The CFIUS may seek to mitigate any national security risk posed by a transaction that is not adequately addressed by other provisions of law by entering into a mitigation agreement with the parties to a transaction or by imposing conditions on such parties (National Archives 2009b).

The CFIUS is composed of the heads of the following departments and offices:

1. Department of Treasury (chair)
2. Department of Justice
3. Department of Homeland Security
4. Department of Commerce
5. Department of Defense
6. Department of State
7. Department of Energy

8. Office of the US Trade Representative
9. Office of Science and Technology Policy.

In addition, the following offices observe and, as appropriate, participate in CFIUS activities:

1. Office of Management and Budget
2. Council of Economic Advisors
3. National Security Council
4. National Economic Council
5. Homeland Security Council.

Finally, the Director of National Intelligence and the Secretary of Labor are non-voting, ex-officio members of the CFIUS (Department of Treasury 2009a).

The CFIUS process generally begins formally when parties to a proposed or pending transaction jointly file a voluntary notice with the CFIUS. Upon receiving the notice, the CFIUS chairperson determines whether the notice is complete and satisfies the requirement stated in the regulations. Then, a review period of up to 30 days begins. During the review period, CFIUS members examine the transaction in order to identify and address any national security concerns that arise because of the transaction. During the review period, CFIUS members may request additional information from the parties. Parties must respond to such follow-up requests.

CFIUS concludes action of the preponderant majority of transactions during or at the end of the initial 30-day review period. In certain circumstances, CFIUS may initiate a subsequent investigation, which must be completed within 45 days. Parties to a transaction may request withdrawal of their notice at any time during the review or investigation stages. Such a request must be approved by the CFIUS and may include conditions on the parties, such as requirements that they keep CFIUS informed of the status of the transaction or that they re-file the transaction at a later time. CFIUS tracks withdrawn transactions.

'If CFIUS finds that the covered transaction does not present any national security risks or that other provisions of law provide adequate and appropriate authority to address the risks, then CFIUS advises the parties in writing' that it has concluded all actions with respect to such a transaction. On the other hand, if CFIUS finds that a covered transaction presents national security risks and that other provisions of law do not provide adequate authority to address the risks, then CFIUS may enter into an agreement with, or impose conditions on, parties to mitigate such risks or may refer the case to the President for action. Where CFIUS has completed all action with respect to a covered transaction or the President has announced a decision not to exercise his authority then the parties receive a 'safe harbour' with respect to that transaction (Department of Treasury 2009b).

Foreign investment and National Security Act of 2007 (FINSA)

On 24 October 2007, the Foreign Investment and National Security Act of 2007 (FINSA), Public Law 110–49, became effective. FINSA aims at further scrutinising foreign investments in the USA and assuring that they do not pose any threat to the nation's national security while simultaneously underscoring the USA's general stance of welcoming foreign investors. In short, FINSA seeks to further improve CFIUS procedures.

Within this context, FINSA allows the President to add additional members to the CFIUS and stipulates that the Director of National Intelligence provides CFIUS with independent intelligence analysis, and the Labor Secretary advises on mitigation conformity with US employment law. Neither participates in policy decisions. FINSA requires CFIUS to conduct an investigation on the effect of the transaction on national security if the covered transaction is a foreign government-controlled transaction, threatens to impair national security or results in the control of a critical piece of US infrastructure by a foreign person. The Act defines covered transactions as any merger, acquisition or takeover that is proposed or pending by or with any foreign person that could result in foreign control of any person engaged in interstate commerce in the USA (Government Track 2009).

FINSA requires CFIUS to submit a report of all investigations to Congress and allows it to negotiate, impose and enforce any agreement or condition with any party to the covered transaction in order to mitigate any threat to the national security of the USA that arises because of the covered transaction. FINSA also requires the President to determine a course of action regarding a covered transaction within 15 days after the investigation is completed. In determining the effects of a foreign acquisition on national security, the President, or his designee, may consider the following factors:

1. Domestic production needed for projected national defence requirements.
2. The capability and capacity of domestic industries to meet national defence requirements, including the availability of human

resources, products, technology, materials and other supplies and services.

3. The control of domestic industries and commercial activity by foreign citizens as it affects the capability and capacity of the USA to meet the requirements of national security.

4. The potential effects of the transaction on the sales of military goods, equipment or technology to a country that supports terrorism or proliferates missile technology or chemical and biological weapons.

5. The potential effects of the transaction on US technological leadership in areas affecting US national security (Department of Treasury 2008a).

Finally, FINSA adds the following provisions:

- Risk mitigation: mitigation agreements or conditions must be based on a 'risk-based analysis'.
- Enforcement and Tracking: requires CFIUS to monitor and enforce compliance with mitigation measures and to track withdrawn notices. The Act also allows for imposition of civil penalties.
- Reopening of Reviews: FINSA allows CFIUS to reopen a review if the parties made a material omission or misstatement to CFIUS, or if the parties intentionally and materially breach a mitigation agreement. Before reopening, CFIUS must agree no other remedy is sufficient.
- Filer Certifications: filers must certify that filings are accurate, complete and comply with the law.
- Confidentiality: FINSA imposes on Congress, with regard to briefings from CFIUS, the same confidentiality rules that bind CFIUS with regard to all information provided by filers (Department of Treasury 2008b).

This brief survey of laws, regulations and institutions indicates that the US regulatory mechanism is a fragmented and complex system of federal and state regulators – put into place over the past 150 years – that has not kept pace with the major changes in the economic system both in the USA and abroad. Generally, the US regulatory system has sought to achieve four broad goals. (1) Ensure adequate consumer protections. US regulators take steps to address informational disadvantages that consumers and investors may face, ensure consumers and investors have sufficient information to make appropriate decisions, and oversee business conduct and sales practices to prevent fraud and abuse. (2) Ensure the integrity and fairness of markets. US regulators monitor markets to prevent fraud and manipulation and to ensure efficient market activities. (3) Monitor the safety and soundness of institutions. Because markets sometimes lead economic institutions to take on excessive risks that can have significant negative impacts on consumers, investors and taxpayers, regulators oversee risk-taking activities to promote the safety and soundness of economic institutions. (4) Act to ensure the stability of the overall economic system. Regulators act to reduce systemic risk in various ways, such as providing emergency funding to troubled financial institutions (Government Accountability Office 2009c).

The financial crisis of 2008–09 dramatically illustrates the ineffectiveness of the regulatory system in overseeing the increasing complexity of US markets, institutions and products that have rapidly evolved over the last several decades. The regulatory system developed in a piecemeal fashion over the past 150 years with some parts of the system created in response to the previous financial crises. The system lacks the comprehensive framework needed to regulate today's highly complex, ever-changing global marketplace (Government Accountability Office 2009d). A close examination of regulating foreign investments (including those from SWFs) illustrates this inadequacy.

Restrictions on SWF investments by sector

There are federal laws with provisions that specifically limit foreign ownership (including from SWFs) in a number of sectors (for example, transportation, communications, natural resources and energy, banking and agriculture). The level of investment permitted or the type of restrictions vary by law and sector.

In the transportation sector, total foreign ownership may not exceed 25 per cent of the voting interest of a US air carrier, under provisions of the Federal Aviation Act of 1958. Some federal laws do not prevent foreign investors from purchasing US assets but instead restrict the activities in which these foreign-owned assets can engage. For example, under shipping laws foreign-owned vessels – meaning vessels more than 25 per cent owned or controlled by foreign investors – are generally not permitted to carry cargo between points in the USA. Foreign investors are allowed to invest in US companies that provide goods and services to the US military, subject to restrictions related to the control of classified information and the performance on classified contracts.

In the communications sector, foreign governments are prohibited from holding broadcast, common carrier (telecommunications services) and certain other radio licenses. These prohibitions may prevent a SWF from being issued such licenses, since such funds are government-owned investment vehicles. Foreign investors may, however, hold up to 20 per cent of the capital stock of licensees, and may hold up to 25 per cent of the capital stock of US entities that control licensees. In the natural resources and energy sector, foreign investors are precluded from directly purchasing and holding mineral extraction leases on US lands. However, the law does allow foreign investors to own these assets indirectly by allowing up to 100 per cent foreign ownership of a US company that holds such leases.

In the banking sector, foreign companies, such as domestic companies, must seek approval for investments that exceed certain thresholds and must meet other requirements once an investment is made above those thresholds. Foreign companies are required to receive approval from the FRB prior to acquiring 25 per cent or more of the voting shares, or otherwise acquiring control, of a US bank. Foreign banks must receive prior approval of the FRB before opening certain types of banking operations in the USA. In general, only foreign banks that are subject to comprehensive supervision on a consolidated basis by the appropriate authorities in their home country are permitted by the FRB to acquire control of US banks or bank holding companies or conduct banking operations in the USA.

Once a foreign company obtains 25 per cent or more, or otherwise acquires control, of a US bank or bank holding company, it becomes a bank holding company and is subject to restrictions on conducting certain banking and non-banking related activities. These restrictions apply to the company and to any company that owns the foreign company. This may also serve to limit foreign investment in banks by SWFs, since many of them would not want to be limited in the other types of investments they could make in the USA.

Finally, foreign investors face no federal restrictions on investments in US agricultural land, but are required to report purchases above a minimum threshold. Under the Agricultural Foreign Investment Disclosure Act of 1978, foreign entities – meaning individuals, organisations and governments – are required to file reports on the acquisition or transfer of agricultural land if it involves more than 10 acres or produces agricultural products of US$1000 or more per year (Office of the Law Revision Counsel 2009a). US entities in which there is a significant interest or substantial control must also file these reports. Significant interest or substantial control is defined as 10 per cent or more direct or indirect interest in the entity if held by a single foreign person or a group of foreign persons acting in concert. This information is compiled by the Farm Services Agency of the Department of Agriculture and is reported annually. A filing must also be made when there are certain changes in circumstance (Government Accountability Office 2009d).

In addition to these federal laws that may restrain foreign investment, there are various state legislations that may affect foreign investors' ability to invest in the USA (including from SWFs). Most state level laws restraining foreign investment appear to be in the insurance and real estate sectors. Many state laws ban a foreign insurer that is owned or controlled in any manner or degree by any government or governmental agency from transacting insurance.

Restrictions on foreign investment in real estate also exist in many states. Many states have enacted laws restraining foreign ownership of real property. These laws vary, with some only requiring foreign investors to register as a company doing business in the state before purchasing property, and others specifically prohibiting foreign ownership of certain types of land. For example, one common type of real property restriction is for agricultural land.

Four conclusions can be drawn from this brief discussion of the laws and regulations that might restrain SWFs' investments both at federal and state levels and that apply to different sectors. First, all foreign investors, including SWFs, must abide by all applicable US laws. For example, all investors (national and foreign), who make substantial investments in US-registered securities, must file proper disclosures with the Securities and Exchange Commission under federal securities laws. Also, mergers and acquisitions by foreign investors face a regulatory review by the Federal Trade Commission or the Department of Justice, if there are concerns about possible antitrust violations.

Second, the sector-specific federal laws that apply to foreign investors vary in the types and levels of restrictions and provisions they contain. However, there is no sector of the US economy within which foreign investors are completely excluded by federal law from any type of investing. Third, generally federal laws do not restrict foreign investment, but place some reporting requirements on foreign investments, regardless of the sector. These requirements include regulating direct foreign ownership in certain sectors or requiring prior approval of foreign investment, restricting certain activities of either the foreign-owned firm or the foreign parent once an investment has been made, and requiring disclosure of ownership.

Fourth, in addition to these laws and regulations, the political environment in the USA post the September 11 terrorist attacks has created and reinforced a 'political sensitivity' towards foreign investments in general and particularly those from SWFs. Because of this political sensitivity the CFIUS review process has come under increased scrutiny and went through significant reforms. Two recent controversies illustrate this political sensitivity and its negative impact on foreign investment. In 2005, China National Offshore Oil Corporation (CNOOC), of which the Chinese government owns 70 per cent, withdrew a US$18.2 billion takeover bid for a California energy firm Unocal Corporation due to political opposition (White 2005). Similarly, a Dubai company, Dubai Ports World, withdrew its attempted acquisition of London-based Peninsular and Oriental Steam Navigation Company, which had operations at six major US ports, including New York and Baltimore (Weisman and Graham 2006). Although initially allowed to proceed by the CFIUS, subsequent congressional and media attention ultimately caused the company to sell the US portion of the business to a US company.

Given this political sensitivity, many representatives from SWFs choose to initiate an informal process under which they meet with members of Congress prior to initiating a formal transaction that might be viewed as politically sensitive to try to mitigate any potential concerns or resistance that could disrupt a planned investment.

Principles for sovereign wealth fund investments

In March 2008, officials from the US Department of Treasury, the governments of Singapore and Abu Dhabi, and their respective sovereign wealth funds the Government Investment Corporation of Singapore (GIC) and Abu Dhabi Investment Authority (ADIA) signed an agreement in Washington, DC. The, then, Treasury Secretary Henry M. Paulson, Jr stressed that 'the USA welcomes SWF investment [and] supports the international efforts to develop a framework for best practices for SWFs and recipient countries.' The signatories agreed on a set of policy principles for SWFs and another one on policy principles for countries receiving SWF investments. The agreement highlights what each side is willing to offer and what to expect from the other side.

Policy principles for SWFs:

1. SWF investment decisions should be based solely on commercial grounds, rather than to advance, directly or indirectly, the geopolitical goals of the controlling government. SWFs should make this statement formally as part of their basic investment management policies.

2. Greater information disclosure by SWFs, in areas such as purpose, investment objectives, institutional arrangements and financial information – particularly asset allocation, benchmarks and rates of return over appropriate historical periods – can help reduce uncertainty in financial markets and build trust in recipient countries.
3. SWFs should have in place strong governance structures, internal controls, and operational and risk management systems.
4. SWFs and the private sector should compete fairly.
5. SWFs should respect host country rules by complying with all applicable regulatory and disclosure requirements of the countries in which they invest (Department of Treasury 2008c).

In short, the agreement calls for transparency, good governance and compliance with the recipient country's laws and regulations. The agreement also emphasises that SWF investments should be driven by commercial interests, not geopolitical considerations.

Policy principles for countries receiving SWF investment:

1. Countries receiving SWF investment should not erect protectionist barriers to portfolio or foreign direct investment.
2. Recipient countries should ensure predictable investment frameworks, inward investment rules should be publicly available, clearly articulated, predictable and supported by strong and consistent rule of law.
3. Recipient countries should not discriminate among investors. Inward investment policies should treat like-situated investors equally.
4. Recipient countries should respect investor decisions by being as unintrusive as possible, rather than seeking to direct SWF investment. Any restrictions imposed on investments for national security reasons should be proportional to genuine national security risks raised by the transaction.

In summary, the agreement called on recipient countries not to discriminate against SWFs and in favour of other investment vehicles such as hedge funds and private equity. Recipient countries should also establish and enforce open and predictable legal and investment environments. Any restrictions should be proportional to perceived national security risks. Most of these principles had been adopted in the voluntary best practices for SWFs, known as Generally Accepted Principles and Practices (GAPP) or 'Santiago Principles'.

Conclusion: the way forward

After the sub-prime crisis, it has become more difficult to finance the US deficit. In contrast to the stock market boom of the 1990s and the post-2001 real estate bonanza, foreign private investors have become reluctant to enter the market. Instead, financing mainly relies on inflows from central banks and SWFs. In 2008, nearly half of all US Treasuries are already owned by foreigners and, according to Ben Bernanke, Federal Reserve chairman, about a third of recent emergency funding for Western financial institutions has come from Asian and Arab SWFs (Woertz 2008). Despite a rise in political sensitivity and a growing suspicion in SWFs' investments, the USA has continued to attract the bulk of these investments.

Some analysts argue that the USA is in a box. By running up large trade deficits and tolerating foreign government intervention in currency markets, the USA has contributed to large dollar overhang abroad – much of it in the hands of sovereign funds. Investments by those funds in Treasury securities helped keep long-term interest rates artificially low, and helped facilitate the real estate bubble and eventually contributed to the sub-prime crisis (Morici 2008).

Foreign investments – governmental or non-governmental – in US financial or non-financial institutions are likely to continue their historical rise. The two sides (SWF holders and the US market) need each other. The challenge facing the USA is how to find the right balance between making the country safe and attractive to SWFs and simultaneously maintaining its open market-based regime in which private sector actors are the dominant players. The challenge facing SWFs is how to address and mitigate growing private and public political suspicion in their operations. The record of SWF investments in the USA and elsewhere indicates that their operations are driven solely by commercial interests (that is, their desire to maximise profit). Still, they have to defend themselves and resist allegations of political objectives. Within this context, voluntary transparency by the two sides is likely to contribute to better economic and political understanding and facilitate the growth of SWFs' investments in the USA.

For several decades SWFs and the USA have engaged in multidimensional and multi-billion investments. This complicated partnership is likely to further grow in the foreseeable future. The economic and financial wellbeing of the USA is in the best interest of SWFs. Meanwhile, the continuing rise of SWFs is good for the US market.

References

Department of Treasury (2008a), 'Section 721 of the Defense Production Act of 1950', available at http://www.treas.gov/offices/international-affairs/exon-florio (accessed 28 January 2008).

Department of Treasury (2008b), 'CFIUS Reform: Foreign Investment and National Security Act of 2007 (FINSA)', available at http://www.treas.gov/offices/international-affairs/cfius (accessed 14 November 2008).

Department of Treasury (2008c), 'Treasury Reaches Agreement on Principles for Sovereign Wealth Fund Investment with Singapore and Abu Dhabi', available at http://treas.gov/press/releases/hp881.htm (accessed 23 March 2008).

Department of Treasury (2009a), 'Composition of CFIUS', available at http://www.ustreas.gov/offices/international-affairs/cfius/members.shtml (accessed 16 March 2009).

Department of Treasury (2009b), 'Overview of the CFIUS Process', available at http://www.ustreas.gov/offices/international-affairs/cfius/overview.shtml (accessed 16 March 2009).

Department of Treasury (2009c), 'Semiannual Report on International Economic and Exchange Rate Policies', available at http://www.UStreas.gov/offices/international-affairs/economic-exchange-rates/pdf/2007_appendix-3.pdf (accessed 15 February 2009).

Federal Communications Commission (2009a), 'Communications Act of 1934', available at http://www.fcc.gov/Reports/1934new.pdf (accessed 10 November 2009).

Federal Communications Commission (2009b), 'Title 47 – Telegraphs, Telephones, and Radiotelegraphs, Chapter 2 – Submarine Cables', available at http://www.fcc.gov/ib/pd/pf/clla.html (accessed 10 November 2009).

Federal Deposit Insurance Corporation (2009), 'International Banking Act of 1978', available at http://www.fdic.gov/regulations/laws/rules/8000-4800.html (accessed 11 November 2009).

Government Accountability Office (2009a), 'Sovereign Wealth Funds: Publicly Available Data on Sizes and Investments for Some Funds are Limited', GAO-08-946.

Government Accountability Office (2009b), 'Financial Regulations: A Framework for Crafting and Assessing Proposals to Modernize the Outdated US Financial Regulatory System', GAO-09-216, January.

Government Accountability Office (2009c), 'Reforming the US Financial Regulatory System to Reflect 21st century realities', GAO-09-216, 8 January.

Government Accountability Office (2009d), 'Sovereign Wealth Funds: Laws Limiting Foreign Investment Affect Certain US Assets and Agencies Have Various Enforcement Processes', GAO-09-608, 20 May.

Government Track (2009), 'Foreign Investment and National Security Act of 2007', available at http://www.govtrack.us/congress/billtext.xpd?bill=h110-556 (accessed 1 March 2009).

Maritime Administration (2009), 'Deepwater Port Licensing Program', available at http://www.marad.dot.gov/ports_landing_page/deepwater_port_licensing/deepwater_port+licensing.htm (accessed 11 November 2009).

Morici, Peter (2008), 'Investments by Sovereign Wealth Funds in the United States', Kiplinger Business Resource Center, available at http://www.kiplinger.com/printstory.php?pid=13367 (accessed 28 February 2008).

National Archives (2009a), 'National Industrial Security Program Operating Manual', available at http://www.archives.gov/isoo/policy-documents/eo-12829.html#201 (accessed 11 November 2009).

National Archives (2009b), 'Executive Order 11858 – Foreign Investment in the United States', available at http://www.archives.gov/federal-register/codification/executive-order/11858.html (accessed 1 March 2009).

National Oceanic and Atmospheric Administration (2009), 'Magnuson-Stevens Fishery Conservation and Management Act of 1976', Public Law 94-265, available at http://www.nmfs.noaa.gov/sfa/magact.html#s2 (accessed 10 November 2009).

Nuclear Regulatory Commission (2009), 'Our Governing Legislation', available at http://www.nrc.gov/about-ncr/governing-laws.htm (accessed 11 November 2009).

Office of the Law Revision Counsel (2009a), 'International Investment and Trade in Services Survey', available at http://USCODE.house.gov/download/pls/22c46.txt (accessed 10 November 2009).

Office of the Law Revision Counsel (2009b), 'Agricultural Foreign Investment Disclosure', available at http://uscode.house.gov/download/pls/07c66.txt (accessed 10 November 2009).

Truman, Edwin M. (2008), 'Do Sovereign Wealth Funds Pose a Risk to the United States?', available at http://www.iie.com/publications/papers/paper.cfm?ResearchID=892 (accessed 25 February 2008).

Weisman, Jonathan and Bradley Graham (2006), 'Dubai Firm to Sell US Port Operations', *Washington Post*, 9 March.

White, Ben (2005), 'Chinese Drop Bid to buy US Oil Firm', *Washington Post*, 2 August.

Woertz, Eckart (2008), 'GCC Needs the Dollar and the US Needs the Funding', *Financial Times*, 29 May.

13
Global Disequilibria

Xu Yi-chong

Sovereign wealth funds (SWFs) have caused a great deal of discussion and concern because of their size, the speed of their growth, their ownership and, more importantly, what they stand for in a changing global economy – a new group of investors controlled, managed and supported by their states. In 2007 and 2008, a scare campaign about the nature of SWFs was rampant in the USA and some European countries: investment from SWFs, it was argued, was threatening some countries' national interest by hollowing out economies and national flag companies, by taking over national resources and by controlling national infrastructures.

By invoking the terms 'national interest' and 'national champions', politicians in many Organisation for Economic Cooperation and Development (OECD) countries successfully created a feeling that SWFs were the Trojan horse of non-democratic countries, undermining their political and economic systems and stealing their national wealth. In France, President Nicolas Sarkozy vowed to protect French businesses from sovereign wealth funds and 'urged a state bank to roll up its sleeves and help France defend its industrial interests' (Emmanuel and Hepher 2008). Along with other members of the European Union (EU), he called on the OECD and the International Monetary Fund (IMF) to draft new rules regulating SWFs. In the USA, Congress held hearings, called for testimonies and directed the Congressional Research Service (CRS) to investigate activities of SWFs and recommend policies to regulate them in the USA. The US government engaged in negotiations with the UAE, Singapore and China, hoping to reach bilateral agreements on the investment made by SWFs in the USA. Demands from politicians, academics and various think tanks for new rules and restrictions on their entry into the OECD markets reached its peak in 2007 and early 2008.

Under these circumstances, SWF-holding countries 'complied' with the demands for new rules. In April 2008, representatives from 26 member countries of the IMF with SWFs met at its headquarters in Washington, DC and formed the International Working Group (IWG) of SWFs. The IMF was asked to co-chair the IWG and served as a secretariat in the following process. A sub-group of the IWG, chaired by David Murray, chairman of the Board of Guardians of the Australian Future Fund, was designated to draft the principles, which then underwent numerous rounds of discussions, reviews and revisions by the whole IWG, with considerable input from a number of recipient countries, including the USA, which commented on the draft of the Generally Accepted Principles and Practices (GAPP) and participated in 'selected sessions at IWG meetings'.

In October 2008, the IWG by consensus adopted the GAPP for SWFs, known as the 'Santiago Principles', in Santiago, Chile. In the process, the financial crisis dried up the credits. Financial and industrial institutions in many OECD countries needed a significant injection of capital and many large SWFs, in 'rescuing' some of the old financial institutions, suffered heavy losses.

By the first half of 2009, the scare campaign against SWFs appeared to wane as the governments of many OECD countries emphasised that their domestic regulation was sufficient to ensure their national economic wellbeing and national security regarding investment from SWFs. Meanwhile, some SWFs were replacing key managers (Norway), reshuffling/combining operations (Dubai World) or shifting away from the financial sector (Singapore's Temasek was a case in point: financials accounted for 40 per cent of its portfolio in early 2008 but fell to 33 per cent a year later). As differences among SWFs widened, the richest countries in the group, either in terms of unused reserves (China) or lower domestic spending needs (Abu Dhabi, Norway, Qatar), had expanded their equity purchases around the world.

Much of the new sovereign wealth activity in 2009 stemmed from China. The China Investment Corporation (CIC) launched an advisory board, allocated billions of dollars to a number of asset managers and made several investments; for example, it purchased a stake in the Canadian mining company Tech Resources, in several Asian resources companies, including one in Mongolia, in the Kazakh oil and gas company Kazmunaigaz, and was on the lookout for US property. The Chinese were, in general, as aggressive in making their investments in overseas markets as in previous years.

Are SWFs 'friends or foes' (Kotter and Lal 2008)? Are they a threat or contributor to national economies? Are they market stabilisers or destructive forces? This chapter argues that these dichotomies simplify a complicated and interconnected global economy. The adoption of the Santiago Principles may have contributed to the changing public debates, yet SWFs are indicative of a much larger feature of the global economy – the global payments imbalances on which, and for which, many SWFs were created.

There are two issues relating to SWFs that are of equal importance: one is about SWFs and the other is about global imbalance. The first section of this chapter discusses the debate concerning the legitimacy, effectiveness and impacts of SWFs. It is argued that SWFs are only one of the many indications of a changing global economy. The second section discusses global payments imbalances and their consequent changing of global power relationships. Global problems need global solutions and collective actions among states. This is the subject of the last section of this chapter. It is argued that the voluntary nature of the Santiago Principles and the informal organisational structure of the International Forum of Sovereign Wealth Funds created in April 2009 in Kuwait may not satisfy many who insist on the formal commitment of SWFs to follow the regulations and rules set by many OECD countries and international financial institutions. Nonetheless, they should be seen as supplementary institutions that, along with a series of others, shape the cooperation from the old-style rich country clubs to more inclusive institutional building.

Sovereign wealth funds and their concerns

Discussions on SWFs are diverse, focusing on various aspects of their make-up – SWFs as investors, SWFs as investments, SWFs as proxy of international rivalries, or SWFs as distinct interests – and various specific subjects, such as the strategies of making investment or the principal and agent relationships between the ultimate owners of the funds and those who manage them.

'What is the problem: S, W, or F?', asked Jonathan Kirshner (2009, p. 311). For many, the most important issue is about 'S' – the ownership of this type of investment funds. SWFs are the current incarnation of the tension between competing forms of capitalism – state capitalism as opposed to market capitalism – and they are the embodiment of rising nationalism. Underlying these claims is the fundamental philosophical debate over the role of the state and the role of the market. Behind the philosophical debates are more practical questions: are SWFs really any different from other investment instruments, both private and institutional? If so, how do they differ? Are they different in their investment objectives or operations?

Many SWF-holding countries argue that SWFs are hardly different from other private or institutional investors as they exist to maximise profits over long-term investment. For some non-OECD SWF-holding countries, the whole argument against their investment lies in the attachment of the word 'sovereignty' to their long-existed investment instruments. Some commodity-exporting countries have had their investment funds for decades: Kuwait established the first post-World War II SWFs in 1953, followed by Kiribati in 1956. These funds had attracted little public attention and caused few concerns in countries where they made their investment. They preferred to keep a low profile. This situation changed, however, not because SWFs altered their behaviour but because 'one day someone woke up in the morning and considered this [SWFs] to be a threat, a danger', as Bader Mohammed al-Saad, managing director of the Kuwait Investment Authority, noted in an interview to a German weekly on 19 May 2008 (Behrent 2008, p. 14).

For others, being 'sovereign' is an issue. First, the recent expansion of SWFs and their cross-border activities have reversed the privatisation trend that swept the globe over the past quarter of a century, and they are undermining the logic of capitalism (Summers 2007). Second, SWFs represent a rising nationalism that threatens liberal democracies as governments are accumulating stakes in what were purely private entities (Lavelle 2008; Lyons 2008). Finally, when SWFs try to invest in private financial and industrial institutions in the developed world, they represent 'cross-border nationalisation of private companies', argued one central banker in Switzerland (Hildebrand 2007, p. 6).

While there is no evidence that such cross-border nationalisation is taking place, labelling these investment funds as 'sovereign' funds has apparently provoked strong emotions from both the supporters and opponents of SWFs. 'Sovereignty is a powerful and deeply emotive word [and] has for centuries been invoked to defend inalienable powers of the state, internally and externally, even as the political organisation of states has been turned on its head' (Steil and Hinds 2009, p. 240). This explains the calls from politicians, media and even some academics in the developed world for their governments to take action to restrict investments from SWFs. Sovereign actions can only be countered by other sovereign actions, they have argued.

Underlying these questions is the assumption that a 'sovereign' state inherently pursues interest maximisation at the expense of others. These interests are broader than those economic interests; they are also strategic and political. The discussions on the political and strategic motivations of SWFs focus on the combination of 'S' and 'F', sovereignty and funds – funds as investment instruments. Given that more than two-thirds of SWFs are in the hands of non-democratic states, it is easy to appreciate some serious concerns that SWF investments could threaten another country's national security and national interests.

Because of these fears, some countries declared that a number of financial and industrial institutions would be out of the reach of SWFs. In 2005, the French government announced that it would include Groupe Danone, a world-renowned dairy producer, on a list of 20 French companies shielded from foreign takeovers and in Switzerland the view was that 'the banking sector is unquestionably of strategic importance for the economy [and] political intervention would therefore be required' if SWFs tried to invest in Swiss banks (Senn 2009). Sovereignty is a problem, according to the argument, because the investment decisions of SWFs can be easily hijacked by governments for political aims. Therefore, it is important to 'ensure that the investment decisions of SWFs are not driven by political objectives' (Hildebrand 2007).

Protecting the 'national security', 'national interests' and 'national champions' raises several issues.

First, cross-border investments are not a new phenomenon and countries, especially developed countries, have long-established legal and regulatory regimes regulating the incoming investment. It is a long-held principle that governments have the right to scrutinise incoming economic activities, be they investment or trade, for security and efficiency concerns. In the USA, for example, an inter-agency committee, the Committee on Foreign Investment in the United States (CFIUS), is mandated to review individual transactions. In Australia, the Foreign Investment Review Board has this authority. According to a report of the US Government Accountability Office (GAO 2008a), all OECD countries have similar institutions reviewing foreign investment. Each country may have its own concept of national security that influences which particular investments may be restricted, and they all share concerns about a core set of national security issues (GAO 2008a). Meanwhile, as a group, OECD members adopted the Code of Liberalisation of Capital Movements as early as 1961, which was based on the belief that global investment is beneficial and necessary to bring economic prosperity. This is also what they have preached to developing countries where lack of regulation is often the case – foreign direct investment (FDI), no matter what sector it is in, is good for much-needed capital, technology, managerial skills and market information. FDI is particularly good for development because investors cannot simply pack up and go, and developing countries have been pushed to open up their markets for capital investment. Some state-owned corporations from developed countries, such as the French EDF and Areva and Atomic Energy of Canada (AEC) in the nuclear industry, have been active investors across a whole range of developing countries. What makes SWFs different from public ownership in OECD countries?

Second, in modern societies, no matter what political system is in place, there is a set of governing institutions that make decisions on behalf of the country. It is more important to understand who makes these decisions and how and why certain decisions are made regarding the 'national interest' – political, strategic or economic – than simply assuming that decisions made by some mysterious 'state' must be designed to undermine the interests of another state.

Third, 'extra-financial' considerations are an integral part of the investment management landscape, regardless of the ownership of these investments. When central banks trade in foreign exchange markets they are making financial decisions based on non-commercial motivations related to their policy objectives. When George Soros short-sold British pounds on so-called 'Black Wednesday' in 1992, he intended to 'discipline' the British government for its over-valued sterling. He succeeded by pushing the British pound out of the European Exchange Rate Mechanism (ERM). There is an assumption that 'good' non-commercial considerations are acceptable but 'bad' non-commercial considerations are not. For example, in June 2006, the Norwegian SWF disinvested more than US$400 million of its Wal-Mart holdings because of the company's treatment of its workforce. The decision was cheered by many. In 2004, the Norwegian parliament adopted ethical guidelines for the Government Pension Fund – Global (GPF-G) – and made certain moral judgements that certain investment should be prohibited (Chesterman 2008). When institutional investors, including SWFs, insist on their 'corporate responsibilities', their investment is often motivated by non-commercial interests (Kyte 2008; Stiglitz 2008). The question becomes: who is the final judge to decide what 'good' or 'bad' non-commercial interests SWFs can or cannot pursue? By what standards, if any, can investment motivations be judged? The issue obviously concerns more than SWFs.

Furthermore, 'extra-financial' considerations are at the core of any government's policies. Indeed, international financial institutions, particularly the World Bank (2002, 2004), and some rich countries are encouraging the commodity export-based economies to establish sovereign savings funds to ease government revenue volatility, manage boom-bust cycles, avoid real appreciation of the exchange rate, preserve capital, transform resources into permanent income and transfer wealth to future generations for transgenerational equity. This involves low-risk as well as high-risk and high-return investments. If sovereign savings funds can achieve multiple long-term objectives, the issues are not about how SWFs are going to invest, but whether a government can resist pressure to spend and set up spending ceilings, whether they are able to garner sufficient political support for saving for future generations and how they can establish institutions to manage these funds as they are designed.

Finally, it is the issue of 'W' – wealth. The first sovereign wealth fund was created as early as 1816, when France set up Caisse des Dépots et Consignations (CDC) to manage the government and overseas tax-exempt funds collected by French savings banks and post offices, however, most SWFs have been created since the early 1970s, mainly in the past decade or so. Except for a few funds that were created with fiscal surpluses, such as the Australian Future Fund, most SWFs were by-products of global financial arrangements or 'global imbalances' – a pattern of large, persistent currency account deficits in the USA and, to a lesser extent, in Britain and some other rich countries, matched by surpluses in oil-exporting countries and Asian developing economies, which have diversified part of their reserve surpluses into SWFs to invest elsewhere (Table 13.1).

The SWF-holding countries vary in many ways: in size (for example, China has a population of 1.33 billion while the Democratic Republic of São Tomé and Príncipe, a Portuguese-speaking island nation in the Gulf of Guinea, has a population of just over 213 000); in wealth (Qatar's GDP per capita is US$110 700 and São Tomé and Príncipe's GDP per capita was $1300 in 2008); and in their political systems. Among the current 48 SWFs identified by the GAO, '28 have been established since 2000 and 20 of these can be classified as commodity funds that receive funds from selling commodities such as oil' (GAO 2008b, p. 11). Some of these funds predominantly invest in domestic economies, while others by their mandate devote all their investment overseas. When countries with relatively low levels of GDP per capita invest in other

Table 13.1   Current account balance

Country	Last 12 months, $bn	% of GDP 2010[†]	Country	Last 12 months, $bn	% of GDP 2010[†]
Portugal	−22.5	−8.6	Norway	+53.5	+14.7
Vietnam	−9.2	−7.7	Saudi Arabia	+20.5	+14.1
Greece	−41.3	−7.0	Malaysia	+32.0	+14.0
South Africa	−11.4	−4.9	Singapore	+34.0	+13.4
New Zealand	−7.9	−4.7	Hong Kong	+18.3	+9.0
Australia	−42.4	−4.4	Switzerland	+48.2	+8.7
Turkey	−21.9	−4.2	Taiwan	+39.8	+7.1
Spain	−77.0	−3.9	Sweden	+29.2	+6.6
US	−419.9	−3.3	Thailand	+16.0	+5.9
Poland	−8.6	−3.1	Netherlands	+42.8	+5.5
Brazil	−36.2	−2.7	Germany	+182.5	+5.3
Italy	63.6	−2.6	Russia	+73.2	+4.4
France	−59.2	−2.1	Philippines	+8.6	+4.4
Canada	−36.6	−1.8	China	+282.2	+4.3
Britain	−28.8	−1.0	Japan	+169.4	+3.2

Note: [†] The Economist poll or Economist Intelligence Unit estimates.
Source: 'Trade, exchange rates, budget balances and interest rates', *The Economist*, 29 May 2010, p. 98.

countries, their SWFs are seen as a threat to free market forces because they are reversing 'a general rule', which is capital historically flowed from the core of an economic system to its periphery. It seems incongruous that these countries remain poorer than rich countries but send their investment out instead of using for domestic development.

Others view SWFs from a different perspective. Because many SWF-holding countries were once poor and suddenly grew rich, some believe their wealth must have come from manipulation of their exchange rate systems or macroeconomic policies not only to obtain wealth but, more importantly, to gain leverage against rich countries. One consequence of their rapid increase in wealth is the shifting of the global economic power equilibrium. For example, the recent expansion of SWFs from oil-exporting countries was clearly the result of rising oil prices during 2003–08. This boom, it was argued, was the product of manipulation 'by financial operators who, reeling from the onset of the crisis, blew out the price from US$70 a barrel to over US$140 in less than a year, before letting the bubble burst', rather than the product of supply-and-demand (Gowan 2009, p. 6). In early 2008, the *Associated Press* reported that while there were no public data showing that sovereign wealth funds invested in oil future contracts, 'government-run investment funds from oil-rich nations might be adding speculative heat to an already red-hot market' (Rugaber 2008). These countries accumulated wealth through building up *their oil bubbles*. For Asian SWFs, the accusation that they manipulated exchange rates has been made loud and clear (Goldstein and Lardy 2005). When 'W' is under consideration, a distinction is rarely made about whether it concerns SWFs, or the current account balance, or foreign exchange reserves, or the associated power in production and politics.

By definition, SWFs are backed by foreign exchange reserves. In practice, because of the large amount of these foreign exchange reserves, some Asian governments decided to diversify part of them for more aggressive investment. Therefore, it is not the wealth of these SWF-holding countries per se that is a threat to currently wealthy countries. Rather, it is the 'global imbalances' that are at the root of the rising SWFs.

Global payment imbalance

SWFs are indicative of the wider problems of the international political economy and they can only be discussed and understood in that context. That is, the global position of the US dollar has provided incentives for the US government to run both budget deficits and current account deficits, and for other countries, particularly oil-exporting countries and Asian developing economics, to hold on US dollars as reserves. It is a point of contention whether low savings in the USA and other rich countries or the savings glut in many developing countries has been the main contributor to the global imbalance. Yet, one undeniable consequence of this imbalance is that double deficits in the USA have affected confidence in the US dollar and caused concerns about the dollar's steadily declining value and its future role as a global currency. It is then not surprising to see countries with current account surpluses diversifying part of their surpluses to higher-risk and higher-return investments rather than making conservative investments in government bonds or treasury bills in the USA. This imbalance is inevitably affecting the power relationships between debtor and creditor countries.

Few would attribute the problems associated with SWFs to 'global imbalances', yet without such imbalances there would not have been the resources or the need to create many of the SWFs in the first place. Economists had long feared that the USA would ruin itself with foreign borrowing on its current account, which measures the balance of investment and saving that has been in the red since 1992. Until 1997, the annual saving shortfall was modest, yet it grew steadily thereafter, reaching a peak of US$788 billion, or 6 per cent of GDP, in 2006. At the end of 2009, the USA ran a current account deficit of $419.9 billion, a significant decline from the previous year of $706.1 billion. The deficits reflected a falling saving rate rather than a rising investment rate. To finance this, the USA needed to borrow from abroad or to sell assets – shares, bonds, property – to pay for the string of deficits. It sucked in savings from abroad at a speed that it could not sustain. The dollar started to decline gradually from 2002, but the current account deficit only became larger. Many economists blamed the 'saving glut' of emerging and commodity-exporting countries that have been financing American consumption habits by acquiring US debts 'at their own risk and accepting the returns accordingly, unlike the debt owed by developing countries where debt service payments are guaranteed in advance' (Jackson 2009, p. 2).

This creates the greatest puzzle in the post-war economy – why have poor countries been so willing to send their savings to rich countries, such as the USA, Australia or Britain? Many American scholars and policymakers have blamed the low saving rate in the USA on the willingness of poor countries to save. As Ben Bernanke, chairman of the US Federal Reserve, explained in 2005, low saving in the USA was a passive response to a global saving glut washing onto its shore; that is, it was not the USA that had lapped up foreign capital, rather foreign capital had been thrust upon it. Even if we accept this argument, several questions remain unanswered. Why is it that some poor countries have had high saving rates but not rich countries, in particular the USA? Why have developing countries not invested savings in their own countries? And what are the political and security implications of this growing global imbalance?

The post-war financial arrangement has placed the US dollar in the position of a global currency. With the US dollar serving as a *medium of exchange* to settle international economic transactions or to intervene in foreign exchange markets, as a *store of value* to be held as an asset for investment purposes or in the form of official foreign exchange reserves, and as a *unit of account* for international trade and investment transactions or as an anchor for pegging the national currency (Helleiner and Kirshner 2009, p. 3), the US government has been in a privileged position to create credits to finance domestic budget deficits and current account deficits without having to suffer high inflation and capital flight. This privileged position was argued to be unsustainable over time under the gold-exchange system (Triffin 1960). Yet the global position of the US dollar survived even with the end of the gold-exchange system in 1971 that removed 'the tenuous discipline which the gold exchange system had imposed on US governments in the management of the dollar' (Strange 1988, p. 16).

The global position of the US dollar remained because in the international system there is no government to decree what should be the international currency, which is decided by a myriad of private traders and market participants. The international currency decision is made based on five basic considerations: (i) the size of the economy; (ii) the depth of its financial market; (iii) a stable currency; (iv) a stable political system; and (v) its external connection as a market and as an investor with extensive networks with market participants elsewhere. The US economy fits all of these categories. It remains the world's largest economy and a large market; it absorbs more oil imports than any other country in the world and maintains the largest trade volumes with other countries. 'The overwhelming majority of commodity prices were denominated in dollars, and in consequence there existed an obvious rationale for many countries to continue to hold reserves in dollars' (James 2009, p. 27). Furthermore, there has not been a plausible alternative reserve currency. Briefly it was argued that the euro might challenge the US dollar's position, yet the euro still 'lacks the political framework and backing sufficient to sustain it through the severe crisis' (Calleo 2009, p. 186).

The combination of free movement of goods and capital and monetary sovereignty – the control of the money supply and the direction and the speed of the economy – of each country has become the driving force behind the global imbalance. Economists have long pointed out the 'unholy trinity' – the trade-off among capital mobility, fixed exchange rate and monetary policy autonomy. Encouraged to open their markets for trade and capital flows, governments in many Asian developing economies have also decided to sacrifice economic efficiency for stability by adopting a fixed exchange rate system. The policy has been politically controversial and economists have had different interpretations of it. Many have argued that the fixed exchange rate system was adopted by Asian developing economies to keep their currencies at an artificially low level in order to boost their exports to the USA; others see it as part of the inevitable rapid development in opening up to the outside world. As the Deputy Governor of the People's Bank of China explained, countries need to have their independent monetary policies. Faced between the choice of a floating exchange rate and free flow of capital, the Chinese government chose the latter so that it could carry out reform. In a sense, it was a choice 'between stability and efficiency'. China chose stability over efficiency with its fixed exchange rate system and trade and capital flows (Yi 2008). This is not a place to discuss policy decisions made by individual countries. The consequence of the combination of free movement of goods and capital along with monetary sovereignty has resulted in a global imbalance as Asian developing countries have run persistent trade surpluses with the USA and some rich Europeans countries. High export growth 'is not the new kid on the block – it is the story of East Asia during the last fifty years' (Aizenman and Lee 2005, p. 3). But it had not always generated current account surpluses. When these countries increased their trade with other countries, they had also opened up their markets to foreign capital. Prior to the Asian financial crisis in 1997, Asian developing countries ran a collective current account deficit of US$78 billion, which was almost at par with that in the USA at the time. Their deficits were financed by other rich countries. This development of Asian economies from having current account deficits to surpluses has prompted some scholars to question whether the fixed rate regime is the only reason for the current account imbalances between Asian developing countries and the USA.

Since the Asian financial crisis, Asian developing economies have expanded their trade and trade surpluses, but they have also seen upward saving rates that has led to a steady rise in their foreign reserves. Because of their experience during the Asian financial crisis of 1997–98, these Asian developing economies initially wanted reserves that were large enough to draw upon if foreign currency financing suddenly dried up to ensure that trade would flow smoothly. Their precautionary measures led to an accumulation of foreign reserves that were predominantly in US dollars, not only because their export to the USA is a lifeline for their continuing economic development, but also because their underdeveloped financial markets have encouraged their savings to go to the USA and the UK where the financial markets are *stable, mature and deep*. Finally, the USA's 'sheriff' role in the region, which may be an annoyance for individual countries from time to time, is acknowledged to be necessary for regional stability and encourages investment flows to the USA.

In the Asian developing economies, it is acknowledged that the size of their foreign exchange reserves exceeds all plausible estimates of what is required for traditional liquidity purposes; for example, they have enough to pay for three months' imports, or to cover short-term foreign currency debt. Even the Central Bank in China admitted that the size of China's foreign reserves is 'sufficient' and that China did not intend to 'enlarge this size further' (Liu and Zhu 2008, p. 5). China diversified US$200 billion into the CIC; Thailand created the Government Pension Fund in 1997 (US$10.9 billion); Hong Kong the Exchange Fund Investment Portfolio (US$186 billion) in 1998; Taiwan the National Stabilisation Fund (US$15.2 billion) in 2001; and South Korea the Korea Investment Corporation (US$20 billion) in 2005 (Lyons 2007; GAO 2008b).

While the Asian developing economies were accumulating their current account surpluses, the USA showed an endless appetite for capital. The world is on a treadmill of global imbalances. In less than a decade, Asian developing countries have not only reversed their debtor status but have quickly expanded their current account surpluses, reaching nearly US$900 billion by 2008. China only started running current account surpluses in 2003 but it has expanded rapidly (its foreign reserves reached US$2.27 trillion by mid-2009). Correspondingly, starting in 1999, the household sector in the USA began dis-saving as individuals spent more than they earned. Part of this dis-saving was offset by the government sector, which ran a surplus from 1998 to 2001. From 2002, both the household sector and the government ran a steady increase in deficits (Jackson 2008), which were financed not only by Asian developing economies, but also by oil-exporting countries.

Oil-producing countries, especially those from the Middle East, were the second largest group of countries supporting the debt-spending habit of the USA. 'America needs both the region's oil and continued support for the greenback; regional governments, in turn, need protection against enemies both within and without, which Washington has promised under a series of unwritten understandings dating back to the first oil shock in the 1970s' (Cohen 2009, p. 161). Middle East oil-exporting countries have accumulated a large amount of foreign reserves in dollars because oil is traded on the international markets in the denomination of US dollars and the USA is the largest oil-importing country in the world.

There are many explanations for these imbalances. Some see them as the fault of the current account surplus countries, that is, as Asian developing economies and Middle East oil-exporting countries dumped their savings at the doorstep of the USA, this savings glut created the perverse incentives for an unsustainable build-up of debts in the USA. In other words, faced with cheap credits at its doorway, the Americans could not resist them but went on over-spending – 'financial obesity'? Others argue that the cheap money policies of the late 1990s and early

2000s in the USA were mainly responsible for fuelling a debt-driven consumer boom, and sucking in record volumes of imports from the industrialising economies of Asia. No matter what the explanation is for its cause, this imbalance cannot be sustained. If policies in Asian developing countries have made a difference in terms of their saving rates, their export surpluses and their accumulated foreign reserves, it is difficult to see the debt-spending US economy as the only natural response to a global saving glut. Changes in this global imbalance have to take place on both sides: the exchange rate is only one of the policies governments can adopt to direct their economies, addressing the imbalance between those with high savings rates and the deficit-spending US economy therefore requires changes on both sides rather than on one side only.

Meanwhile, all parties involved are aware that since the global position of US dollars has helped boost the US hegemonic political, strategic and economic status, 'any decline in that role will also have important distributional consequences among states in the international system' (Helliener and Kirshner 2009, p. 5). No one is ready to challenge the status quo. Short of undermining the global position of the US dollar, countries with surplus reserves have found another channel to make their surpluses more profitable – SWFs, which provide a natural channel for the proposed shift of surplus reserves from passive liquidity management to active profit-seeking investment.

Oil-exporting countries have always sought financial and industrial assets in the USA and other countries. Abu Dhabi, for example, with 0.02 per cent of the global population, has 10 per cent of global oil reserves and 5 per cent of the world's gas reserves. With the significant rises in oil prices in 2005–07, its SWF, the largest in the world, swelled to an estimated US\$750–900 billion. The similar story could be told about the total assets of Saudi Arabia and Kuwait, estimated to equal those of Abu Dhabi, and the newly created SWFs in Qatar (2005), Russia (2008), Venezuela (2005) and Nigeria (2004).

The main reason for the creation of these SWFs was to establish more active management of foreign exchange reserves with a view towards maximising risk-adjusted returns rather than preparing for shortages of international liquidity. The global imbalance was, therefore, the root and consequence of these SWFs as 'the world has moved robustly toward liberalisation of both trade and capital flows while governments have asserted a historically unprecedented sovereign right, and indeed responsibility, to control the supply and price of national money' (Steil and Hinds 2009, p. 9).

While SWFs might be the by-products of the global imbalance, their emergence is also an indication of a broader shift in the balance of power. The global position of the US dollar is not only an economic matter; it has helped boost US hegemony by allowing the US government to fight major wars in Iraq and Afghanistan with bills partially paid by Middle East oil-producing countries and Asian economies that hold a large amount of US debt. It has also permitted Americans to maintain their lifestyle. More importantly, 'Americans, it appears, have grown deeply habituated to our exorbitant post-war privileges [and] our political elites are addicted to managing the world' (Calleo 2009, p. 186). When US Congress raised concerns about investments made by SWFs from developing countries (even though it had frequently been courted by businesses from these countries), Treasury officials brought the matter to the attention of the OECD, IMF and the Bank for International Settlements (BIS) and demanded action be taken in drafting new rules and regulations over SWF investments. The US Treasury, meanwhile, engaged in bilateral negotiations to press SWF-holding countries to subject their investment to a new set of rules for 'best practices'.

The global solution

If SWFs are the by-products of a global financial imbalance, any concerns about SWFs would also be 'global'. To address any related issues would require changing the behaviour of both current account surplus and deficit countries. That is, according to customary laws of economics, countries with surplus reserves should diversify their reserves, increase spending on domestic economies and float their exchange rate, while the USA should 'reduce consumption, give incentives to exports, and squeeze funding for military interventions' (Calleo 2009, p. 186). Obviously, none of these actions could be taken unilaterally without there being serious consequences for other countries. More importantly, the global financial imbalance is not a simple economic issue, it is a geopolitical one. In an integrated world, issues concerning SWFs require a global solution and collective action. Yet so far, instead of seeking a global solution and collections, the recipient countries – those where SWFs made their investment – imposed the discriminatory pressure on SWF-holding countries and preferred to subjected themselves to a set of disciplines that were designed especially for them. This led to the creation of the IWG and the acceptance of the Santiago Principles.

While the IWG, GAPP and the Kuwait Declaration that created the Forum of SWFs might not satisfy everyone, they can be seen as part of the efforts to build 'a global constitutional order that is pluralistic rather than hegemonic, one that better accommodates the increasingly diverse world in which we actually live' (Calleo 2009, p. 188). This may help explain the shift from the initial reluctance to introduce regulatory rules on SWFs only to the willingness of participants to engage in rule-making.

In 2009, SWFs of developing Asian and Gulf countries became actively involved in the process of drafting the GAPP and creating the Forum. This was the reverse of the position they had adopted a year earlier. At that time they had preferred to keep a low profile and were surprised when world attention focused on them. The Chinese were among those who complained about this unwanted attention. In an interview with the US current affairs show *60 Minutes*, Gao Xiqing, president of CIC, told American television journalist Lesley Stahl, 'You know, the Chinese culture is [one of] being self-effacing, trying to hide yourself, don't stick your head out for people to knock on. We do not want all this attention.' Preferring to be on the periphery of global public attention, the Chinese did not think new codes of conduct would be necessary. 'Why should SWFs be singled out when American hedge funds and private equity firms do not have such a code?', asked Gao Xiqing. 'It would only hurt feelings; it is not economic, it does not make sense, and it is politically stupid.'

The Gulf SWFs made similar comments in 2007–08 when pressure was increasing among OECD countries for 'regulating' and even 'restricting' SWFs from investing in their countries. The US Congress passed, and President Bush signed, the Foreign Investment and National Security Act of 2007, which increased congressional oversight over acquisition of US businesses by foreign governments. At this time, the EU called for the development of a set of common European policies to respond to SWF investments.

Once they realised that they would have to 'cope with a far-from-hospitable reception by a number of Western leaders and their public' (Behrendt 2008, p. 3) and face potential protectionism against their investment in some Western countries, SWF-holding countries decided to sit at the negotiation table in writing the rules rather than resist efforts to face unilaterally determined restrictions. Once at the negotiation table, they would be able to express their concerns and make their voices heard. Given there is no one 'higher authority' over the 'sovereign' investors, politicians in some OECD countries pushed for 'tough control' over these investments. Several OECD countries demanded the IMF and OECD study the concerns. The IMF embraced the opportunity to restore its credibility that had suffered disastrously after the Asian financial crisis and to revive its business that had been declining to the extent that profits from its lending could hardly cover its operations or support its staff. SWFs offered a good opportunity for it to revive itself. The meeting of November 2007 became a catalyst for SWF interactions with international institutions and governments which were on the receiving end of investments. The negotiation of new rules on SWFs was conducted among officials from SWFs, but members of IWG also held three rounds of discussions with recipient countries.

To address rising concerns, the GAPP highlighted four objectives of SWFs:

1. To help maintain a stable global financial system and free flow of capital and investment.
2. To comply with all applicable regulatory and disclosure requirements in the countries in which they invest.
3. To invest on the basis of economic and financial risk and return-related considerations.
4. To have in place a transparent and sound governance structure that provides for adequate operational controls, risk management and accountability (IWG 2008, p. 4).

The GAPP is a voluntary and non-binding agreement, given that there is no enforcement agency over sovereign states. Several points need to be highlighted regarding the GAPP.

- It explicitly specifies which market participants should *not* be classified as SWFs: they 'exclude, *inter alia*, foreign currency reserve assets held by monetary authorities for the traditional balance of payments or monetary policy purposes, state-owned enterprises (SOEs) in the traditional sense, government-employee pension funds, or assets managed for the benefit of individuals.'
- It acknowledges that the threats presented until now are all hypothetical even though the negative perception of some SWFs persists.

In April 2009, 16 out of the 26 members of the IWG met in Kuwait city and adopted the Kuwait Declaration, which established the International Forum of Sovereign Wealth Funds. The Forum is designed to serve as a platform where members can exchange ideas and views among SWFs and with other relevant parties, share views on the application of the Santiago Principles including operational and technical matters, and encourage cooperation with investment recipient countries, relevant international organisations and capital market functionaries to identify potential risks that may affect cross-border investments and to foster a non-discriminatory, constructive and mutually beneficial investment environment.

The Forum is not an international organisation in the sense that members are not direct representatives of their governments but officials with corporate mandates from the SWFs. Behind each SWF, there are a number of conflicting interests between those who manage these funds and those (the citizens as a whole) who are the ultimate shareholders who do not have direct control over the management of the funds. The creation of developing Asia's SWFs was driven by popular pressure for more active, profit-oriented management of the region's large surplus reserves and the loss of some of the investments in turn was openly criticised by the public too.

It would be a serious mistake to presume that SWFs in countries with less pluralistic systems do not face questions about their investment strategy or performance at home. Increasingly, domestic opposition regarding poor investments made by some of these funds is not only heard in democratic countries such as Norway – where some complained that insufficient efforts were made to address the integrated challenges of climate change and sustainable development as promised – but also in non-democratic countries, such as China. When, for example, CIC suffered heavy losses in its investment in Blackstone, one of the largest US private equity firms, the Chinese public was outraged. The fact that SWFs are custodians of national wealth is a double-edged sword in the sense that they might create accountability problems, but they can also encourage more risky investment behaviour when initial losses occur.

Negotiating new regulations and rules was strongly encouraged by the rich countries. Bringing the non-OECD SWFs under the umbrella of the IMF was considered an effective way to monitor and manage their activities and investment in the recipient countries. It is too early to tell whether this group of players in the Forum can adopt a united position when faced with complex issues. Yet, 'be careful what we wish for'. The establishment of the Forum may have signified the emergence of a new and powerful collective player in the international financial world, whose control of large amounts of assets can have important impacts on both sides of the investment.

When the Latin debt crisis erupted in the early 1980s, most creditors were private commercial banks in a few developed countries, mainly in the USA, while debtors were sovereign developing countries. To get their money back, private commercial banks in the USA enlisted the government for help and the Reagan administration readily jumped in for fear of the potential collapse of its banking system. To ensure creditors could squeeze everything out of the debtors, the Reagan administration enlisted governments in Europe and adopted a strategy of 'divide and conquer' – they (with the IMF as a front-man) would negotiate with each debtor country on a one-to-one basis. Diverse and often conflicting interests prevented developing debtor countries from adopting a united front. This made it much easier for conditionalities to be imposed.

This time around, while it is still too early to tell how far this collective effort will go, there is no doubt that drafting and adopting the GAPP and the following establishment of the Forum indicates a desire for cooperation. As the co-chair of IWG, H.E. Hamad Al Hurr-Suwaidi, the Under Secretary of Finance of UAE, explained, 'from the outset, there was agreement that the developing criticism in the media and in certain recipient countries, questioning the investment objectives and practices of SWFs, deserves a collective response so as to preserve the benefits of an open and stable global financial system' (2008, p. 2).

The differences are clearly indicated in the GAPP and the following statements were made by various SWFs. These differences, however, are not only natural but also an indication of a changing global economy. While the recipient countries of investment from SWFs still insist that the responsibilities of SWFs be 'transparent' and their investment not be for political or other strategic objectives, there is no consensus on what transparency and non-commercial objectives mean in operation. In explaining to the public about the GAPP, Hama Al Hurr Al-Suwaidi said:

> Accountability and transparency are key elements of the Santiago Principles. The IWG members have affirmed their commitment to openness and disclosure to the owners of the SWFs and also to provide information to recipient country regulators and make disclosure as applicable under local laws and regulations. The IWG members have also agreed to publish relevant financial information that demonstrates the economic and financial orientation of SWFs' investment operations.
>
> (2008, p. 4)

This statement highlights the fundamental problems of 'regulating' SWFs from a multilateral perspective. First, there is a distinction between disclosure of information to the owners and disclosure of information to the receiving end of SWF investment. The governing structure and operations of a given SWF are under a set of rules defined by its government. So long as the management of an SWF follows the legal and regulation requirements in its own country, it is difficult for other governments to demand changes in its governing structure or operation, especially demand to follow the Norwegian example. When an SWF's operation goes beyond its country's border, it may face legitimate concerns from national regulators, politicians or even from members of the public in recipient countries. While it is important to ensure that SWFs follow the rules and regulations of other sovereign countries, it is also a legitimate concern that SWFs would not suffer from discriminatory restrictions. Both sides must agree on a reciprocal arrangement. Until now, both sides have been restrained from pushing their argument too far. Instead of challenging the rules and regulations in the countries where SWFs want to make their investments, they have tried to avoid direct confrontation by contacting the relevant authorities in the target countries well before any review process is even triggered (Barysch et al. 2008, p. 9).

Adopting the GAPP by consensus has undoubtedly legitimised the existence of SWFs. The creation of the Forum particularly needs to be taken seriously when one tries to understand the nuances of SWFs. The Forum is not an organisation and its work is coordinated by its chair, David Murray of the Australian Future Fund, and his two deputies from ADIC and CIC, assisted by the secretariat provided by the IMF. It is a forum where SWFs, not states per se, exchange information, not about their investment strategies but rather of the changing rules in countries in which they are interested in making investment. This exercise of exchanging information is considered important for SWFs because , as one member stated, 'the US Congress can be illogical, irrational and political from time to time'. 'Politicians can be short-sighted too', said another. The Forum can provide SWFs with some predictability, thus circumventing the unpredictability of some politicians. The Forum and the Santiago Principles, however, would not be able to deal with all the concerns about SWFs because they are not designed to regulate the behaviour or coordinate actions of states. They are about SWFs – government-owned investment instruments, operating largely independent of their governments.

Conclusion

The issues and concerns about SWFs cannot be dealt with until the international community settles the issue of the 'reserve currency' status of the USA. Clearly, 'in a global world, there is no reason for current accounts to be balanced' (Blanchard and Milesi-Ferretti 2009, p. 3). We may even be able to 'live with global imbalances' for some time because 'the large US current account deficit is both comprehensible and welfare-enhancing from a global point of view' (Cooper 2007, p. 104). The imbalance, therefore, is one of 'good imbalances' (Blanchard and Milesi-Ferretti 2009, p. 3) and will adjust as countries with large surpluses revalue their currencies and increase their domestic spending.

Others are not so optimistic about the 'natural forces' of the market. They point out that the global financial disequilibrium has deeper and broader political and economic implications for world politics. Current account surplus countries have argued that the system based on the currency of a single country is unstable and unfair when it provides the top currency-holding country with an 'exorbitant privilege' in running its policies, sometimes at the expense of others. They demand changes to the rules and the current international financial arrangement. Current account deficit countries insist that it was persistent surpluses that created their 'financial obesity' and therefore the main responsibility to address the global imbalance lies with countries that have surplus reserves. For many countries that occupy the middle ground, the real issue is how to change the current 'non-system' into a global financial system that can provide stability and reflect the changes (Lago et al. 2009). Restructuring and recreating a new international arrangement is a question of politics, not economics.

References

Aizenman, Joshua and Jaewoo Lee (2006), 'Financial Versus Monetary Mercantilism: Long-run View of Large International Reserves Hoarding', IMF Working Paper 06/280.

Al-Suwaidi, H.E. Hamad Al Hurr (2008), 'Statement at meeting of the International Monetary and Financial Committee', International Working Group of Sovereign Wealth Funds, Washington, DC, 11 October.

Barysch, Katinka, Simon Tilford and Philip Whyte (2008), 'State, Money and Rules: An EU Policy for Sovereign Investments', Centre for European Reform, London, December.

Behrendt, Sven (2008), 'When Money Talks: Arab Sovereign Wealth Funds in The Global Public Policy Discourse', *Carnegie Papers*, 12, October.

Blanchard, Oliver and Gisn Msria Milesi-Ferretti (2009), 'Global Imbalances: In Midstream?', IMF Research Department, 22 December.

Calleo, David P. (2009), 'Twenty-first Century Geopolitics and the Erosion of the Dollar Order', in Eric Helleiner and Jonathan Kirshner (eds),*The Future of the Dollar*. Ithaca, NY: Cornell University Press, pp.164–90.

Chesterman, Simon (2008), 'The Turn to Ethics: Disinvestment From Multinational Corporations for Human Rights Violations – The Case of Norway's Sovereign Wealth Fund', *American University International Law Review*, 23(3), pp. 577–615.

Cohen, Benjamin J. (2009), 'Toward a Leaderless Currency System', in Eric Helleiner and Jonathan Kirshner (eds), *The Future of the Dollar*. Ithaca, NY: Cornell University Press, pp. 142–63.

Cooper, Richard N. (2007), 'Living with Global Imbalances', *Brookings Papers on Economic Activity*, 2, pp. 91–107.

Emmanuel, William and Hepher, Tim (2008), 'Sarkozy vows to defend France against wealth funds', *Reuters UK*, 9 January.

GAO (2008a), 'Foreign Investment: Laws and Policies Regulating Foreign Investment in 10 Countries', GAO-08-320, February.

GAO (2008b), 'Sovereign Wealth Funds: Publicly Available Data on Sizes and Investments for Some Funds are Limited', GAO-08-946, September.

Goldstein, Morris and Nicholas Lardy (2005), 'China's Role in the Revived Bretton Woods System: A Case ff Mistaken Identity', Working Paper 05-2, Peterson Institute for International Economics, Washington, DC.

Helleiner, Eric and Jonathan Kirshner (2009), 'The Future of the Dollar: Whither the Key Currency?', in Eric Helleiner and Jonathan Kirshner (eds), *The Future of the Dollar*. Ithaca, NY: Cornell University Press, pp. 1–23.

Hidebrand, Philip (2007), 'The Challenge of Sovereign Wealth Funds', Speech at the International Centre for Monetary and Banking Studies, Geneva, 18 December.

Jackson, James K. (2009), 'The United States as a Net Debtor Nation: Overview of the International Investment Position', Congressional Research Services, RL32964, 3 August.

James, Harold (2009), 'The Enduring International Pre-eminence of the Dollar', in Eric Helleiner and Jonathan Kirshner (eds), *The Future of the Dollar*. Ithaca, NY: Cornell University Press, pp. 24–44.

Kirshner, Joshua (2009), 'Sovereign Wealth Funds and National Security: The Dog that will Refuse to Bark', *Geopolitics*, 14, pp. 305–16.

Kotter, Jason and Ugur Lel Ugur (2008), 'Friends or foes? The Stock Price Impact of Sovereign Wealth Fund Investments and the Price of Keeping Secrets', International Finance Discussion Paper, No. 940, Board of Governor of the Federal Reserve System, August.

Kyte, Rachel (2008), 'Balancing Rights with Responsibilities: Looking for the Global Drivers of Materiality in Corporate Social Responsibility and the Voluntary Initiatives that Develop and Support Them', *American University International Law Review*, 23(3), pp. 559–76.

Largo, M, R. Duttagupta and R. Goyal (2009), 'The Debate on the International Monetary System', IMF Strategy, Policy and Review Department, 11 November.

Levelle, Kathryn C. (2008), 'The Business of Governments: Nationalism in the Context of Sovereign Wealth Funds and State-Owned Enterprises', *Journal of International Affairs*, 62(1), pp. 131–47.

Liu, Pand and Junbo Zhu (2008), 'The Management of China's Huge Foreign Reserve and Its Currency Composition', Working Papers of the Institute of Management Berlin, Berlin School of Economics, No. 37, 04/2008.

Lyons, Gerard (2007), 'State Capitalism: The Rise of Sovereign Wealth Funds', *Law and Business Review of the Americas*, 14(1), pp. 1–62.

Rugaber, Christopher S. (2008), 'Analysts: Government Funds Heat Up Oil Prices', *Associated Press*, 18 March.

Senn, Myriam (2009), 'Sovereign Wealth Funds as Public-Private Challenge for Institutional Governance', paper presented at Sovereign Wealth Funds: Governance and Regulation, organised by the Faculty of Law, National University of Singapore, 9–11 September.

Steil, Benn and Manuel Hinds (2009), *Money, Markets & Sovereignty*. New Haven, CT: Yale University Press.

Stiglitz, Joseph (2008), 'Regulating Multinational Corporations: Towards Principles of Cross-Border Legal Frameworks in a Globalised World Balancing Rights and Responsibilities', *American University International Law Review*, 23(3), pp. 451–558.

Strange, Susan (1988), *States and Markets*. London: Pinter Publishers.

Summers, Lawrence (2007), 'Funds that Shape Capitalist Logic', *Financial Times*, 29 July.

World Bank (2002), 'Striking a Better Balance – the World Bank Group and the Extractive Industries: The Final Report of the Extractive Industries Review', The World Bank, Washington, DC.

World Bank and International Financial Corporation (2002), *Treasure or Trouble? Mining in Developing Countries*. Washington, DC: The World Bank.

Yi, Gang (2008), 'Renminbi Exchange Rates and Relevant Institutional Factors', in Wang Mengkui (ed.), *China in the Wake of Asia's Financial Crisis*. New York: Routledge, pp. 59–67.

Index